Strategic Intelligence

A Handbook for Practitioners, Managers, and Users

Don McDowell

THE SCARECROW PRESS, INC.
Lanham, Maryland • Toronto • Plymouth, UK

FOUNDATION® BOOKS
Delhi • Bangalore • Mumbai • Kolkata • Chennai • Hyderabad • Pune

Published by
Cambridge University Press India Pvt. Ltd.
under the imprint of Foundation Books
Cambridge House, 4381/4 Ansari Road, Daryaganj, **New Delhi** 110 002

Cambridge University Press India Pvt. Ltd.
C-22, C-Block, Brigade M.M., K.R. Road, Jayanagar, **Bangalore** 560 070
Plot No. 80, Service Industries, Shirvane, Sector-1, Nerul, **Navi Mumbai** 400 706
10 Raja Subodh Mullick Square, 2nd Floor, **Kolkata** 700 013
21/1 (New No. 49), 1st Floor, Model School Road, Thousand Lights, **Chennai** 600 006
House No. 3-5-874/6/4, (Near Apollo Hospital), Hyderguda, **Hyderabad** 500 029
Agarwal Pride, 'A' Wing, 1308 Kasba Peth, Near Surya Hospital, **Pune** 411 011

This edition was published by arrangement with Scarecrow Press.

ISBN 978-81-7596-744-1

Published by Manas Saikia for Cambridge University Press India Pvt. Ltd. and printed at Sanat Printers, Kundli.

Contents

Preface *vii*

Acknowledgments *ix*

PART I: **General Concepts**

1 Using Strategic Intelligence 3
Organization and Focus of This Book 4
Background on Strategic Intelligence and Analysis 5
Approaches and Processes 6
The Future Use of Strategic Intelligence 7

2 Strategic Intelligence: Role, Definitions, and Concepts 10
Basic Concepts about Intelligence 11
The Strategic Intelligence Process 17
The Role of Strategic Intelligence and Its Impact on Management 24
Conclusion 28

PART II: **Critical Observations**

3 Overview of the Implementation and Impact of Strategic Intelligence 33
History of the Early Years 34
Progress in the 1990s and Beyond 35
Current Situation: Challenges for the Profession 38
Problems for Analysts 45

Summary of Observations 48
Conclusion 49
4 The Case for Establishing a National Strategic Intelligence Apparatus 51
Concepts, Application, and Management 52
Development and Application of Strategic Intelligence 55
Management and Resource Requirement 59
One Future Approach: A National Strategic Crime Intelligence Unit 62
Requirements of a Separate National Strategic Intelligence Service 65
Conclusion 68

PART III: **Issues for Clients and Managers**

5 Why Managers and Executives Need Strategic Analysis: The Law Enforcement Model 73
Enforcement and Strategic Intelligence 74
Strategic Analysis Input to Policy Making 76
Implementing Strategic Intelligence Programs 77
Challenges for the Executive to Accept Strategic Intelligence 79
Conclusion 81
6 Management Models and Behavior: Impact on Intelligence 84
Intelligence as the Servant of the Executive 84
Historical Perspective on Management Style 85
Contemporary Management Approaches 87
The Present Situation 88
Blending Analytical Support and Management Thinking 89
7 Management and Self-Management of Strategic Projects and Processes 95
The Role of Intelligence Management 96
Issues and Principles 96
Managing Strategic Intelligence Projects 98
Strategic Analysts and Self-Management 99
Conclusion 100

PART IV: **Processes and Techniques**

8 Developing Concepts: Understanding the Topic 103
Processes and Techniques for Strategic Intelligence 103
Conceptual Frameworks 105

Identifying the Features of a Strategic Topic 109
How to Develop the Conceptual Model 110
Conclusion 113
9 Defining the Task: Prescribing the Boundaries of the Project 115
Assessing the Scope of the Assignment 117
Developing the Terms of Reference 123
Additional Aspects of the Problem Definition Phase 126
Conclusion 128
10 Strategic Project Work Plans 133
Structuring a Strategic Project Work Plan 134
Designing and Presenting Work Plans 145
Conclusion 149
11 Generating Hypotheses 151
Hypotheses: Basic Concepts 153
Techniques for Generating Hypotheses 159
Using Hypotheses 162
Conclusion 166
12 Developing Indicators for Strategic Topics 168
What are Strategic Indicators? 169
A Process for Developing Indicators 170
Conclusion 175
13 Data Collection Plans for Strategic Projects 177
The Information Imperative 178
Sources of Information 179
Planning the Collection Activity 184
Strategic Research and Its Impact on Intelligence Collection Planning 190
Conclusion 192
14 Collation and Evaluation of Data 195
Collation Principles and Practice 197
The Evaluation Process in Strategic Intelligence 205
Conclusion 211
15 Deciding on Analytical Approaches 213
Preparation for Analysis 216
Resources for Analysis 217
Approaches to Intelligence Problem Solving 223
Analytical Approaches to Specific Problem Issues 227

Probability Theory: A Brief Comment 230
Conclusion 231
16 Developing Strategic Reports 234
General Concepts and Preparation 235
Presentation and Format 238
Finalizing the Report for Distribution 242
Conclusion 243

PART V: The Analyst

17 The Role, Responsibilities, and Functions of the Analyst 247
The Analyst's Role and Function 247
The Analyst's Responsibilities 255
Special Challenges for the Analyst 259
Conclusion 262

Final Thought 265

Further Reading in Intelligence Analysis 267

About the Author 271

Preface

This reference book is the result of several long years of considerable thought, experiment, research, and practical experience. Throughout this time I have been developing my own views and concepts on the doctrine and practice of strategic intelligence and analysis, as well as lecturing, teaching, speech making, and writing on the topic. To some degree, there is also an element of frustration invested in the book, since comparatively few of our intelligence brethren attempt to write down their experiences and thoughts to help create the "body of learning and opinion" so necessary for the development of any profession. Thus, I have used this book as the medium to finally put into a much wider and more accessible form my thoughts on strategic intelligence doctrine and experience in its usage.

I admit that the focus of this book appears to the casual reader to be directed primarily at the law enforcement community. However, one should make no mistaken assumption about this; strategic research is absolutely just as relevant to the public and private sectors of any society. Strategic analysis is applicable to every field of corporate, government, or individual endeavor, because the techniques facilitate the in-depth planning that is the key to developing grand plans and strategies. The test I offer to readers who are not part of the enforcement community is this: Wherever the discussion focuses on policing, try substituting terms and scenarios that relate to areas that interest you—policy formulation, marketing, investment and takeover planning (or avoidance), and the like. The concepts translate easily to these other areas of endeavor.

In developing this book, I have drawn not only on my own rather long and fortunately broad experience but also very much upon the wide range of knowledge and experience held and shared by others. The discerning reader/researcher will find, as I did a decade ago, when the previous edition was published, that there is still very little reference material available on the specialized topic of strategic analysis. Of course, current literature is useful in understanding basic intelligence and analysis concepts and their application in achieving tactical and operational outcomes. There is a growing tendency to publish strategic analysis books with a military or national security focus; these nonetheless provide insight into how the lessons might apply to the enforcement and compliance field as well as the corporate world. However, the development of the strategic intelligence ideas and the process adaptations included in this book represent my own way of applying research methods to the specific needs of government and corporate intelligence work. While the general ideas are obviously not new, this "packaging" of the concepts and the proven success of applying the methodology to real-world strategic problems and issues is itself an advance on existing intelligence processes available within enforcement.

I feel a need to stress the following important point, though. I do not claim to have "invented" anything new. What I have done is search out those tried and tested skills, techniques, and models of research that seemed to suggest that they could be shaped and recast for use in the real intelligence world. No such model existed at the time of my research, nor had any apparently been tried with total success in the field of law enforcement planning and crime trend forecasting. What was needed was a single model, principled and logical, that could be followed with confidence and yet, if used flexibly to suit changing circumstances and constraints, would more than adequately meet the analytical requirements of each and every project.

I am sincerely thankful for the support, help, and critical appraisal I have received from my professional colleagues and students throughout the world of intelligence analysis and research. I hope they, and those new to the subject, will benefit from the ideas expressed in this book. In particular, I hope readers will go on to extend the application of strategic analysis within their own organizations, whatever they might be.

Acknowledgements

This book would not have been possible without the contribution and inspiration of many intelligence professionals, colleagues, and friends. Throughout my experience in developing and teaching strategic intelligence and analysis, I have had the opportunity to meet and discuss these concepts with a wide range of practicing analysts across several continents.

For this new edition, I am indebted to Jan Goldman of Scarecrow Press for his continued encouragement and support.

In particular, I wish to acknowledge the input and encouragement I have received over the past several years from Marcel Scholtes and Paul Minnebo (the Netherlands); Pascal Wautelet (Belgium); Tom Haney, Howard Clarke, and David Neely (Canada); Mark Boyce (New Zealand); Dalene Duvenage (South Africa); Lesley Wheatley, Amanda Hopkins, and Kenneth Matthews (United Kingdom); Bob Heibel (United States); and Anthony Nolan (Australia).

My research into the theory and practice of strategic intelligence has, of course, been generally educated by comprehensive reading, even though, to the best of my knowledge, there are no direct quotes or extracts from the works of other authors in this book. On the other hand, I am fortunate to have been given many opportunities to work on the application of the principles and processes outlined, inspired by the work I have done in various corporate and government organizations around the world.

And finally, special thanks go to my wife, Beverley, for her continuing encouragement and assistance in bringing the book to fruition.

I

GENERAL CONCEPTS

1

Using Strategic Intelligence

While this may well be the first major reference book about strategic intelligence and its application in a nonmilitary context, of course it is not a book about an entirely new concept. After all, intelligence and analysis have existed in various forms for many years. Depending upon one's view of history and assuming a certain generosity in ignoring some of the semantics now investing this genre, intelligence practice can be tracked back to biblical times in the Christian world as well as to the ancient writings of Eastern and Oriental military philosophers such as Sun Tzu.

There is a growing body of literature on intelligence practice in the world of enforcement. In this work, the term *enforcement* is taken to include policing, compliance, and regulation. The bulk of this intelligence literature has been generated over the last decade and is a significant manifestation of how the field is increasingly being accepted as a legitimate part of enforcement community responsibilities worldwide. While not all of the topic literature is innovative or instructive, the vast amount of informative material on applications and experiences serves to assist the development of the profession. As yet, though, intelligence still lacks some of the essential components that ought to accompany its claims to be a "profession." There is not yet agreement on what constitutes a doctrine, a common language, and standardized approaches to staff selection, training, and development. The ideas of *best practice*, desirable as an essential element within any modern management environment, have not yet been clearly articulated within the intelligence sphere, at least not in a way that is universally accepted by the practitioners.

Intelligence is a field of activity that has a rich history, yet it still lacks clarity of definition and agreement. This is not to denigrate the performance of many of its practitioners; rather, these comments are designed to point up the fact that, despite the length and breadth of its historical practice, there is still much to do to explore the boundaries, opportunities, and limitations of the application of intelligence in the world of enforcement.

Much work is being done by various intelligence coordinating groups in Europe and North America to overcome this deficiency. For example, many agencies have developed or contributed to the establishment of standardized approaches on intelligence training programs, crossing the boundaries between practitioners and academics to provide the best possible blending of skills training and education. However, to some observers, while tackling the training issues is a relatively easy starting point, the fact remains that little has been done to comprehensively bring together a set of protocols and values that could become the accepted "intelligence doctrine" of the community. There is no lack of ideas about what might be included in such a code, in my opinion. Rather, the concept of agreeing on and then accepting a generic code is not necessarily one that can easily be embraced by agencies striving to achieve excellence, recognition, and competitive edge.

ORGANIZATION AND FOCUS OF THIS BOOK

While the foregoing remarks apply to the world of intelligence in a generic sense, the setting of this book is aimed at that specific subset of intelligence: strategic intelligence and research. Readers will note that this book includes both critical appraisal of the intelligence scene and a number of chapters on practical issues of particular interest to managers.

In addition, one whole part of the book is devoted to processes. These are designed to ensure that any strategic research project is well organized and imaginatively conceptualized to meet the needs of the assignment. The process steps themselves are not difficult to comprehend, and many readers will not only recognize them but may be in the habit of applying them in their workplace. It would be a mistake, though, to trivialize the process as being "common sense" or "merely structural." The fact is that no research project of worth can start without the appropriate visioning and plan; nor can it hope to succeed if attention to detail is significantly absent.

As will be discussed later in this book, much of the teaching regimen for strategic intelligence does indeed emphasize the process, but only in the context of concurrent critical, creative thought about applying that process in a specifically strategic setting. Moreover, what has emerged from the teaching experience over a decade and many hundreds of students is that this disciplined and orderly—yet creatively conceptual—approach is precisely what is needed in all intelligence work. It is an unfortunate deficiency that such teaching strategies figure rarely, if at all, in basic intelligence techniques training worldwide.

BACKGROUND ON STRATEGIC INTELLIGENCE AND ANALYSIS

In the nineteenth and twentieth centuries, intelligence practice evolved toward the form that is now recognizable in the context of current practice. To its detriment, the intelligence milieu is somewhat misunderstood by many observers. The concepts of espionage and critical analysis are often confused as if they were all part of the same activity. *Espionage* is about gathering data in the intrusive and invasive environment of spying. *Intelligence and analysis* is a wider process of problem solving that involves data gathering and analysis, interpretation, and speculative consideration of future developments, patterns, threats, risks, and opportunities.

Strategic intelligence analysis can be considered a specific form of research that addresses any issue at the level of breadth and detail necessary to describe threats, risks, and opportunities in a way that helps determine programs and policies.

Strategic intelligence is not a new form of analytical practice. Strategic intelligence and analysis is a well-established form of the craft of intelligence with a recorded history that goes back more than two millennia. Yet despite this, its acceptance within modern enforcement practice is comparatively recent, and even now, in the early twenty-first century, its development is still slow and patchy. A broad definition of strategic analysis in an enforcement setting is shown below. Note that even though the words used are those consistent with enforcement responsibilities, the ideas are so simple that the reader can readily see its adaptability to other environments as a policy and planning tool for government and nongovernment organizations and in the corporate world. The key definitional issues are the depth of study, the development of futuristic and holistic explanations and projections, and the purposeful use of analytical results as the basis for actively planning for such a future.

In modern usage, bringing into being this "new" form of intelligence and analysis has not been easy. It is often considered a specialization that seems to take up considerable resources in terms of the types of people and the esoteric range of information involved. In addition, there is a fairly widespread perception that strategic intelligence dwells on issues that have little relevance to daily operational needs. In these circumstances we have an explanation for the hesitation of agencies to take up strategic analysis as a legitimate—even fundamental—function of their intelligence activity.

Whereas the other, more established forms of intelligence (tactical and operational) have been codified and accepted for at least two decades,[1] the push to similarly categorize and codify strategic intelligence doctrine and principles of practice began only in the early 1990s.[2] These efforts have already achieved demonstrable results, although they do vary from country to country, and these variations tend to reflect the different levels of acceptance and commitment to using strategic research for better planning and improved preparedness.

The code of practice for strategic intelligence has been fully developed and successfully tested for several years now. Like most routines and protocols, it needs constant maintenance and fine-tuning, but the reality is that the process works well. It sets out a highly disciplined approach to crime research, whether it is on particular groups, laws, or criminal behavior phenomena. The approach defines every element of the activity necessary to undertake a form of "conceptual" analysis. It demands that practitioners accept the need for highly disciplined and orderly processing of data, whether hard or soft, yet at the same time encouraging the development of intuitive and creative thinking to enable a high degree of reasonable speculation about topics that are often vague and data-poor.

APPROACHES AND PROCESSES

The activities involved in strategic intelligence research are easily recognizable as part of the generic family of intelligence processes. Yet, because they have to be adapted to suit differences in focus and purpose, the overall approach and its process components have their own quirks and challenges. It is true that strategic analysis involves considerably more care and attention to planning and data gathering, and to analysis and inductive thinking, than might be expected for traditional operational intelligence.

However, it would be wrong to differentiate strategic from other forms of intelligence as if it were merely a question of process. What sets it apart is more basic than that: It is the underlying issue of purpose, and how that in turn defines and reshapes the process, that is important.

Strategic intelligence and analysis practice focuses on being able to creatively think one's way through issues at a macro level, yet constantly retain pragmatic links to the inevitable tactical and operational impact and outcomes. Even allowing for the depth of research that may be appropriate to some subjects, the activity always remains driven by a need to address just how the eventual results, conclusions, and recommendations can be anchored into operational readiness and response mechanisms. Certainly any strategic intelligence product that doesn't answer the question "What can we do about it at a practical level?" is incomplete.

Regardless of whether the consumers and clients of strategic intelligence are managers at force, government, or regional and district levels, the outcomes of the analytical work always have to be relevant in terms of what one does, how one does it, and what legal framework is appropriate. These are not just terms for use at national or state headquarters level; they are relevant to every level of decision making where programs and policies are planned and implemented. Nor is strategic intelligence necessarily the stuff of a future many years ahead. To be relevant and useful in modern policing and thereby foster an ability to adapt to changing criminal behavior and threat to public security, strategic planning must be flexible and adaptive to changing situations. The key to strategic planning is intellectually rigorous research. Just as important is the recognition that, to monitor continuing crime problems that loom large, strategic research should be conducted on a continuing—or, at the very least, recurring—basis.

This is all covered in considerable detail in the following chapters.

THE FUTURE USE OF STRATEGIC INTELLIGENCE

Strategic intelligence is a manager's tool. In the context of policing, for example, it is about decision making on important and overarching issues, not simply about targets for arrest. No manager can expect to function with full effectiveness if she doesn't have all the factual data; nor can one hope to properly proceed with enforcement unless there also exists a wide level of understanding of relevant problem issues. Strategic intelligence and analysis is key to providing this enhanced level of understanding, and it is always pitched at the level of command being exercised, an aspect of strategic product development not always understood by managers.

Far from the myth that strategic research is appropriate only to top level executives, it is in fact always relevant to those who need to have a strategic plan. If managers at district and regional centers need a planned approach to deployment and utilization of their forces, they also need a strategic understanding of the crime problems facing them, expressed in terms relevant to their own context.

If strategic intelligence continues to be regarded with hesitancy, perhaps even wariness, executives may look to tactical and operational results to provide direction toward the future. If this occurs, as it already does in some areas, then police forces everywhere run the risk of underachieving. For example, there can be little doubt that if we simply measure arrests as the prime indicator of success, then we have lost sight of the need to make sure that those arrests signify the most important and effective way of dealing with a particular type of crime. Antidrug activity, for instance, is typically a high-profile and intensely busy area for both intelligence and investigative activity. Yet without the broader understanding of how drug markets are changing and the impact of such changes in terms of user groups, user behavior, and so on, police antidrug squads are at risk of remaining busy at the expense of maintaining focus.

Sometimes this preoccupation with results competes with the real need to understand that some of our efforts could be put to better use in the sense of long-term outcomes. This is an area that continues to delay the introduction and acceptance of strategic intelligence practice into enforcement circles. Serious concern about crime and society cannot be fed by a diet of targeting intelligence alone. In times of resource constraint, there is a need for an intelligence service that delivers both types of outlook, not just one.

Strategic intelligence is different enough to demand that it be identified and programmed separately from targeting intelligence at the tactical and operational levels. Yet the two are complementary, not competitive. They need to closely interact and preferably, where organizational circumstances permit, they can actually integrate. The sharing of operational, target-driven perspectives can only serve the useful purpose of "educating" strategic specialists to street reality. The counter-flow of strategic overview can only aid targeting analysts in better understanding the sort of environment in which their criminal targets operate.

Senior executives in all walks of life, policymakers and lawmakers—including politicians—could gain benefit from the understanding that such insights, though occasionally unpalatable, provide real gain in illuminating the problems and providing both warnings of changed threat and forecast of potential opportunity. It is not uncommon for changes to come from the bottom up. However, in the case of strategic intelligence, the experience of the past several years has tended to show that unless "management" is committed to acquiring strategic insights into problem solving, there is little likelihood of real change driven by analysts themselves doing strategic research.

NOTES

1. Intelligence training for law enforcement was first codified and marketed by the U.S. Corporation Anacapa Sciences Inc. in the mid-1970s. Even now, much of the worldwide basic training in intelligence techniques owes its foundation to the continuing usefulness of the so-called Anacapa model.

2. This refers to the work done by my own company in Australia and subsequently in Canada and Europe.

2

Strategic Intelligence: Role, Definitions, and Concepts

Strategic intelligence and *strategic analysis* are terms used to describe a certain type of intelligence and analysis practice. If all intelligence is concerned with analyzing issues so that forecasts can be made, then strategic intelligence takes on a specific aura, that of aiming to provide the type of analysis that relates directly to achieving the overarching—that is, strategic—objectives of organizations, corporations, and governments.

This book aims at introducing the reader to ideas that may, in some cases, be new. In doing so, its intention is to avoid the semantics that sometimes obscure, rather than clarify, meaning. One school of thought holds a view that strategic intelligence is a tool, though one that is exclusively for the use of the upper levels of management. Indeed, many organizations would support a definition of strategic intelligence along the following lines, lending truth to this widespread but erroneous belief:

> One view is that strategic intelligence is the specific form of analysis which is required for the formulation of policy and plans at agency, corporate, national or international levels.

We certainly couldn't argue with this view, but is it the only valid one? Why limit strategic intelligence only to groups at those levels stated? Everybody has experience with the difference between major aims and en route problems to be addressed. Success in any endeavor is dependent upon a collection of activities to prop it up. To put this in a different way, it is common to note that while we may have major aims that voice our overall intentions, there are also sets of "smaller" objectives and goals that have to be met along the way if we are to achieve overall success. This applies as much to starting and running a business as it does to managing a department. By any definition, a *strategy* is directly concerned with the development and use of an overall plan that encompasses all the details necessary to arrive at the main aim. Certainly, organizations such as federal or provincial law enforcement agencies have overarching objectives to achieve. For them, some form of intelligence analysis that addresses all the features that might inhibit their achievement is an essential feature of forewarning and forward planning.

The development of strategies, however, is not necessarily confined to this higher level of organizational headquarters planning. Every organization or group that can separate its goals and objectives into the two streams of upper and lower decision making needs a strategy to reach success. All organizations, big and small, deserve such a service. Thus, for law enforcement strategic intelligence is as much a local commander's tool as it is a tool of the main capital city or national headquarters command. In sum, strategic intelligence serves the needs of all those groups who want to plan carefully for mainstream achievement in the foreseeable future, whether they are corporate, regional, familial, or social.

BASIC CONCEPTS ABOUT INTELLIGENCE

Defining the Terms

The word *intelligence* is commonly used in several ways, but, apart from the contexts involving intellect, two meanings stand out as being quite different:

- Intelligence can be used to describe both a *process* and an *activity*; therefore we talk about "doing intelligence work."
- On the other hand, intelligence is also used to denote the *final product* of that process. In other words, we can speak of "developing" or "possessing" or "having produced" intelligence.

Perhaps we should start with a definition. At its simplest, intelligence might be described as processed information. This is meant to convey a sense that raw information must be processed before it can be interpreted. But the word *process* does not convey any real sense of substance or exactitude. Indeed, if there is a key element that is missing in any definition that revolves around the idea of *processing*, it is that intelligence demands a high degree of *interpretation*, coupled with some inevitable, considered *speculation*. What we are really talking about is something rather more like *applied research*. No matter what field of work we are involved in, we have the following concerns:

- problems to solve;
- a need for good planning;
- data to search for, gather, and amalgamate; and
- answers to find.

No matter who your employer is or what topics and interests hold your attention, all intelligence practice has those key elements in common. Yet another definition in common use that embodies these ideas could be crafted from various entries in the *Concise Oxford English Dictionary* and others, and suggests that intelligence can be thought of as being described in the following terms:

> Intelligence is the sum of what is known, integrated with new information, and then finally interpreted for its meaning.

Intelligence is often described in terms of where and why it is being done. So terms like *military*, *political*, *economic*, or *crime* intelligence are commonly used worldwide. What does this terminology mean? Without doubt, these separate applications have some impact on both the way in which intelligence processing is carried out and the type of product being developed.

Types and Levels of Intelligence Activity

No matter how it is generated or used, it is conventional wisdom that intelligence is a practice driven by established principles. However, the practice does hold an integral flexibility that allows for modifications to suit the environment in which intelligence is to be applied. What this means, in essence, is that while intelligence doctrine is an established body of knowledge, intelligence practice is ever changing to meet emerging needs.

Apart from identifying differences in the organizational settings in which intelligence is used, intelligence also differs demonstrably in accordance with its intended purpose. Intelligence product used by managers and senior executives is clearly more likely to deal with issues that relate to their responsibilities than to those of line supervisors. Conversely, intelligence used in everyday routine operations will necessarily find little application at the corporate headquarters level.

In fact, it is this ability of intelligence practice to shape itself to fit the changing and particular needs of organizations and parts of organizations that, if properly used and flexibly applied, make it an extremely useful tool. It is a feature of intelligence, in almost every application, that it serves two distinct ends: One focus is for management, and the other is directed at the operational and functional level. Intelligence that is generated purely for management and executive use—and therefore deals with the overview questions of mission, goals, objectives, programs, and resource planning—is termed *strategic intelligence*, for it aids in the development of organizational strategies.

At the other end of the scale, intelligence that services the daily needs of supervisors and line managers and focuses on immediate, routine, and ongoing activities of the organization—the frontline functions, as it were—may be called *tactical* or *operational intelligence.*

Why does this apparent contradiction exist? The development of intelligence doctrine and practice, for enforcement use particularly, can be linked directly to its use in the military. In that environment, the most practical, intimate application of intelligence to identifying and dealing with target individuals and organizations has always been termed tactical. Activities involving operations against multiple targets of like or related character, where coordination of effort is the key, is called operational, and the intelligence designed to support it is operational intelligence. Typically, these operations might demand a high degree of comprehensive integration of input and preparedness (including intelligence) simply because of the organizational or geographic span of criminal/enemy/opposing activity.

In translating military doctrine to enforcement applications, intelligence terminology has undergone a shift in meaning. Routine, day-to-day activities in the world of enforcement are commonly called *operations* and, hence, target-oriented intelligence tends to be termed *operational intelligence* rather

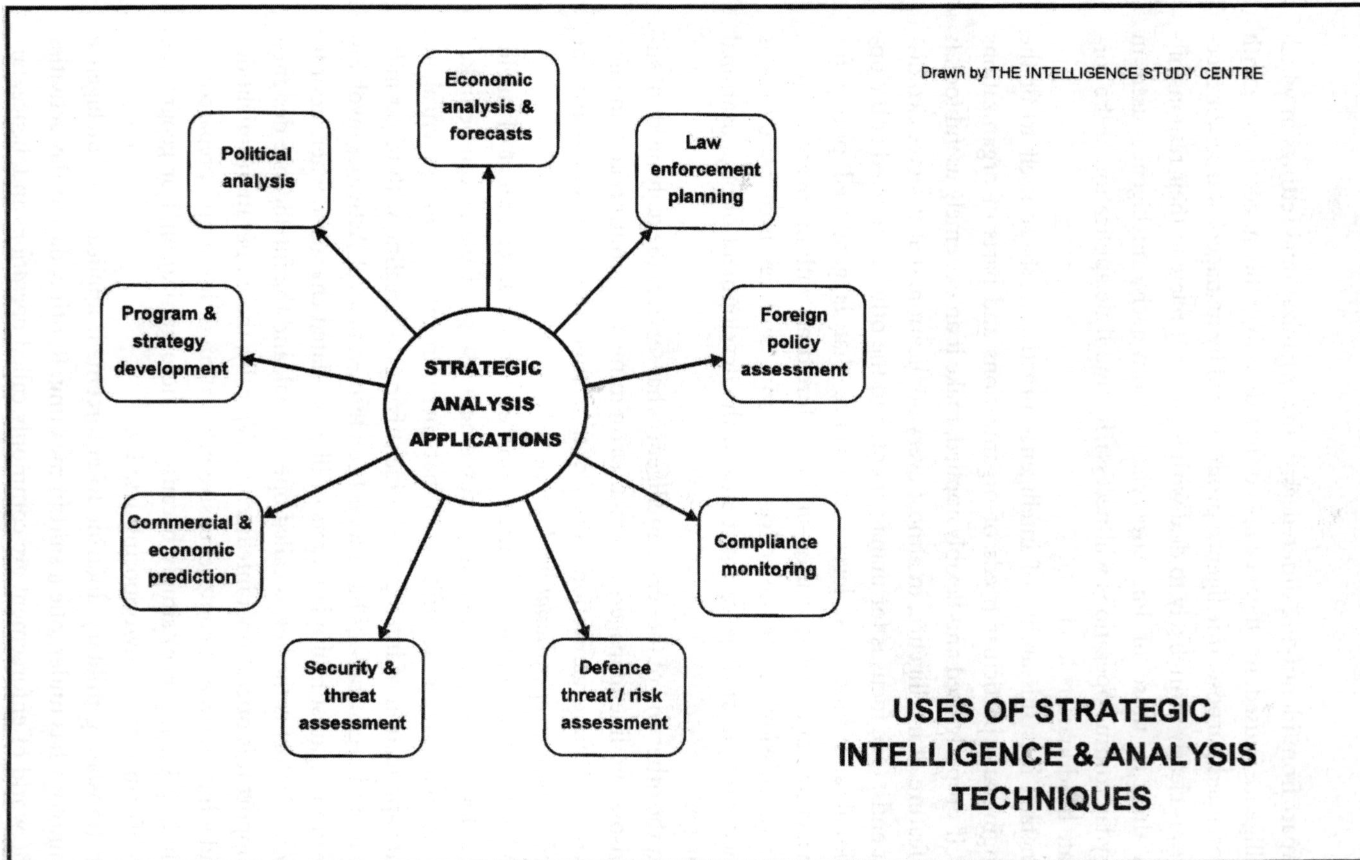

FIGURE 2.1
Uses of Strategic Intelligence

than *tactical* as military parlance would have it. Conversely, when it comes to more coordinated requirements for intelligence involving multiple targets and perhaps multiple jurisdictions, enforcement practice is to continue the reversal of military terminology and call it *tactical* (instead of *operational*). Even so, enforcement agencies rarely seem to take to this term *tactical* easily or comfortably, since it has little relevance to the way they naturally describe their activities. Instead, its use seems to be based on an acceptance that there are three tiers of intelligence, two of which—operational and strategic—have already been labeled, and thus the remaining category needs to be given a separate label: tactical.

The differing ways military and enforcement agencies describe their work is natural and understandable. But how should we deal with the apparent problem of terminology? One way is simply to accept that, for enforcement agencies, it might be more useful to stick to two tiers of intelligence: target-oriented, or operational; and deep, phenomenon-focused research, or strategic. This would mean that there is a need to recognize that some operational intelligence needs a more overarching, coordinated, and expansive view of the criminal world. Nevertheless, that may be a more sensible and acceptable approach than using the term *tactical* in a context that many find uncomfortable or obscure or even ambiguous.

I am not advocating wholesale change to long-established doctrine. In these circumstances, one solution can hardly be argued to be "more correct" than another. What we should accept is the practical reality that enforcement organization and activity is one for which the notion of operations is an all-encompassing idea free from divisions according to scale. In truth, there are small operations and large, multifaceted ones. In this setting, there is no need to establish what would be, for enforcement, somewhat artificial divisions and accompanying terminology labels. Operational intelligence can logically be accepted for what it is to police, customs, and similar agencies: a form of intelligence in which the prime focus leads toward action, whether it be against one or several targets.

Operational (or Target) Intelligence

In the field of law enforcement, for example, operational intelligence is generally concerned with the identification, targeting, detection, and intervention (or interdiction) actions taken against specific criminals or wrongdoers. Often,

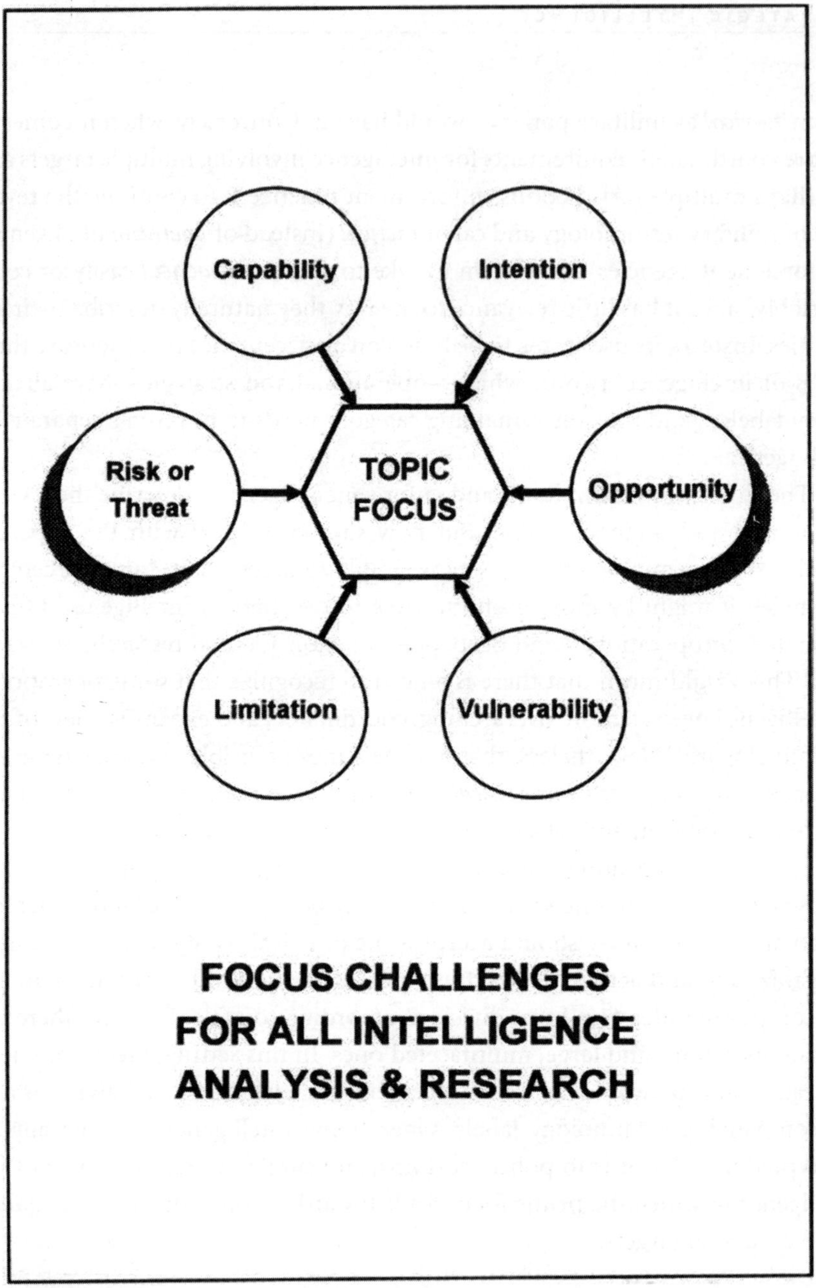

FIGURE 2.2
Focus Challenges

this intelligence involves identifying specific elements of illegal operations of any sort. These include, but are not limited to, syndicate networks; individuals or groups involved in unlawful activities; methods used (modus operandi, or MO); specific details about the capabilities, limitations, vulnerabilities, and intentions of the likely perpetrators; and their sources of support and finance.

Target intelligence, regardless of whether it is called tactical or operational, functions best when it is undertaken at close proximity to the grassroots working activity, and in conjunction and cooperation with local officers of that organization. This type of activity demands collection and input of routine data that cover current actions and reactions of both the target group and the organization's enforcement staff and follows the process shown in figure 2.3.

Strategic Intelligence

Strategic intelligence deals not with individual targets so much as with the overall trends that can be interpreted by looking at a large range of target activities. It is best considered as applied research into a particular phenomenon so that, in due course, the knowledge gained will help focus ongoing operations and provide the basis for policy and legislative review. These concepts are defined and explained in this section, and you should keep in mind the diagram of the basic intelligence process cycle shown in figure 2.3.

This basic model is the "standard" intelligence process taught formally to operational and analysis personnel from all around the world. It is easy to understand and easy to utilize; it is just as useful in intelligence and research work as it is to detectives and investigators. It is important that the analyst fully understand the steps as a precursor to going on to consider its adaptation toward the strategic intelligence process.

THE STRATEGIC INTELLIGENCE PROCESS

Intelligence and Law Enforcement

The process outlined in the previous section is taught as intelligence practice throughout the world. Any close study of that model will inevitably lead to the conclusion that good intelligence practice depends on having several common denominators:

- a properly structured and systematic process;
- orderly and disciplined application; and

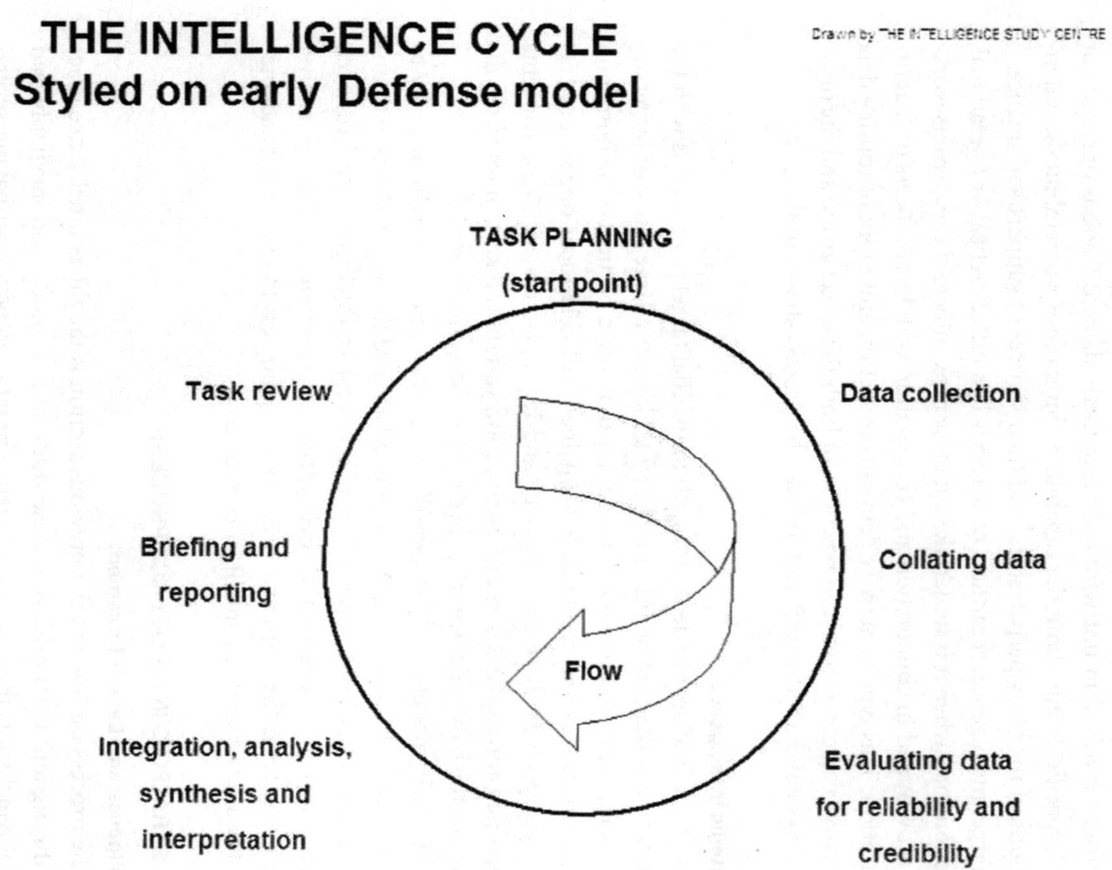

FIGURE 2.3
Intelligence Cycle

- a visible and established mandate by the organization's management to carry out this role.

Political, national security, and military intelligence might be thought of as being concerned with well-defined "enemies" and threats. This is not necessarily the experience in other areas of intelligence research. For example, there are certainly differences when it comes to applying intelligence in the areas of enforcement and compliance, regardless of whether it is in policing, immigration, customs, taxation, or any other of the myriad agencies having such functions. Those types of agencies have to meet quite different challenges. The tasks typically concern monitoring and detecting criminal activity carried out within the communities that could be described as being "under protection." Within this role, agencies deal with the entire community, the majority of whom may normally be basically honest and law abiding, some of whom are unscrupulous and greedy, and a few of whom are clearly criminally inclined. The role in enforcement intelligence has but a few basic similarities with other forms of intelligence, particularly in defense, since enforcement organizations are charged with identifying antagonists and adversaries, and only then evaluating their intentions, capabilities, limitations, and vulnerabilities.

However, regardless of the type of enforcement agency—regulatory or compliance—involved, it is elemental that the principal intelligence tasks will revolve around providing advice to assist officials in their ongoing role to protect the integrity of particular sets of responsibilities and laws.

Adapting the Intelligence Process for Strategic Purposes

The intelligence process outlined in the preceding section on basic concepts is a system that generally suits any intelligence task and purpose. What is special, then, about strategic intelligence? The simplest way to examine this question is to compare the two, point for point, and search for both similarities and differences. The result of this will be an adaptation of the intelligence process that, by adding or strengthening certain aspects, makes it suitable for consideration as a strategic intelligence plan.

To help understand these differences as well as the similarities, examine the diagram in figure 2.4 and compare it to that for the more "basic" intelligence processing, shown in figure 2.3, earlier.

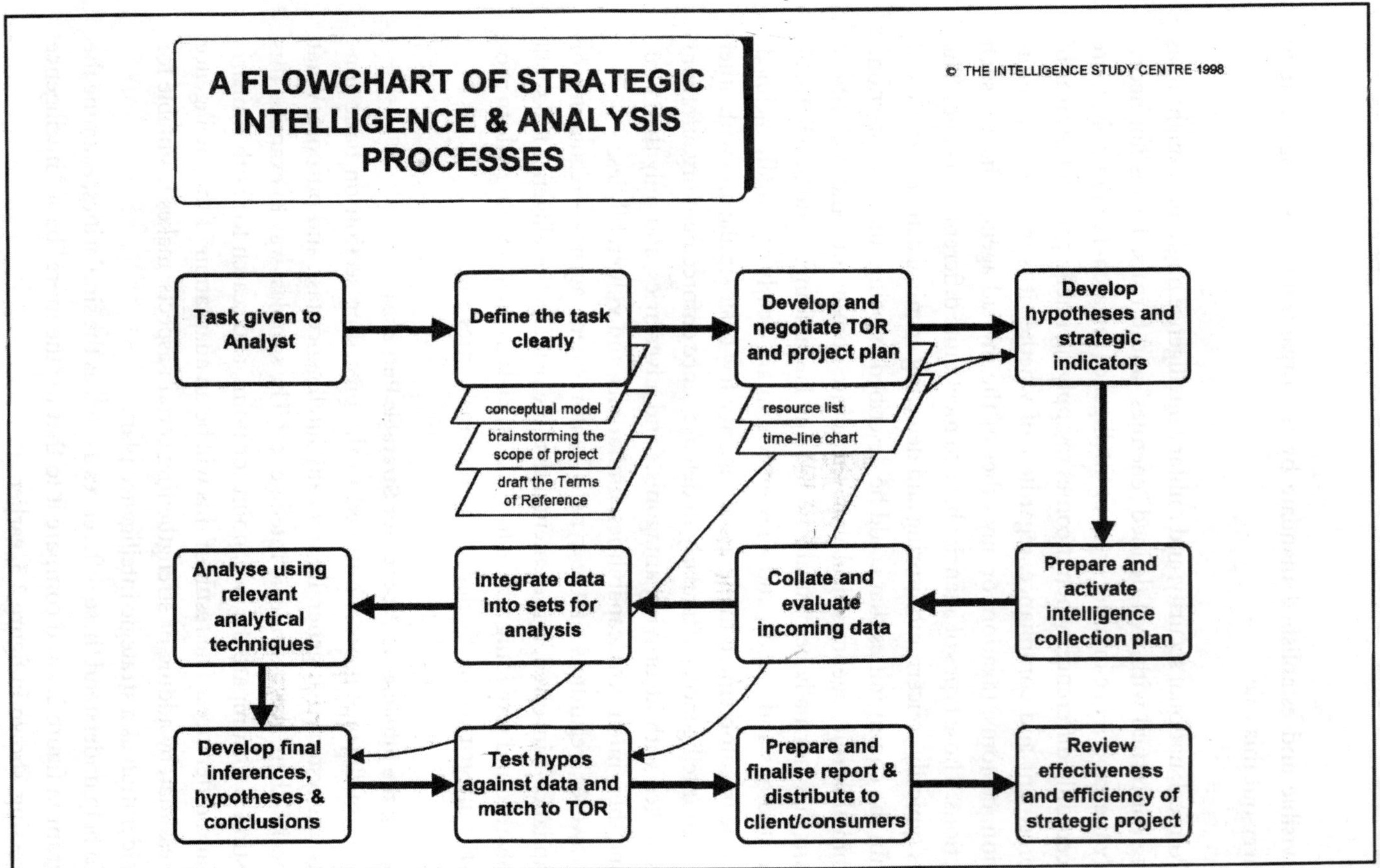

FIGURE 2.4
Strategic Process Flowchart

Differences between Strategic and Other Intelligence Processes

1. Tasking and Focus

Let us start the comparison by looking at tasking. Tactical intelligence deals with targeting specific wrongdoers; strategic intelligence is more concerned with examining problems in a way that provides understanding of the structure, purpose, and nature of the topic so that organizations can develop comprehensive plans to deal with it, not merely react by targeting individuals. However, there is even more to the differences than merely the nature and breadth of the task, as shown below.

- In tactical intelligence, the topic is usually one very well understood by those concerned with both the operations and intelligence services. Many of the staff will have had deep and continuing experience of the particular sort of crime being probed.
- For strategic intelligence topics, there is quite a high likelihood that the subject may be unfamiliar, or at least that you are being asked to investigate it to a depth far beyond the norms of your experience. In this climate, you need to think carefully about exactly what is wanted, in what depth of research, and with what limitations or constraints.
- It is essential that you explore the parameters of the topic in outline form, by way of initial research (what will be discussed as *conceptual modeling* later in this book), and negotiate an agreed directive (Terms of Reference) with your manager and the ultimate client.

While tactical intelligence is usually done in support of ongoing operations, and the analyst is thus answerable to the operational commander for quick and specific advice, strategic intelligence often serves the needs and interests of persons far removed from operational responsibilities. Strategic intelligence more commonly provides advice to executive-level "clients," not tactical commanders.

2. Planning the Strategic Research Project

Any intelligence plan will cover the timing and resources needed to undertake the task that has been assigned. In strategic intelligence work, the emphasis will change as the planner realizes the complexity involved in covering all the research necessary to deal with a major analysis project. Forward planning in this activity is absolutely essential if the analyst is to be able to bring together the required resources as needed.

By contrast, tactical planning may well be detailed, but an inherent feature of it is that as events unfold, the most important requirement may well be the ability to act quickly and flexibly to meet urgently changing operational circumstances. In this latter milieu, a tactical plan provides a starting point for guidance, and is rarely followed slavishly to its preordained conclusion.

3. Information Collection

There is a fundamental difference between tactical and strategic intelligence data collection planning and information gathering, primarily in terms of scope. If tactical intelligence is concerned with target identification, then the data collection challenge tends to be focused on individuals and their associations, plans, and capabilities. Strategic intelligence looks more toward gaining a deeper understanding of all the aspects of a particular crime phenomenon and its impact, near and far. For this purpose, data collection is aimed at gathering all sorts of data from every source imaginable, both within and outside of government circles.

4. Collating and Evaluating Data

Collating and evaluating data tends to follow much the same set of principles and practice, whatever the form of intelligence. Many analysts moving into strategic work will already have had experience of these parts of the process, and, in any case, they are reviewed and explained in greater detail in later in this book.

- If there are distinct differences, they are to be found in the fact that strategic intelligence demands the collection of a far greater range of "soft" data than would be the norm in tactical intelligence.
- Since you must gain an understanding of the nature, extent, and impact of a particular crime, and then make forecasts about future impact and options for handling it, there is automatically a high likelihood that you will find yourself collecting and analyzing qualitative, anecdotal, and impressionistic information.
- In many cases, the chances are that the analyst will encounter very high volumes of such data, unable to "measure" it in traditional ways, yet equally unable to reject it. These matters have implications for the way in which one

plans the collation (storage and recording) mechanisms, and in the approaches one might need to adopt for evaluation purposes.

5. Analysis

These same challenges flow into the analysis step in strategic intelligence. If the issues are complex and the data of widely varying quality, then it follows that the analyst needs to spend some considerable time working out just what types of analysis suit what categories of information. There is a much greater need to be able to handle particularly the qualitative information in a way that allows you to see meaning, even where no substantive proof or statistical reliability can be found.

6. Developing Some Workable Concepts and Hypotheses

As a continuation of this theme, the whole business of arriving at (or deliberately generating) strategic hypotheses is again less positive and conclusive than may be the case in tactical intelligence.

- There is a strong case for "taking an inspired gamble" on the balance of data currently available, producing useful hypotheses, and using them as a means to do further data gathering and checking.
- Where this differs from tactical intelligence is in the complexity, yet again, of trying to find the right sort of data to support or invalidate hypotheses. While it may be simple to assert, in a tactical case, that "X is involved in providing weapons to a gang," the reality in strategic projects will be that your statement of hypothesis is much more generalized and all embracing. Thus there is a demand for more extensive and wider data collection for the testing phase.

7. Reporting the Results of Strategic Research

Finally, there is the matter of reporting. Tactical intelligence is often an ongoing affair in support of an operation, and reports are generally given verbally in the form of briefings to commanders. Written reports are used much less often, since the operational requirement of the "client" at that level is for immediate, persuasive advice.

In strategic intelligence projects, the outcomes are almost certain to be written reports that provide a wealth of detail and comment. However, you may take the opportunity to provide an additional verbal briefing by way of introduction to the report, or to clarify and comment upon particular matters covered in it.

Summarizing the Differences

The specific objective for strategic intelligence is to provide accurate, long-range intelligence to enable effective high-level planning and management of law enforcement resources to meet the overall perceived threat. It is not an activity that is geared directly toward tactical law enforcement goals. Adaptation of the standard intelligence cycle, rather than wholesale change, is needed. The techniques and skills of intelligence officers are readily applicable to being used in solving strategic problems of analysis, providing that additional care is taken relative to the breadth and depth of the strategic topic being examined.

THE ROLE OF STRATEGIC INTELLIGENCE AND ITS IMPACT ON MANAGEMENT

Role

Strategic intelligence focuses on the longer-term aims of agencies, groups, organizations, and governments. It deals with important objectives and overall plans, and while it may or may not need to function in an operational environment close to the day-to-day action, this is dependent upon the level at which the strategic client is located. This form of intelligence may be localized at district or regional level, or it may be conducted at a headquarters level close to the organizational and national clients, whether they be corporate executives, senior government officials, group commanders, or politicians. In essence, in the law enforcement context strategic intelligence provides senior managers and executives (at *all* levels) with insight and understanding into the following:

- current and emerging trends;
- changes in the crime environment;
- threats to public safety and order;
- opportunities for controlling action and the development of counter-programs; and
- likely avenues for change to policies, strategies, programs, and legislation.

Unless strategic analysis is used as a legitimate component of decision making, there is a danger that managers will be unable to achieve their full potential in determining how to consider and resolve major issues. The whole purpose of strategic intelligence is to support the effective achievement of organizational objectives. From the point of view of providing a workable understanding of strategic intelligence, it really is irrelevant that these objectives be confined to a single

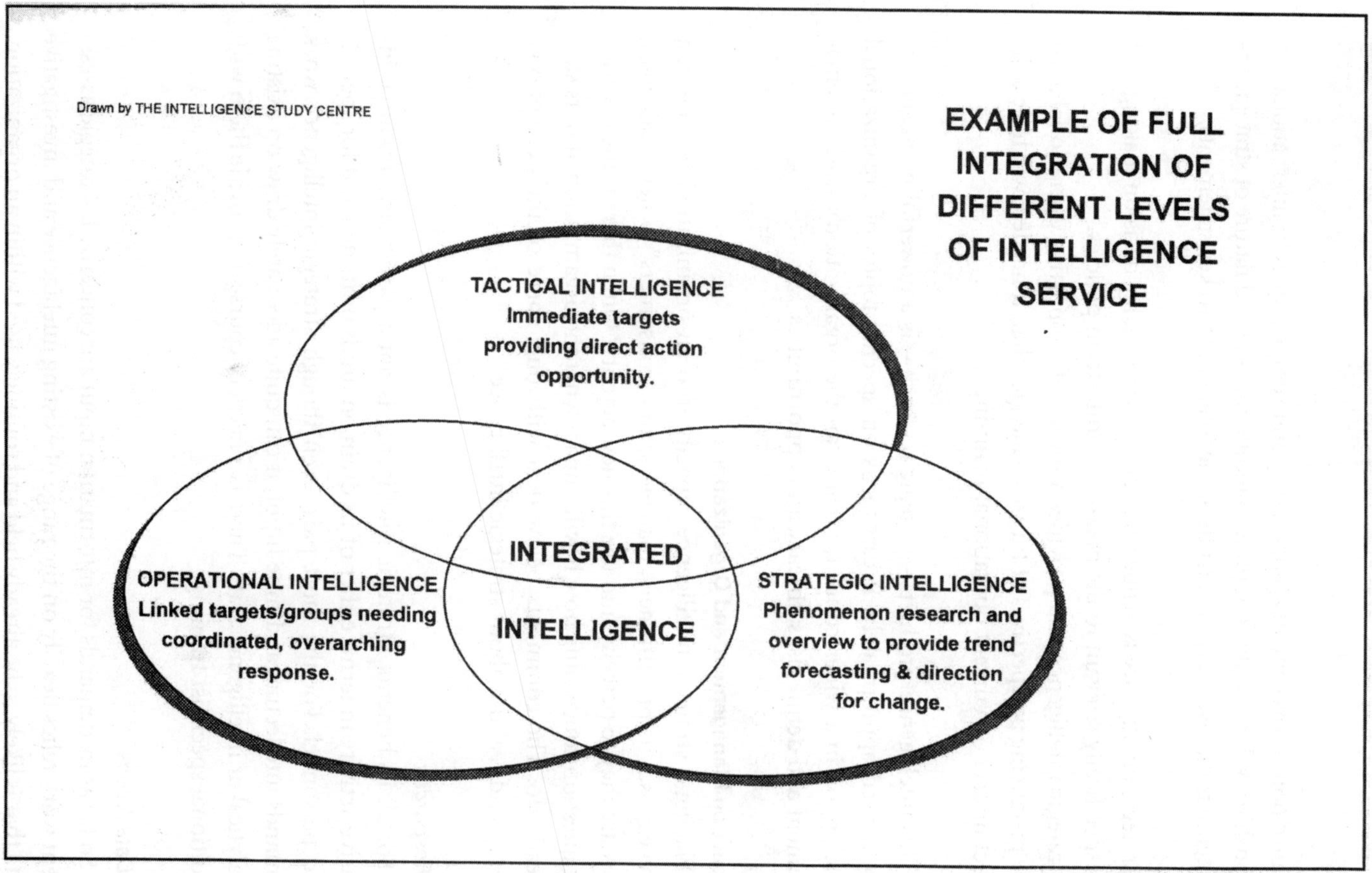

FIGURE 2.5
Intelligence Integration

organization, a government agency, a corporate empire, or even international relationships. What is critical in understanding the role and nature of strategic intelligence is that we accept the truth of the following two key statements:

- Strategic intelligence is deliberately designed to enable decision making that is specifically relevant to the making of long-term policies.
- Strategic intelligence also provides a means of supporting operational aims by producing perspectives of future challenges that, if heeded, will have a direct impact on current operational planning.

This intelligence product—strategic research—is a powerful management tool if used appropriately. It can focus on specific topics of organizational concern, or, in a wider context, it can scan the organization's working environment and define risks, threats, and opportunities.

Impact on Management and Organizations

Placing a strategic intelligence capacity into an organization for the first time exposes its practitioners, managers, and "consumers" to new challenges. How are they to perceive and use this new activity? Often there is the overriding question concerning how it will impact what the organization and its staff already do. The comments below deal with only some of the perceptions, myths, and realities about strategic intelligence.

1. Resources

For all its benefits, strategic intelligence is not a particularly resource-intensive activity in terms either of its drain on funds or its demand for specialized personnel. For the most part, even though strategic intelligence work demands intellectual and time input, it can quite adequately draw on existing analytical or intelligence staff. There is a need, of course, to provide them with additional specialist training.

2. Data Needs

So far as its demands for information input are concerned, strategic assessment work relies heavily on the range of existing intelligence and investigative data that is likely to be already held and routinely used within an organization.

- This information, regardless of the purpose behind its collection, will always provide a prima facie data bank for the commencement of strategic assessment activities.
- In fact, if there is a distinct difference in the use of data for strategic purposes, it lies in its application for different and wider purposes that relate specifically to corporate expectations, not operational ones.
- It is unlikely, however, that strategic analysis can survive only on information already being collected within or by an organization. The very nature of the topics likely to be of strategic interest is such that there will be a requirement for the collection of additional data from a wide range of sources.

3. Creative Thinking

Much of the background topic-related information often sought has been shown to be able to be obtained, not unsurprisingly, from open sources. The key to this rests with the creative thinking applied by the strategic analytical staff to their plans for exploring the topic.

- Indeed, it can often be observed that if strategic research within government suffers qualitatively in a recurring way, this can be linked to the standardized and routine approaches to the collection planning that seems to accompany the type of operational thinking prevailing within these organizations.
- In effect, strategic thinking demands a capacity and, more importantly, a willingness to conceptualize issues and plan research that deliberately is set up to go beyond organizational norms.

4. Bonding between Practitioners and Management

Strategic analysis activity provides the opportunity to forge close bonds between executive, managerial, and intelligence staff. At the same time, the nature of the activity actually demands this sort of "closeness" among the players.

This is pivotal to ensuring that those who need the service (the "clients") can relate effectively to its practitioners and providers, so that a candid exchange and negotiation of information, views, and suggestions can be facilitated. A close and professionally respectful understanding in the client/practitioner relationship is directly beneficial to meeting the objectives of all the stakeholders involved.

5. Reliability of Judgments and Forecasts

In all strategic intelligence work, the breadth and detail of the study being done inevitably means that the intelligence staff have to rely on their powers of judgment in developing assessments and projections. This is directly caused by the demands placed upon them to comprehensively analyze issues that are not only complex, but will usually have far-reaching impact.

The outcomes of a strategic intelligence project are *not* likely to be easily measured, certainly not in any close time frame. Indeed, their purpose is to inform the management decision-making process in such a way that managers and executives can consider issues against a set of considered, but nonetheless speculative, perceptions of change and opportunity.

CONCLUSION

Strategic intelligence has a key role to play in every area of management and corporate determination of future plans. Law enforcement and the related areas of compliance monitoring in governments everywhere are obvious areas for deployment of strategic analysis capability. The direction of operational policing against crime is absolutely dependent upon the focus that strategic analysis of issues can give in helping shape enforcement programs, policies, and strategies.

While intelligence practice is not particularly difficult, strategic intelligence is a relatively new phenomenon for enforcement. In this milieu, it has yet to be fully understood, both in terms of what it involves with regard to commitment and sheer hard work, and in the context of just how to get the best use out of it. Strategic intelligence and analysis is fundamental to good planning, and yet its practical and physical demands are small, particularly if your organization already has a commitment to intelligence to support operational activity.

What is required is a flexible understanding that this unique product follows a somewhat different path in terms of processing. Moreover, to handle the challenge of analyzing strategic issues demands a commitment to dealing with projects in an imaginative and creative way to facilitate the research involved. Any attempt to reduce strategic analysis to a highly regimented and process-driven approach, with all the traditional reliance upon measurement of activity to "prove" that the project is proceeding well, will just not work.

It is true that strategic intelligence and analysis is a highly disciplined and orderly form of the genre, but it requires nurturing, understanding, and a supportive environment if this form of research is to provide truly useful outcomes for senior executives.

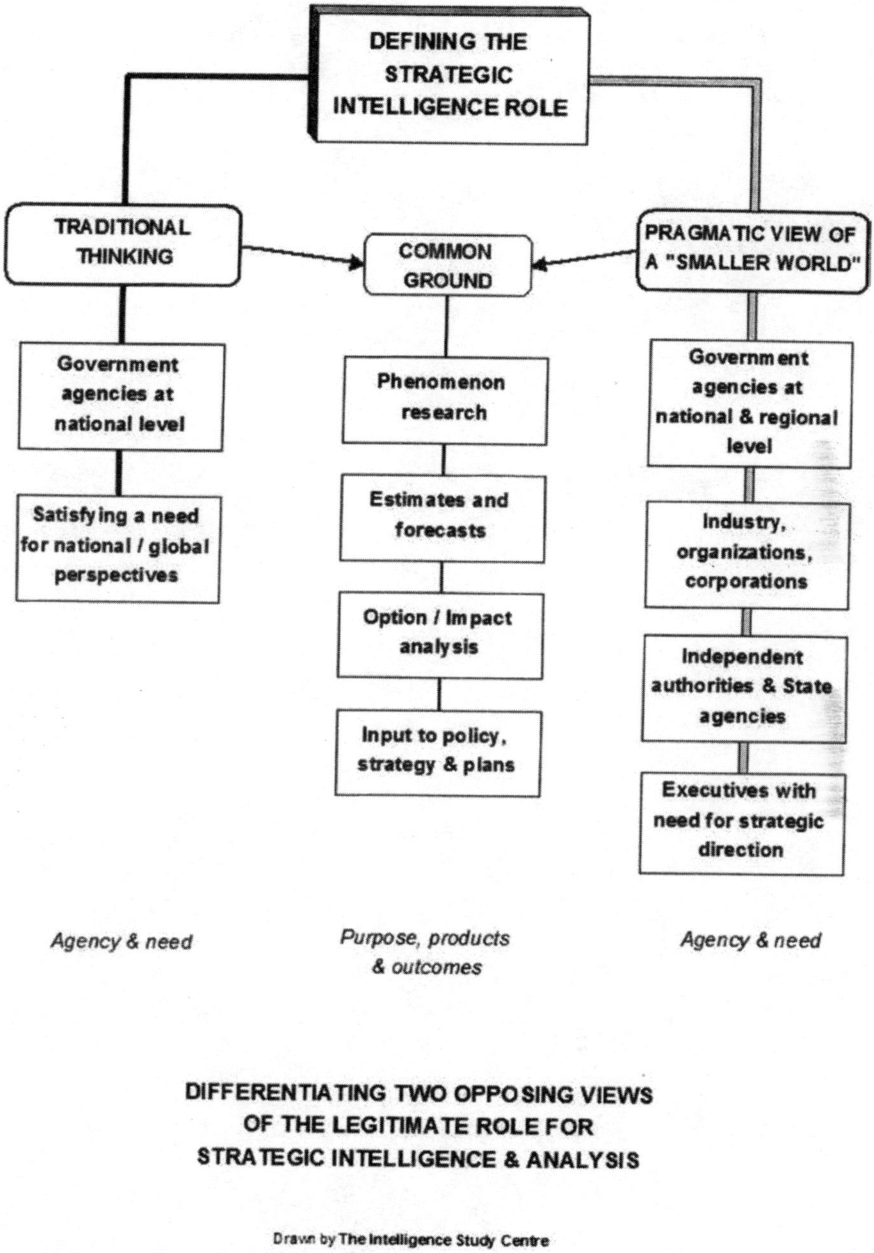

FIGURE 2.6
Defining the Strategic Intelligence Role

II

CRITICAL OBSERVATIONS

3

Overview of the Implementation and Impact of Strategic Intelligence

This chapter[1] covers an international view of the development, introduction, and implementation of strategic intelligence within law enforcement. The opinions are derived from the author's personal observations and close working association with specific intelligence units and their parent organizations. The purpose of this chapter is not simply to provide information about the background and the current situation concerning strategic intelligence. While this sort of information giving is essential to ensure that we remain up-to-date about what is going on around us, the real focus here is inevitably on working out how to improve the current state of affairs to the benefit of our clients and ourselves, as professionals in the field of intelligence.

Many adaptations of strategic intelligence mentioned in this chapter go beyond traditional law enforcement applications, and the purpose of citing them here is to indicate the universal flexibility and usefulness of strategic intelligence. However, the main focus remains concentrated on enforcement in all its aspects, and on probing the relationship between strategic intelligence and our ability to both better understand and explain the present and to explore and prepare ourselves, as well as our clients, for the future.

A dose of real honesty is relevant here. It can be fairly claimed that, at least in some countries, strategic intelligence has either been successfully introduced or is in the process of being introduced. These countries and agencies are mentioned in comments and notes elsewhere in this book and, while pleasing from a professional advancement point of view, it should be of concern that so few of the major agencies are committed to the objectives of properly establishing a strategic intelligence capability. It seems to be the case that the original enthusiasm is in some danger of being diminished, blunted, and marginalized.

HISTORY OF THE EARLY YEARS

A useful starting point for this chapter may be to provide some brief background that explains how strategic intelligence came to be introduced formally into enforcement and my role in this. In 1989 I wrote my first paper about strategic intelligence and its essential application to law enforcement planning. My belief at that time was that strategic intelligence had barely been given a mention in any of the available literature about law enforcement and its intelligence support structures and mechanisms. The popular and respected intelligence authors of the 1980s (Maartens, Morris, and Peterson, to name but a few) rarely, if ever, mentioned strategic intelligence, and, even then, in no substantive detail. Of course, intelligence journals from the military and national security areas frequently referred to the genre. However, it was and to some degree still remains my observation that no one had bothered to focus on this topic, to think it through, and to articulate the concepts and their potential application in modern law enforcement or any other activity of government.

Early articles were aimed at consciousness raising by writing about the usefulness of strategic intelligence for meeting increasing demands that law enforcement become less reactive to the changing world crime scene and instead focus more positively on looking forward and forecasting (the concept of *proactivity* so often mentioned). Hand in hand with this was a program of research that resulted in the development of the core of what has become an accepted "model" for strategic research in law enforcement.

Perhaps more important than merely providing training was my then agency's commitment to using strategic intelligence to develop risk-and-opportunity analysis of certain crime phenomena in Australia using the strategic intelligence model developed.[2] The first real test of the concepts and doctrine came during 1990 and 1991, when the government requested a strategic assessment of the relationship between the criminal and social environment involving illegal drugs. The purpose was to examine these issues and recommend changes to health, education, social, and police policies and to the entire body of Australian law affecting such issues. A by-product of the task was to test the model itself as the basic research mechanism. We were to make it available for peer-group review and critical appraisal, and then publish it in the form of a guidance handbook for use by Australian enforcement agencies—which we did in 1991 and again in 1997 following a substantial rewrite.

Finally, it is appropriate to point out that I had—and still have—no illusions that the model is static or "carved in stone." The research model is constantly being fine-tuned with the benefit of increasing experience in applying it to a growing variety of applications. It is worth noting, though, that no other model was offered as alternative thinking, then or since, by member agencies of the law enforcement community.

PROGRESS IN THE 1990s AND BEYOND

Since 1990, the cause of strategic intelligence has been advancing steadily on several fronts in terms of diverse applications and international acceptance. A consistent theme, though, is that there are two principal objectives that need to be jointly achieved if strategic intelligence is to become as successful and useful a component of law enforcement planning as it has to national defense and security.

- First, there is still a continuing need to convince senior managers and executives that good planning must be preceded by good analysis, and that strategic intelligence is a particularly apposite tool for this purpose.
- Second, there is of course the need to ensure appropriate training be given as widely as possible in order to educate and empower analysts—at all levels and from all walks of life—to understand what is involved in applying their skills to strategic issues.

Changing Managers' Beliefs

To meet the main objective—that of developing management conviction—many speeches and papers have been presented and published, explaining and praising the pivotal nature of strategic research as the foundation for understanding and preparedness for changes in criminality. For some agencies, educating and persuading managers about this vision has been achieved through special training workshops conducted specifically for middle to senior staff who, in their normal work situations, become the "clients" of strategic analysis. Such workshop opportunities are generally few and far between, with significant differences among the approaches taken by different executive "boards of management." For example, of the major police forces in the world, very few have had access to the sort of familiarization that is essential to change thinking and open up an opportunistic view of the value of strategic analysis.

One major inhibitor to spreading this doctrine has been the lack of availability of managers and executives to participate in training that has been largely described as "unnecessary" because of existing levels of management awareness. It has been interesting to observe that although it can fairly be said that all senior police managers have some familiarity about intelligence and its potential, few indeed have more than a superficial level of understanding about the specific benefits of strategic analysis and, as a balancing element, their obligations (as clients or managers) to help make any strategic research system function effectively. On the plus side, wherever the manager workshops have taken place[3] there has been a direct increase in their interest in acquiring strategic intelligence product to aid in operational and policy decision making.

Helping the Analysts

As to the preparation and nurturing of analysts to undertake strategic research, there has been a continuing program to bring practitioner-level training to intelligence agencies throughout Europe, Canada, and Australasia. Courses have attracted attendance from a wide variety of agencies, law enforcement as well as others, involving many hundreds of trainees. It is pleasing to note that the course design and teaching strategies used have become increasingly acceptable as "benchmarks" for several agencies of world repute,[4] and that the high demand for such training reinforces the belief that the strategic intelligence "message" is getting through. These courses focus on principles as well as application. They are directed toward getting analysts to become skillful at conceptual analysis, relying on other, more quantitative "tools" only as the requirements of any particular case dictate. In terms of applying strategic intelligence to real-life problems in law enforcement and regulation, it now has an established track record of use in examining and recommending strategies for handling many major enforcement and compliance problems. Examples include:

- illegal drugs;
- domestic violence;
- exploitation of minors (including child abuse and pedophilia);
- violent crime;
- immigration and the illegal movement of refugees;
- terrorism and other forms of politically motivated violence and crime;
- organized crime in its many forms and ethnic groupings;
- financial crime, including money laundering;
- large-scale fraud of many varieties; and
- environmental crime, including pollution control and protection of endangered wild flora and fauna.

It is worth looking further at the contrast between law enforcement and its utilization of strategic intelligence, comparing it with other adaptations and applications, and taking note of the way in which the strategic intelligence concepts and principles, as they are taught, have been picked up and adapted by nonpolice organizations. This is important as a signal of the universal usefulness of proper research at this level—providing analysis and illuminating issues above the level of our usual daily preoccupation with operational matters. Such projects and applications have included the following:

- in the field of environmental regulation, the examination of wildlife issues in the context of the impact of crime and other forms of loss on conservation and protection policies and laws;
- consideration of the broad trends in industrial development and the potential risks associated with pollution control regulations and compliance mechanisms, and their abuse, negligence, incompetence, or deliberate avoidance; and
- in the area of government tax regulation, the use of strategic intelligence to both chart the trends in avoidance and minimization schemes and to conduct impact analysis associated with potential changes to tax systems—looking at all aspects including economic implications and criminal opportunities.

Overall, there seems to be no real argument that strategic intelligence and analysis are useful tools for addressing enforcement interests and facilitating forward planning and threat minimization. But reality falls well short of promise, even after these past several years of experience and growth. Mere statements of support and understanding by police agencies for this "new" intelligence tool demonstrably overreach the realities involved in commitment to effective implementation. This is not a phenomenon limited particularly to any country but rather one that can be universally observed. The key issue here is that while the acceptance of strategic research within enforcement circles in Europe has gone well beyond the experience of other countries, there are nonetheless continuing difficulties in matching the hyperbole of the language of commitment with the reality of resourcing and management everywhere.

CURRENT SITUATION: CHALLENGES FOR THE PROFESSION

Even given the experience of some ten years of implementing strategic intelligence programs, there are many issues that can almost certainly be improved upon. We should recognize and acknowledge just how much ground has been made in the last several years to bring the image of strategic analysis to the forefront of law enforcement intelligence thinking. There are many positives to be proud of, but, as with anything new, there are still many attitudes and behaviors that need to be improved or altered if strategic analysis is to deliver its promises. This is possible only if we face up to the deficiencies and try to develop strategies for change.

A basic issue in explaining and justifying the use of strategic intelligence to law enforcement managers hard-pressed for results and resources has always been the nexus between strategic intelligence and operational[5] intelligence. A fundamental principle of our profession is that all intelligence activity serves specific needs, but the total effort must support the whole of the agency's role and responsibilities. In other words, to be most effective, intelligence must provide help for all that agency's interests. Operational intelligence is fine in its place. However, it does little for upper-level planning, and vice versa.

There can be no real argument that any one form of intelligence is in competition with any other, or is more useful or meaningful than any other. Each is part of a whole, and each contributes in its own way to specific vested client interests and goals within the organization.

It seems that this principle is still seen as both logical and acceptable, and indeed the marketing and advertising of intelligence—and we should acknowledge that part of intelligence functioning is to sell itself—are effective in reaching out to responsible and concerned audiences, such as managers and executives. However, something is still seriously deficient, for it is obvious from the way in which strategic intelligence is being implemented that there are, in fact, tensions between the two separate, sectoral intelligence interests.

Tensions and Pressures

What is the problem? This section is hardly the place for a lengthy dissertation on all that is wrong in this respect, but there are some main points that can and deserve to be made and considered. The issues involved include the following.

Expectations of police accountability for expenditure and performance outcomes are often interpreted as meaning that units are expected to report "satisfactorily" on quantifiable outcomes and activities such as:

- cases;
- prosecutions;
- arrests;
- seizures; and
- charges.

The vision of policing and regulation as a protective deterrent for society is thus sublimated in favor of measurable "hit rates."

- This leaves intelligence to be judged specifically—and almost solely—on the basis of its worth in terms of input to the hit rate.
- Those who measure and judge the success and usefulness of intelligence are increasingly encouraged to find a direct link between the intelligence product and the resulting investigative successes (arrests, for example).

Wherever strategic intelligence has been introduced into a police culture, it has largely been accorded some special status consistent with its focus on in-depth research into issues of significance to upper management levels.

The results from such special treatment can be often observed to include the following:

- The selected analysts are, for the most part, "different" from the norms ordinarily associated with operational intelligence. This is understandable given the purpose and demands of strategic intelligence, but there is a consequence that may be as unintended as it is unfortunate: that such selection practices can impart an image of elitism that tends to distance the strategic analyst from the concerns of everyday intelligence functioning.
- In almost every intelligence unit visited across various continents, strategic intelligence is organizationally separate from operational intelligence activities. While it is understandable that there is some separation from the norms by virtue of the level of client and the types of topics and depth of focus, this isolation often extends to intellectual and emotional separation of the various parts of the intelligence apparatus.
- The end result is one in which each "half" of the intelligence effort may end up with diminished contact with the other, a decrease in mutual understanding and sharing of ideas about different aspects of common issues, and a loss of mutual respect.

This separation of the intelligence interests also tends to drive a wedge between the respective client groups themselves, and field commanders and central office executives can easily develop a highly parochial and partisan view of the whole world of intelligence, depending on their respective needs for intelligence support.

Finally, it is quite commonly observed that field units, for example, and their attached, supporting intelligence cells are ignorant of the relevance and potential value of strategic intelligence. By the same token, strategic intelligence units and their client groups can—and do—develop a disdain for acknowledging any value in the information and interpretations that derive from operational intelligence.

The fundamental truth in all of this is that such situations, if allowed to go unchecked, can create two mutually exclusive intelligence apparatuses within an organization. Two outcomes would be likely in such circumstances. Each would be deprived of the real input and support of the other. The client organization would thus be ultimately deprived of the total intelligence services it both needs and deserves.

Management Understanding and Awareness

As senior executives and managers change, so does an agency's consciousness and awareness levels about strategic intelligence and all it can stand for. Such changes may simply be limited to a lessening of enthusiasm, and a slow (or perhaps not-so-slow) reduction in real levels of resource support for strategic intelligence work.

From a professional intelligence standpoint, often the changes in the level of understanding and awareness of strategic intelligence concepts are arguably even more serious. They can be marked by a shift in the pattern of topic tasking operated by the agency, with a noticeable movement away from truly strategic issues requiring comprehensive and meticulous research, toward projects that have more in common with complex operational matters (and their recommendations for immediately useful operational by-products). Every time this happens, it is the agency that is the poorer—by underachieving at the strategic end of the spectrum in favor of enhancing input into the operational focus of activity.

It is pointless to argue with any rational decision by an agency's executive to shift resource allocation to meet changing priority needs. But doing so in the manner described, where the decision can be based to a significant degree upon ignorance of the opportunities likely to be missed, is neither logical nor, in the long run, beneficial to that agency's best interests.

Time Horizons

None of the foregoing observations and criticisms, however, should be confused with the very real issues of "timeliness" that now increasingly affect our entire approach to strategic intelligence servicing of an organization.

Perhaps the least understood issue relating to the development of strategic intelligence is the time horizon that must be addressed in the forecasting process. It should be recognized that many different belief systems have grown up in the world of intelligence concerning this issue, with the impact of polarizing intelligence thought to no good end. The most common point of difference surrounds the nature of strategic intelligence and its definitional setting. One belief system suggests strategic research is only relevant to "supreme commanders" (for want of a better term) and top-ranking executives and that, in consequence, such research is meant to provide typically five- or ten-year outlooks.

The fact is that these "definitions" are neither accurate nor applicable universally to all users of strategic intelligence. There can be little argument with such views, providing that they are always understood strictly in the context from which they stem. These opinions are based within the relatively limited framework of defense (and perhaps, at a stretch, national security) considerations. In these settings, lengthy forward warning on changing risk pictures was historically tied to the time periods needed for nations to prepare themselves to cope with threatening change.

We generally acknowledge that the development of intelligence culture in law enforcement and other related areas of government and business thinking owes its genesis to military practice. However, these historical links should not, in any way, constrain the flexibility of adapting that model to best meet enforcement requirements. Certainly the military definitional thinking about strategic intelligence as providing five-to-ten-year (and beyond) strategic preparedness thinking cannot seriously be accepted as the norm for agencies that have to be much more pragmatic and reactive to ever-changing circumstances in the criminal environment.

The urgent and pragmatic requirements of government agencies and big business have to "drive" the application of strategic intelligence doctrine to produce strategic outlook assessments that suit their decision-making time frames. What cannot be supported is the sort of inhibited thinking that suggests that the original military model discussed above is applicable in all circumstances. Plainly it is not. If, for example, the enforcement community needs urgent and early warning of major change and, once warned, needs to be able to react within the pragmatic constraints of budgets and resourcing issues, then the strategic intelligence service has to devote at least a significant component of its outlook to meet these very real user requirements. This is not to say that the long-term five- and ten-year outlooks about social change and criminal development are unnecessary. Rather, an equally relevant focus for strategic research must be to provide commanders (particularly field executives) with the sort of strategic warning that matches their time frame demands. If this means that intelligence units must start to provide both long- and medium-term outlooks to allow for long- and medium-term strategy and program development, then how could one argue with such logic?

The polarization of views mentioned previously and the passionate arguments that accompany it do nothing for the profession and even less in real terms for the client. It is surely time for the intelligence community to remind itself that our role is to provide service, not to adopt precious and lofty points of view that prevent this.

Managing the Strategic Process

To the uninitiated it might seem that the easiest part of setting up and running a strategic intelligence service is the business of deciding what topics to explore. This is far from the truth, and although many agencies already have strong corporate-like structures that provide for a group approach to operational and intelligence planning, many others do not. In these latter circumstances, the problem that emerges is that any client may approach the strategic intelligence resource with a problem to examine. Typically, the single most important determinant of the type and amount of work that unit will undertake is often a question of "volume" and the place of a topic in the queue of work awaiting attention.

- This does not address the organization's need in any total sense; it merely deals with those clients who take the time to make an approach to the strategic intelligence service.
- What is needed is some mechanism for the organization corporately to consider the competing ideas and requests of its senior executive clients and determine the limits and priorities of the list of work to be transmitted to the strategic intelligence cell.
- Unless such a scheme is established, the outcomes will inevitably disappoint at least some clients and end up creating frustration for the strategic analysts themselves. On the other hand, any scheme to effect control over strategic tasking should not operate solely on a directive basis—that is, one that limits the strategic intelligence staff to doing only those things that are "approved." Indeed, one of the significant strengths of strategic research is its capacity to identify useful leads for further examination, and this initiative should be applauded rather than inhibited. Fostering this sort of sense of intelligent adventurism is a key task for the close levels of supervisor/manager, and yet, without it, those at the corporate peak would likely be ignorant of developing themes and prospects.

In providing these observations on developmental and implementation shortcomings in the history of applying strategic intelligence to law enforcement, the focus so far has been on the key role of managers and executives. There is one last such issue to discuss before I move on to talking about the difficulties created, or at least perpetuated, by strategic intelligence analysts themselves.

Intelligence, like any other activity, has to be "managed," in the broadest sense of that term, if it is to become and remain an effective pursuit. In many areas of law enforcement, the introduction of strategic intelligence has fostered strong expectations. These surmise that this vital new intelligence product will illuminate issues in such a way that agencies can plan their future to cope with the good and the bad—the challenges, risks, and opportunities mentioned elsewhere in this section. Strategic intelligence for law enforcement is, after all, about analyzing and forecasting shifts and changes in crime patterns, and in social attitudes and societal vulnerabilities to crime. It is about providing governments with a direct capacity to identify and take advantage of opportunities to combat or minimize or even forestall criminal enterprise.

In the case of operational intelligence, the unit and its officers and analysts operate in close proximity to their clients, which are the operational unit leaders, detectives, and investigation cells and the like. Such proximity tends to facilitate the feedback mechanisms essential for guidance of that sort of intelligence effort.

Strategic intelligence presents a far more difficult challenge. While field commanders will ultimately gain some direct or indirect benefit from strategic analysis of issues, they are not the real clients of this service. An agency's senior management and executive level is the absolute client for strategic analysis. Yet, because of the nature of hierarchical structures, there will always be some "distance" in structural terms between the strategic intelligence staff at the lower end of the organizational spectrum, and the executive at the upper end.

Effective management is pivotal in making sure that executive interest in a strategic issue is able to be translated into clearly understood project tasking. The mere hierarchical "distance" between the parties must not inhibit the communication so essential between client and provider. Yet, in this context, some common problems occur.

- There is often some actual physical separation of the client from the strategic project leaders and staff, forcing a reliance on translation of information and orders through successive layers of intermediate managers and the vagaries of communication systems and protocols. There are obvious delays in this process, with messages filtering down—and back up—between those communicating. Moreover, the time lost and the sheer effort of trying to communicate clearly without the ability to respond and react quickly brings its own sense of being "detached" from each other's reality, with the result that the work may not quite address all of the concerns of the client. On the other hand, the client may never get to properly understand exactly what might have been achieved had the communication mechanism been more able to facilitate the exchange of views so essential to planning strategic research.

- There is also some considerable difficulty for managers and supervisors at all levels in being able to comprehend that the interaction between client and strategic intelligence provider is a dynamic one. Both parties absolutely need to share and explore ideas and understanding not only of what is required, but of the purpose to which it will be put and the opportunities and costs (in all terms) associated with specific issue study. Transmission through intermediaries creates an environment of oversimplification and potential misunderstandings that will—and do in real life—threaten the quality and usefulness of the strategic study.

PROBLEMS FOR ANALYSTS

Perhaps it is useful here to begin with a provocative view about strategic intelligence. Contrary to the opinion of some observers, who are often not strategic practitioners, I believe that strategic intelligence activity is not really "hard" to do. The techniques and mechanisms are relatively simple and generally well within the competence levels of good analysts and researchers. Conversely, if there are problems about implementing strategic intelligence programs within agencies and governments, they are problems that have little connection with the intellectual difficulty of the milieu itself.

The difficulties are those of acceptance that such an intelligence service is even necessary, let alone possible and practicable. The law enforcement community seems too easily capable of losing sight of some of the lessons of history, of events in which strategic analysis has played an important role in shaping the future planning of national agencies and large organizations. For whatever reason, the law enforcement environment seems to create its own expectations that everything can—and should—be done immediately, with outcomes that are certain, or at least highly predictable over a short time span.

One may think that this attitude is something that is the concern solely of managers and executives, but the fact is that these feelings transmit themselves all too easily to intelligence practitioners who have to live in this sort of "real world." It is the impact of this thinking on them, and their reaction to it, that is worth considering.

In a teaching environment, it is relatively easy to get agreement from student strategic analysts that the model and techniques will work and should be put to use. Why is it, then, that so many examples of strategic analysis and its reporting fall short of expected standards? It is now commonplace to find units and organizations in which certain strategic studies are held up as shining examples of useful input to organizational decision making. In others, the concepts, the process, and the potential outcomes are scorned as being too vague, too imprecise, too far-reaching, too indirect in meeting organizational needs, and so on.

There are probably two main reasons for this phenomenon. First, from a management perspective the notion of "usefulness" is a shifting standard, and can change from month to month as organizational stresses increase and priorities change to address new requirements. Any strategic study project is likely to be started on the basis of assuming a certain set of interests and priorities exist. Thus, those who are doing the analytical work must be notified of any changes to this setup, since they have the potential to affect the direction and even the entire rationale for the project.

Second, many analysts become influenced by managerial and client pressures to find quick solutions to what are complex problems. Their solution to this dilemma is often found and solved (if such is the word) by the analyst truncating the project design, limiting the search for appropriate data, and changing the entire careful methodological approach. The purpose of doing this is to substitute a single hypothesis-driven direction to achieve desired outcomes (by management) in lieu of the more sensible, wider approach that involves examining all dimensions of the issues.

Certainly it cannot be argued that strategic projects are immune from normal organizational tensions of time, funds, resources, and data; these are unavoidable elements of law enforcement intelligence life. If these issues create stress for the project, then the solutions that ought to be considered by the analyst must be handled in such a way as to solve the problems but nonetheless maintain a pragmatic hold on the original visions and horizons. Changing the methodological approach to a particular strategic project is not the problem; the research doctrine is quite flexible in all respects. However, when the research requirement is accompanied by any strongly directive approach—most often from clients or managers who may be acting personally or, conversely, giving voice to institutional beliefs—this will suggest answers and so inhibit real analysis in favor of justifying views already held. This sort of action-and-response cycle will almost always pervert the capacity of intelligence to produce proper research-driven outcomes.

The analyst is in an invidious position in these cases: trying to meet the genuine expectations and requirements of clients and yet being expected to ensure that balance and a sense of perspective are maintained, avoiding being led to unwarranted conclusions merely because of the client's prejudices. In trying to deal with such pressures, it is most often the analyst personally who has to suggest corrective action and, at the same time, try to find "acceptable" ways to inform the client of the rationale for effecting change to his original directives.

The message that deserves reinforcing here is simply that the model is a useful and highly adaptable framework for tackling any strategic analysis or research project. It requires careful planning to implement properly and effectively, and yet it is flexible enough to handle strategic issues, whether they be in law enforcement or any other analytical environment. At the same time, this inherent element of flexibility should not be mistaken to mean that parts of the process can easily be excised or substantially altered without creating some significant—and often disappointing—outcomes. As mentioned above, because the strategic project needs to be carefully planned at the outset, the analyst should address any subsequent changes equally carefully. New or revised plans must be made to take account of the changed circumstances. This is no one's responsibility but the analyst's.

Another issue that we should recognize is the propensity of some—perhaps many—individual analysts to turn their newfound responsibilities and skills for strategic analysis into something of a permanent, specialized job that could be misinterpreted as relieving them of the bothers of daily office routine.

Perhaps it is based in the institutionalized uniqueness or elitism of strategic intelligence that seems to pervade some organizations (mentioned earlier), but, whatever the reason, many analysts can be observed to act as if their responsibilities are solely tied to the development of long-term assessments. In these units, the staff often actively discourage any attempt to have them report regularly on their progress or utilize their growing specialized knowledge on specific issues to answer questions or provide briefings. Instead, such personnel operate as if an assignment to strategic intelligence is tantamount to gaining permission to become involved in academic research, free of the tensions and demands of organizational demands except in the very broadest sense. While one might imagine that this is a very individual phenomenon, there are certainly whole units devoted to strategic analysis where these models of behavior are the norm rather than the exception.

SUMMARY OF OBSERVATIONS

This summary section serves as a quick reminder of some of the elements of strategic intelligence practice and application that have either "gone wrong" or at least have strayed from the path of sensible best practice. These are all issues that can and should be improved if organizations are to acquire what should be a serious and effective strategic assessment support service. I have chosen to write them up as specific recommendations for change or reinforcement.

- Place emphasis on ensuring that managers and other organizational clients develop a strong awareness of the use of strategic analysis as a fundamental tool for future planning and decision making.
- Task and use strategic intelligence and operational intelligence in such a way that they complement each other, rather than compete for resources and attention.
- Structure and place the strategic intelligence unit or cell so that its location in the organization does not distance it from would-be clients and consumers of the product, or from other intelligence functions.
- Administer strategic intelligence with sensitivity to avoid any misplaced sense of elitism or behavioral arrogance.
- Establish workable tasking mechanisms to ensure that strategic intelligence resources are applied to issues of genuine concern and importance to the organization's role and responsibilities.
- Continue to provide expert strategic intelligence training not only to practitioners, but adapted to suit the awareness needs of other intelligence officers and of supervisors, managers, and executives.

- Ensure that analysts and clients work together to conduct projects in such a way that even where substantial changes are required to earlier plans and expectations, both cooperate to develop revised project plans that still achieve organizational needs.
- Encourage supervisors and managers to oversee strategic assessment projects to provide a continuing level of input of necessary information, guidance, and leadership.
- Ensure that analysts follow the logical processes taught in strategic intelligence training, and apply these to all strategic problem-solving issues, flexibly adapting them to suit specific project needs.

CONCLUSION

For over a decade we have seen a remarkable breakthrough in gaining endorsement for strategic intelligence and analysis practice within the world's law enforcement community. Naturally, progress is both slow and patchy, since this relatively new tool takes time to be accepted fully by organizations that do not have a strong existing involvement in intelligence analysis work. What is important, though, is that the ideas have taken root, and implementation is slowly but surely following.

However, there are already some serious lessons that we can learn about using strategic analysis. We need to find the strength to commit ourselves to a strategy of remedial action—one that would involve increased, better publicity; further training and familiarization for practitioners and their managers; and a sense of vigilance to ensure quality control over the strategic products being produced. If not, then our profession is in some danger of having this essential exciting technique become devalued and marginalized. A lot of criticism directed toward strategic intelligence even now, at this relatively early stage, is born of ignorance of what it is and how it should work.

As intelligence professionals, we simply cannot divorce ourselves from responsibility for such criticism. Frankly, no one else will fix these situations, and we need to take a strong hand in showing how better to do things and achieve useful strategic results. The inescapable thing is that successful law enforcement simply must have strategic assessment as a tool. It is up to us, individually and collectively, to make it work.

NOTES

1. This chapter is my personal appraisal of the development, introduction, implementation, and outlook for strategic intelligence within the international law enforcement community. It was originally delivered at the EUROPOL International Conference of Intelligence Analysts in the Netherlands in October 1996 and has been updated frequently since then.

2. At the time, I was director of the Strategic Crime Studies Unit of the Australian federal Attorney-General's Department.

3. For example, there has been a heavy concentration of these in the Netherlands, the UK, and Canada in recent years.

4. Europol, H. M. Revenue and Customs (formerly H. M. Customs and Excise UK), the National Criminal Intelligence Service (UK), the Royal Canadian Mounted Police, and the Dutch National Police Service are among the committed adherents to the training doctrine.

5. Throughout this chapter the term *operational intelligence* has been used to suggest intelligence activity that provides close levels of support to line units. While many intelligence organizations use and differentiate between the terms *tactical* and *operational*, such terminology is by no means universally accepted nor are the same definitions applied across agencies. In these circumstances, I have chosen to settle on the single term *operational* simply to distinguish it and tactical intelligence from strategic intelligence.

4

The Case for Establishing a National Strategic Intelligence Apparatus

While much of this book seeks to spread the word about strategic intelligence and encourage its application at all appropriate levels in all elements of society, this chapter makes a complete shift in emphasis. It promulgates a vision that every nation should seriously consider establishing a focused, specialized strategic intelligence research unit to examine trends and futures. Although the chapter talks mostly about enforcement as the basis for this model approach, the approach itself can be adapted to other forms of government or corporate endeavor without difficulty. The model's focus is on "excellence through specialization," and discusses one method of arranging to deliver intelligence at this level free from the functional "contamination" that comes from loading this mega-responsibility onto organizations that already have other practical and operational responsibilities.

This chapter is divided into two parts. In the first, some basic ideas about intelligence and its general role in a law enforcement environment are discussed and revised, with specific emphasis on strategic intelligence. This focus is essentially directed toward describing the provision of intelligence services within individual agencies and, in doing so, covers the following areas:

- the rationale for production of intelligence;
- definitional statements on types of intelligence;

- users and their application of intelligence products;
- resources required to produce intelligence; and
- management of the intelligence process.

While it can be assumed that many readers of this chapter will already be familiar with "the Craft of Intelligence,"[1] the first part of this paper is intended to provide an informed discussion of the rationale for (and workings of) the strategic intelligence arena. The second part of the chapter moves away from the discussion of agency-specific arrangements and looks to national and state issues for intelligence. In accepting that law enforcement agencies can carry out their own intelligence support programs, including the generating of corporately supportive strategic intelligence, legitimately and effectively, this part examines the argument for generating a centrally coordinated strategic intelligence service. Such a service could provide an overall focus on law enforcement (as on other issues) for a national or state government or major corporate empire, to enable the development of overarching policies, direction, plans, and strategies.

CONCEPTS, APPLICATION, AND MANAGEMENT

Organizational Decision Making

The basic premise in any discussion of intelligence is that, however it may be defined, it is an essential component activity of every rational decision-making process. In the context of this book, a useful starting point in understanding intelligence is to examine the relationship between the identification of organizational needs and the decision-making process to meet those needs. In simple terms, any organization's decision making falls into two principal dimensions:

1. decisions concerning overall direction and purpose of the organization; and
2. decisions affecting implementation of these "direction statements" of the organization.

This concept holds true for all organizations: law enforcement bodies, defense agencies, commercial and industrial corporations, and public sector organizations. Determining agency goals, deciding what objectives the organization ought best to develop, deciding upon operational routines and priorities—these are all steps essential to the establishment of the working "rules" for the organization.

To do this effectively demands a high degree of knowledge and awareness of the environment within which the organization is to work. Information is the key to this process, and yet information by itself is not necessarily enough to ensure that decision making is a wholly rational and logical activity. What is really needed is a set of forward-looking perspectives of those events, activities, and trends that are likely to affect the organization's achievement of its goals—in short, intelligence.

Information is essential to the intelligence process. Intelligence, on the other hand, is not simply an amalgam of collected information. It is instead the result of taking information relevant to a specific issue and subjecting it to a process of integration, evaluation, and analysis with the specific purpose of projecting future events and actions, and estimating and predicting outcomes.

Strategic Intelligence

Just as decision making operates in the two main dimensions discussed above, the total intelligence effort operating in support of any organization is most effective if it addresses these two separate—but necessarily linked—levels of interest and focus. At one end of the scale, implementation of an organization's operational responsibilities is clearly the role assigned to line units. At the other extreme, corporate executives have the prime responsibility for development of the organizational guidelines and direction statements that chart the overall direction of the organization. In the necessary process of developing and reviewing policies and strategies, the provision of up-to-date knowledge and forecasts of future trends is not just important; it is key to the success of the development/review process. This essential support service is a particular sort of intelligence, termed *strategic intelligence.* While it acts in direct support of the policy-making function, it does usurp that responsibility from the organization's decision makers.

Two useful definitional statements about strategic intelligence, applicable to a law enforcement environment, are shown here:

- Strategic intelligence provides the law enforcement organization with an overview of criminal capabilities, vulnerabilities, trends, and intentions in order to allow for the formulation of organizational policies and plans to combat criminal activity.

- Strategic intelligence and analysis, in the fields of enforcement and compliance, focuses on comprehensively describing and assessing a phenomenon, its history, and its likely future changes, in order to allow the review and development of policies, programs, legislation, and strategic direction.

It is important to note that many different forms of these definitions exist, since many agencies feel a need to produce a modified version to suit their organization's particular circumstances. All the variations, however, include the common notions of width of overview and the intention to feed into macroplanning activities. Finally, since much of the practice of law enforcement intelligence owes its genesis to the military intelligence model, it is appropriate to include here a comparable military definition of strategic intelligence in order to note the similarities and differences with the above enforcement statements.

Strategic intelligence is that intelligence required for the formation of nationai defense policy and military plans at both the national and international levels.

It is relatively easy for a well-established and appropriately sourced intelligence unit to provide comment on the "real story" behind current events as well as noting emerging developments in previously established patterns of activity. These sorts of intelligence product are variously described as basic, or background, intelligence and current intelligence. Since both are clearly removed from the immediacy of tactical line-support intelligence, this type of intelligence effort becomes part of the strategic intelligence activity. However, it must be remembered that if the intelligence product becomes severely limited, it can also comment upon the impact of the likely medium- to long-term outcomes of these developments.

Tactical and operational intelligence is aimed at directly meeting agency objectives and responsibilities by focusing on criminal (or other threatening) organizations, individuals, and modus operandi.

This type of intelligence is targeted at specific risk and threat activity with the goal of immediately neutralizing it.

In short, intelligence must be able to offer advice to answer the "So what?" question likely to be posed by the organization. To do this, the intelligence unit must be prepared to look beyond the immediate period for interpretation of the picture in terms of its future impact. By doing this, corporate executives will be able to review plans and policies that define the organization's approach to issues of purpose, direction, resource, and materiel management. One particularly apposite term for this value-added dimension of strategic intelligence product, coined by the military, is *indicators and warning intelligence.*

A Brief Word on Operational/Tactical Intelligence

Beyond the type of deep intelligence support needed for input to the development and review of corporate strategies and policies, there also exists a clear need to provide intelligence that will aid the organization in implementing its operational tasks. Law enforcement and military bodies commonly use two terms[2] to describe this sort of close-support intelligence: operational intelligence and tactical intelligence. It is possible to draw some distinction between the two, based, for example, on issues like the level of threat identified, the size of the organizational unit likely to be involved in reacting to the product, or the immediacy of the target or threat identified. However, common practice in law enforcement agencies is to simply see this type of intelligence as generically serving line functions and supporting operational activity, hence terming it operational intelligence. The standard definition shown above may appear in various forms although all carry the common denominators of service and support to line activity. I have taken the liberty of paraphrasing the statement to include both operational and tactical terminology.

DEVELOPMENT AND APPLICATION OF STRATEGIC INTELLIGENCE

Every organization has its legitimacy of purpose based on a statement of its established role and function. Law enforcement organizations and others in the public sector rely on government legislative prescriptions for their focus, for example, administrative arrangements orders and the like. It follows, therefore, that each organization has a legitimate requirement for strategic intelligence support in moving to accomplish effective development and review of its own very specific corporate plans, policies, and strategies.

Production of Strategic Intelligence

Strategic intelligence activity has as its clients corporate planners and senior executives of the organization, and the product is delivered in the form of continuing or special strategic intelligence assessments. These assessments encompass a range of subjects that have particular importance for that agency. They may cover, for example, analysis and interpretation of such medium- and longer-term, broad-based issues as changes in the type and nature of threats posed by organized criminal groups, as well as trends and developments in avoidance methodologies, with forecasts for change to the pattern of criminal behavior.

Intelligence Development to Cover National/State Needs

As indicated elsewhere, it is a comparatively recent phenomenon that any law enforcement agencies have become involved in the production of strategic intelligence product in any truly effective, structured fashion. The understandable preoccupation of all agencies has been to set up information-gathering and recording networks and focus on the production of operational intelligence likely to be of more immediate use. This preoccupation with events and risks at the operational end of the spectrum has not, of course, been limited to any one national law enforcement community. The development of agency and government awareness of the need to develop strategic intelligence services is a relatively universal phenomenon.

In a typical national setting, the federal law enforcement agencies have regulatory, enforcement, and crime prevention responsibilities that transcend state, territorial, or provincial boundaries. While the need for maintenance of an operational intelligence capacity is obvious, each federal agency also has a justifiable need to develop and review corporate policies and plans to meet the changing crime scene. In other words, each needs a strategic intelligence service to point the way of change and enable policy decisions to be made in a climate of awareness and forewarning. By and large these national agencies have, to varying degrees, acted to develop this capacity.

Yet in some countries, a few of the state or regional law enforcement agencies have also become interested in the production of strategic intelligence product. It is argued in these circumstances that knowledge of strategic intelligence developments and warnings may assist the formulation of policies and conduct of operational responsibilities at the state or regional level. However, it has remained the generally held view internationally that it is "more appropriate" for the development and dissemination of strategic intelligence product to remain in the hands of federal agencies. The caveat to this statement is usually that the federal strategic intelligence capability can and should also provide such strategic warnings as the states or territories need.

There is no uniform agreement on what is the best policy in this regard. In some countries, the above model applies and appears to work more or less successfully in that the states and territories do receive strategic intelligence outlook and warning products. In other situations, however, it is clear that the amount of urgent tasking required for national government purposes simply precludes any opportunity to focus on jurisdictional interests and needs at the level of state and regional government.

If one considers what strategic intelligence truly represents—a focus on producing intelligence product that underpins and informs the process of policy formulation—then how is it possible to argue that the logical answer is a single national strategic intelligence production service? The answer lies in recognizing that strategic analysis and research is needed at several levels—not just one—and that to establish an appropriately multilayered strategic intelligence system is not impossible. For some readers and officials, such an idea may be uncomfortable because it seems a solution for dissipating scarce resources. Clients at all levels of government and corporate responsibility may understandably disagree with such an observation.

Focus of Strategic Intelligence Tasking

It is a truism that intelligence tasking within any organization is—and, to be organizationally effective, must be—tasked to address defined organizational goals. Intelligence doctrine universally teaches that all intelligence effort is directed in pursuit of defined "problems," these being conceived in terms that directly address established organizational concerns. What this means is that, for both tactical and strategic intelligence development within an organization, intelligence tasking can legitimately focus only upon those areas of activity that fall within the defined parameters of that organization's role. Thus, the intelligence effort is truly agency specific, although there is considerable scope for sensible and cooperative pooling of effort and sharing of resources between agencies when the intelligence "problem" can be seen to impact upon more than a single agency, each extracting only that which is appropriate to its needs.

The following statement, then, summarizes the inevitable—and appropriate—outcome: Unless spurred on by wider interests, an agency intelligence unit will tend to collect and process a wide range of data to produce strategic intelligence assessments that specifically address only issues of concern to that agency's specific role.

Information Sources and Collection

There are many important requirements for the effective production of useful intelligence. It is appropriate here to briefly consider the issue of sourcing and use of information relevant to the intelligence effort. The intelligence process cannot survive without the input of data. While items of information themselves may have little or no intrinsic worth, providing that the data gathered meet the criteria of relevance, accuracy, and timeliness, then the intelligence process has the potential to provide a value-added holistic product, greater in the whole than merely the sum of its contributing parts.

Data collection is as disciplined a component of the intelligence process as any other. It is neither efficient nor effective for intelligence operations to rely merely on gathering everything possible about every conceivable subject of interest. Rather, there must be an orderly approach to defining subject areas of interest, identifying the sort of information that is likely to illuminate those issues, selecting the most likely (existing and potential) sources to provide that information, and, finally, accessing the sources and collecting the data.

The key element of this part of the process is the definition of the information to be sought; the vehicle for this is the intelligence collection plan. It is generally the rule that, accepting and allowing for the focus that needs to be applied to the final intelligence product in terms of organizational imperatives, the collection plan must nonetheless examine the subject in the widest possible context. This is necessary if we are to ensure that the fine-tuning of the assessment is both rational and logical. One cannot expect to effectively develop the final product unless the analysis and interpretation components of the process have taken place in an atmosphere of broad but detailed awareness of all the issues surrounding the intelligence "problem."

For national law enforcement agencies involved in developing strategic intelligence, much of the emphasis on major crime developments is tied in with international developments and, indeed, may be initiated by crime groups either located abroad or connected with overseas criminal organizations. Certainly, changes in the international scene have been shown to have significant impact on such issues as money laundering and transfer, and production and transportation of illicit drugs. Most federal law enforcement agencies have already established wide networks of international sources of information of use in the intelligence arena. The information thus made available is not only useful in the development of tactical intelligence in direct support of law enforcement operations, but also contributes importantly to the ongoing strategic intelligence study of threat assessments in respect of major categories of crime.

MANAGEMENT AND RESOURCE REQUIREMENTS

The Cost of Intelligence

Worthwhile intelligence cannot be produced without cost. It is appropriate to consider the key requirements of intelligence activity and the various forms of cost associated with them. The most obvious example of cost is the intelligence unit's demand for high levels of continuing input of every sort of conceivably useful, relevant information. However, the overall "cost" associated with intelligence work is quite extensive and may include, but is not limited to, those components listed below.

1. Measurable Costs
    - human resources
    - training and development
    - equipment
    - administrative funds
    - time
    - information collection mechanisms
    - dissemination and reporting resources
2. Other "Costs" (the impact of changed priorities)
    - unfulfilled expectations
    - frustration

As a starting point in the discussion of intelligence resource requirements, it is well to recognize that it is an accepted maxim of the discipline of intelligence that there are three principal prerequisites for the effective production of all intelligence. These elements are:

- a clear understanding of the organization's goals and objectives coupled with a detailed knowledge of the organization's operational activities and routines;

- access to information that is appropriate to the nature of the assessment work envisioned; and
- the availability of necessary resources—appropriately trained personnel, funds, and equipment.

These requirements generally hold good for production of intelligence, regardless of whether the final product is to serve a strategic or operational purpose. Having said this, there are some significant differences in the way in which these three prerequisite requirements are approached and defined, depending upon the ultimate outcome and consumption of the intelligence product.

Staffing and Development

Like any other endeavor, the "cycle" of intelligence activity[3] demands application of a particular set of skills and techniques. These can be easily learned, although in their application within the discipline of intelligence, it is often considered that the practice demands going beyond the question of mere technical ability, requiring extra performance qualities that include, for example, imagination and flair (though these notions are, at best, ill defined even by those arguing in their favor). Perhaps for this reason, selection of personnel to carry out intelligence assessment functions has often seemed to be more difficult than expected and has not always been as successful as hoped.

It should be noted that training and development programs for intelligence analysis are already well tried and established, initially for basic intelligence techniques and later for advanced and strategic intelligence assessment. Intelligence doctrine is dynamic, however, and training and development cycles need to provide opportunities for staff to refresh and gain new skills and techniques.

Accepting the arguments—and the difficulties outlined earlier—any detailed study of the intelligence process unequivocally points to the necessity of careful selection and training of personnel, if they are to be able to master the intricacies of the intelligence process and become effective in the production of intelligence. Various selection and recruitment strategies to fill the intelligence ranks have been tried. These run the gamut from reassignment of experienced line staff, who understand the organizational milieu and, it is felt, "only" need additional, specialized training; to direct recruitment of tertiary qualified staff to function as analysts, based on an assumption that tertiary training provides an adequate demonstration of applicable research-based skills.

Neither the examples given above nor their many variations necessarily succeed fully or on every occasion. One important, often overlooked, factor is that intelligence itself is not a single stream activity. The craft is a specialized, disciplined one, embodying technical and intellectual ability, but it *is* composed of a number of equally specialized subactivities that make the intelligence process work.

Successful strategies for selection and training for intelligence work recognize the necessity of defining "the job" and preparing the right staff with the appropriate tools, skills, knowledge, and technical ability to handle the particular role assigned to them. On the other hand, staffing intelligence units by relocating personnel for any reason other than their desire and ability to work in intelligence is risky. It invites a probable risk of failure, even though this may be seen only eventually, as an inability to realize the full potential of both the individual and the unit against a background of opportunities lost.

The essence of intelligence work is the ability to process vast volumes of data against a background of need—as defined by the intelligence "problem"—to describe both what is happening and what is likely to be the outcome. The demands placed on individuals to forecast in what is inevitably an uncertain environment places its own stresses on those employed in intelligence. Operational urgencies add to the pressure, and yet offsetting this is the sense of achievement that buoys the spirit and encourages and enthuses the practitioners.

Material and Administrative Costs

In general terms, intelligence units represent high-cost activities, particularly where the emphasis is on data collection, storage, and communication. This is particularly the case for those agencies with operational responsibilities that demand the production of operational and tactical intelligence.

The development of strategic intelligence creates different demands for resources. The intelligence collection plan takes every opportunity, when appropriate, to utilize data that has already been collected *by other agencies.* The home agency then holds this data for the limited time necessary to develop and complete specific projects. By this means, much of the more "traditional" data storage and related cost burden is substantially diminished. It is essential, however, to provide for the temporary collection, maintenance, storage, and retrieval of data relevant to particular projects.

Similarly, the high travel and other administrative costs that typify the production of tactical/operational intelligence, with the aura of operational immediacy surrounding its processes, are diminished since the production of strategic intelligence functions in an environment somewhat removed from this sense of immediacy. The development of strategic intelligence product has its own pressures, but they are rarely able to be translated into the magnitude of administrative costs associated with operational matters.

Other Costs

The production of strategic intelligence is almost never a task that is simple or quick. The requirement is for an assessment of the "long view" of a problem, encompassing the widest possible view consistent with the particular subject. The selection of appropriate staff, the collection of relevant data, and the development of properly constructed project plans for each and every assessment are essential components of the activity, each having its own intrinsic cost.

By any measure, the management of time is one of the most difficult and demanding elements within the strategic intelligence process. Research, evaluation, analysis, and interpretation inevitably take up considerable time and effort, and, unlike tactical intelligence production, the strategic intelligence chain of activity has an extra dimension to it that is much more cerebral than merely process based.

The point to be made here is that, allowing for what might appear to be a less "urgent" environment for the production of strategic intelligence, there are high levels of expectation to be found not only from clients and consumers of the product, but from the intelligence staff themselves. Indeed, once the basic processing of data has been completed, the emphasis in the next phase is on intellectualizing the intelligence problem and beginning the task of interpretation—activity that can create high degrees of stress, expectation, and frustration. Management of strategic intelligence units must be structured to recognize and respond to these conditions.

ONE FUTURE APPROACH: A NATIONAL STRATEGIC CRIME INTELLIGENCE UNIT

Background

In the earlier part of this chapter we discussed the established, legitimate role of strategic intelligence developed within and for agency use in determining corporate plans and policies. This section argues the potential of providing a national level of strategic crime intelligence analysis, separate from existing agency-based strategic intelligence activities. By providing strategic intelligence assessments of the total crime environment, such an initiative would support national objectives in the establishment of integrated law enforcement policies, strategies, priorities, resource deployments, organizational requirements, and training needs.

In a typical national law enforcement context, the federal police force and other major agencies (such as customs) have established strategic intelligence programs within their intelligence units. The focus of these strategic "cells" is primarily on issues relevant to their own separate, agency-specific areas of responsibility. Increasingly, however, it can be noted that there is a move toward joint resourcing and direction toward examination of those issues in which the different agencies share common enforcement interests. But the acceptance of a "task force syndrome," combining forces and focusing the synergy toward solving specific problems, is not the whole answer. Certainly these arrangements can be hugely successful given the right combination of circumstances, people, and mandate; however, they remain essentially short- to medium-term groupings of individuals with the same goal. A larger step is needed if governments are to gain strategic intelligence and analysis advice that transcends the agency interests of stakeholder organizations at the federal and state/regional levels.

Development of Government Policies

Given that many federal law enforcement agencies are organizationally established within different departmental responsibilities, government policy making in the law enforcement arena requires input from several portfolios, each with its own perspective of roles and responsibilities. It is a logical extension of these arrangements that wherever policies affect single agencies,

> One solution for providing the national government with strategic outlook on crime is to establish a separate, discrete strategic research unit within the enforcement community but outside of established agency boundaries.

such policies tend to be developed almost solely within the portfolios handling those agencies. Even allowing for the fact that a "cabinet submission" mechanism, which requires interagency contact, normally allows for some cross-pollination of ideas, this sole-agency approach tends to dominate government policy development within law enforcement. Police write submissions on policing; customs, on import/export matters; and so on.

This scenario presents an acute dilemma for those ultimately responsible for the development of enforcement policies and strategy. Although it still remains an established and accepted model of how policies are shaped in some societies, there is a growing realization that these arrangements are not at all consistent with what needs to be known about the nature of criminal endeavor. What we have had is a system of independent, individualistic, and discrete law enforcement agency strategies, a system that lacks congruence with the present state of awareness of the intricacies of criminal organization and activity.

Realistic perceptions of crime and its impact on society suggest that the approach described above has reached the limits of its usefulness. The complexity of crime and its far-reaching impact upon society is already well understood and documented. In this context, maintenance of the existing approach to national law enforcement policy making and strategy setting, based on the singularity of agency perceptions of the crime "problem," is unlikely to achieve the full measure of national—that is, federal and state—potential to combat the overall threat. Each of the law enforcement agencies involved in this arena of policy development will almost certainly draw on its own integral strategic intelligence capability for its assessment of the intelligence problem. This is certainly understandable, but an assessment nonetheless that is drafted from the agency's singular perspective of the threat to and impact on its areas of responsibility.

Government policy making has, as a principal objective, the establishment of comprehensive strategies that suit society as a whole. It follows that the analysis of crime and its overall impact similarly must go well beyond traditional limitations that are imposed, however inadvertently, by the vision imparted by individual agencies involved in the strategic intelligence assessment process. The result of the existing chain of activity, as described above, is that national law enforcement policies run the risk of being—or becoming—a collection of individual agency strategies focused toward goals. These are unable to be properly articulated because no single, complete definition and description of the crime environment is available to the combined justice agencies or to governments.

If what is required is a process that results in determining a truly national approach to establishing comprehensive law enforcement policies and strategies, then it follows that reliance upon a set of individual agency-based intelligence assessments as the basis for understanding the totality of the crime environment is flawed. There is clearly a justification for the provision of this holistic level of strategic intelligence assessment service, one that covers the entire criminal environment. This is essential if governments are to understand the nature and scope of crime and, as a result, be able to develop the appropriate matrix of law enforcement policies and strategies.

REQUIREMENTS OF A SEPARATE NATIONAL STRATEGIC INTELLIGENCE SERVICE

Basic Outline

The essential components of any planned arrangement to deliver a national level of law enforcement strategic intelligence product for executive-level government consumption will remain very similar to those already in existence at agency level. Of necessity, there will be some obvious differences of the sort listed below. Some additional explanatory comments have been added in the following paragraphs, as well as those made earlier in the chapter.

Role

In essence, what is needed is a national law enforcement intelligence service for government decision makers, one that is capable of carrying out comprehensive strategic intelligence assessments of the criminal environment and its impact on society. The output of such a service will ideally provide both definitions and descriptions of the crime "problem" as well as forecasts of trends and developments. Any such intelligence service has two key features:

- To be effective, its purview of data (as might be defined by type or source/origin) cannot be limited simply to law enforcement information concerning what is known about criminals and crime. What is needed is the capacity to develop a clear grasp of the totality of the impact of crime upon society, in all its aspects. This would be the basis for focusing upon the development of sensible law enforcement strategies that "fit" into national policy making.

- Since the rationale for this service is solely to generate strategic intelligence assessments, it will be detrimental for those involved to have any role related to operational activities. Indeed, those involved in the strategic intelligence service proposed should remain absolutely divorced from other organizational units or agencies involved in operational activities. To do otherwise is to run the risk of skewing the focus of the service away from its necessary isolation and "neutrality" and impart, instead, some sense of the parenting body's responsibilities and views.

Organizational Setting and Mandate

As discussed above, organizational placement and establishment of the strategic analysis unit needs to take into account the requirement that the unit be separated from the normal run of law enforcement agencies, with their ongoing operational responsibilities, and exist, instead, in a more neutral and isolated environment. This concept accepts that existing law enforcement agencies already have a legitimate role in producing and consuming strategic intelligence in order to develop or modify their operational strategies and plans.

While it could be hypothesized that one or other of the existing enforcement agencies could set up and provide the type of strategic research service envisioned in this chapter, the reality is that few existing agencies have a mandate that goes beyond the individual agency and into the realm of wider national service on behalf of all stakeholders. Nor do many agencies have the focus or the commitment necessary for the development of strategic intelligence that looks comprehensively at all areas of criminal impact on society. Most importantly, the very nature of the agencies, their task orientation, and the staff resources typically available to them by and large militates against their being able to sensibly assume the national strategic servicing role outlined herein.

Organizational placement should take into account the need for the service unit to have a level of freedom to develop and conduct its assessment activities, separate from pressures related to information/intelligence-collection activities or operational urgencies that occur in existing law enforcement agencies. The essence of the strategic unit is that, to be effective, it must be an intelligence *assessment* unit in its own right, not a service adjunct to support some defined operational function elsewhere.

Tasking of the Assessment Activity

The focus of a truly national strategic intelligence service should be to examine and provide assessment on all areas of the criminal environment that threaten public order. Much work has already been done within the law enforcement community to identify and list priorities of subjects deserving urgent attention for examination and assessment. Throughout these developments, there has been a tendency to focus on deciding which of the existing agencies should carry out the role, ignoring the principles espoused above. This difficulty in identifying a suitable agency to undertake this essential work is not only evidence of the deficiencies in the present system but further argument in support of establishing the type of crime assessment service discussed in this chapter.

An additional and equally important feature of tasking will be to not only examine those areas of established criminal activity, but maintain a continuing overview of activities. These latter may not necessarily be "criminal" under existing statutes, but could well represent modes of behavior that are considered aberrant, antisocial, or otherwise unacceptable to society.

The strategic intelligence unit must be equipped with a wide mandate to access data and conduct research to provide assessment on the projects decided upon. This will necessitate access to data already held within the law enforcement environment that can be made available, subject to security provisions and prevailing operational requirements. If the full range of criminal impact areas is to be effectively canvassed, it will also be necessary for the service unit to have access to a much wider range of state and territorial agencies than might normally be the experience of existing intelligence units.

Legitimacy and mandate can be provided in several ways. For example, these notions can be addressed in the drafting of a definitive role for the strategic intelligence unit by government and in formalizing information access arrangements with all the relevant agencies (law enforcement and others). However, much of the success of the unit's activities in information collection will derive not so much from these *formalized arrangements* but also through *effective and sensitive liaison* between the unit and those agencies. In addition, a positive, proactive program of sharing the final, value-added intelligence product with the contributors is a strong positive reinforcement of the value inherent in the relationship among all these parties.

Establishment Options

Whatever the shape and placement of the strategic assessment unit, it is feasible to consider the following prescriptions as options.

- Staff numbers and attendant equipment can be kept to a minimum, since intelligence assessment and research activities, rather than active collection-related functions, make up the predominant requirement.
- The amalgamation of skills and experience to conduct highly specialized national assessments could well be met through a combination of permanent posting plus temporary assignment to the unit, with other law enforcement agencies providing the pool of short-term assignment personnel from within the ranks of their intelligence organizations.
- Budget support for the strategic assessment unit will not place high demands on government—apart from the provision of essential worktable equipment (computers, etc.), the principal recurrent costs will be for salaries, travel both domestically and internationally, and communications costs.
- Management of the functioning of the unit should operate at three levels:
  1. task direction and overall reporting to and through a nominated "peak" agency, department, or committee;
  2. the senior officer of the strategic unit, directing the programs of assessment and day-to-day management of human and financial resources, responsible for reporting to the governing body; and
  3. project management, effected through team leaders operating within project groups.

CONCLUSION

The role of strategic intelligence within law enforcement communities is generally recognized and accepted to some degree, and in some cases the capability already exists. It is well understood that individual law enforcement agencies have a legitimate need for strategic intelligence capacity to meet their own organizational objectives.

National governments may determine that it is necessary to move toward development of law enforcement strategies that are integrated to meet the totality of the criminal environment threat in all its aspects. If this is so, then it is essential that an intelligence support capacity be developed to provide holistic strategic intelligence product to define and map the criminal environment.

Of the several options available, on the basis of accrued experience to date, one thing is certain: Inevitably, there are *no* benefits derived from mandating such a role to an existing agency. All already have their own functions and responsibilities and, in some cases, the strategic intelligence capacity to support them. To add a new role—one that transcends normal law enforcement intelligence capacity—would act as a negative force impinging upon the traditional, established intelligence needs of the agency selected. In addition, the existing traditional role would impact the potential for the production of what should be a truly national level of strategic criminal assessment.

Various other models have been tried and are still in existence, for example, in Australia, Canada, and the United Kingdom. In these models, a typical national police agency, with responsibilities for providing intelligence in support of its existing legal powers and responsibilities, will be asked to take on the extra burden of the super-production of overall national strategic analysis for the benefit of other agencies. The burden of merging two discrete roles has generally proved that an agency in these circumstances is not able to do either role comprehensively.

The decision of which solution to adopt is one that must be guided by principle and pragmatism. Translation of what is an accepted national requirement into reality means, in essence, that decisions and choices must be made free from the noise generated by competing interests. However, what is needed is not merely a quick decision, but a planned, comprehensive approach to the development of the capacity to undertake the role expected.

NOTES

1. In describing the discipline of intelligence, this phrase was coined by Allen Dulles, former head of the CIA, in his book of the same name.

2. This differential approach to both the concepts and the semantics involved in intelligence product multilayering is discussed elsewhere in the book.

3. The terms *cycle* and *process* are used equally within intelligence circles to describe the chain of action that encompasses the steps of collection, collation, evaluation, integration, analysis, interpretation, reporting, dissemination, and review.

III

ISSUES FOR CLIENTS AND MANAGERS

5

Why Managers and Executives Need Strategic Analysis: The Law Enforcement Model

Strategic intelligence is an essential tool for the development of modern law enforcement policies, plans, and programs. It is a form of intelligence applicable at all management levels, whether it assists in the deployment and use of resources by helping managers understand the complex matrix of competing public order requirements or provides analytical support at corporate and government levels to aid in overall justice policy planning.

Over the past few years, there has been a noticeable upsurge in the application of intelligence services within various civilian fields: law enforcement, policy planning areas of government, criminology and other academic study centers, and industry. Many would assert that the reasons are linked to increasing pressure within the community for "better" planning in the public sector, coupled with high expectations of accountability in the public and private arenas. Whatever the truth of this, while this present focus on intelligence is a new and—to the profession—welcome development, we should remember that there is in fact nothing really "new" about the practice of intelligence. Indeed, it has been with us for many centuries in many different guises, serving a variety of military, political, and social objectives.

During war and peace alike, in seeking to understand and interpret the action of others—and, to be honest, to gain advantage from such understanding—nations, organizations, and individuals have historically used intelligence to provide or enhance awareness of issues, to seize opportunities, and to prepare for the future.

ENFORCEMENT AND STRATEGIC INTELLIGENCE

The focus of the chapter is the field of intelligence in law enforcement, and the issues raised here are discussed in the broad context of policing, justice administration, and maintenance of public order.

A suitable starting point is the conviction that, in enforcement, there is a long-held "popular" belief that the predominant role for intelligence is to support tactical and operational objectives. This does not sit well with the lessons of history, in which intelligence has consistently reached well beyond the confines of operational activity. In fact, from the Bible onward, the record of human endeavor is repeatedly marked with significant shifts in power that could not have taken place without the support of an intelligence capacity to look over the horizon of tactical concern and focus instead on vision, strategies, and plans for the future.

Views are changing, and strategic intelligence is becoming increasingly accepted within the enforcement community as a desirable—even essential—extension of traditional intelligence support. But why have there been delays? The most likely explanation is that "intelligence" has been seen as an operational tool, while "planning" has long been viewed as some special and distant prerogative of managers and staff, generally excluding intelligence groups. Rightly or wrongly, intelligence has been too useful to operational concerns to allow its mandate to extend into other areas of activity and service. Indeed, applied to law enforcement interests, it is hard to imagine any persuasive argument that could deny such a valuable future tool to organizational executives and managers holding responsibility for developing and reviewing enforcement policies, plans, strategies, and programs.

As a way of demystifying the aura that surrounds strategic intelligence in some areas, it can be thought of simply as *an application of intelligence practice that is used specifically to examine and illuminate classes of threat, risk, or opportunity.*

One of the principal myths that surround strategic intelligence is that the product belongs only to "top management," a view derived from memories of its place in wartime as the upper echelon, "headquarters" form of intelligence. From an enforcement perspective, holding on to this view clearly ignores the realistic requirements of the typical district or regional commander. Just as legitimately as others above her, this officer needs a comprehensive plan to determine the way in which different resources can be applied to changing crime needs in her own area.

The value of strategic intelligence in this example is that it is able to go well beyond what tactical intelligence can see, simply by standing back and taking a longer and broader snapshot of what is and what has been, and, by so doing, forecast what might be. This form of intelligence activity, of course, is deliberate in ensuring that there can be a planned approach, well ahead of time, to resource deployment, equipment changes, development or adaptation of different skills and techniques, and variation of regulatory and compliance mechanisms.

At its best, strategic intelligence can be a truly proactive form of intelligence activity working directly in support of management planning, regardless of the level of management one sees as the client. In this way, strategic intelligence is not "competing" with tactical intelligence; rather, it complements it, but at different levels within organizations. In any typical law enforcement agency, therefore, the development of strategic studies that are specific to agency interests is obviously a legitimate pursuit for intelligence. It would be unthinkable—even irresponsible—for any agency to ignore the need to develop an awareness and understanding of enforcement issues, examining them for their impact on that agency, so that corporate plans can be developed appropriately. However, this form of agency-relevant planning cannot logically occur in a conceptual vacuum. While the practice has often been for agencies to investigate and analyze issues within their own organizational boundaries, looking solely at "policing issues" and "police data," there are considerable dangers in adopting any approach that leaves out consideration of other views, aspects, and features of the area of crime study.

It is perhaps understandable that in times of resource limitations, enforcement agencies have to be seen to concentrate only on the issues at hand, but this cannot be taken to an extreme where important matters outside of traditional policing areas are ignored in the name of expedience or apparent irrelevance. To do so almost certainly means a shortfall in the quality of outcomes, plans, and programs. In fact, it is obvious that law enforcement, justice, and public order concerns do not and cannot operate in a vacuum. At the single agency level, the same could be said of agency aims and objectives. It is hardly possible for any police force or similar group to argue that its role is independent of other concerns, for there are always points of contact—and the potential for tension—between the agency and the community, and among agencies themselves. Inevitably, enforcement concerns interact with a wide range of social policies and community interests. If planning has to take account of these expanded dimensions, so too must the practice of strategic intelligence. To be effective, strategic intelligence activity within enforcement agencies must therefore be allowed—even encouraged—to consider issues on a broad plane, examining all relevant aspects of the crime problem, if it is to provide an appropriate and useful level of service.

STRATEGIC ANALYSIS INPUT TO POLICY MAKING

The need for strategic intelligence support for planning activities can also logically be taken even further than just providing a service for individual enforcement groups. While it is possible for a single enforcement agency, acting independently of others, to develop a strategic view of the issues on which it is—or should be—focusing, the reality is that it is becoming increasingly difficult to conceive of issues that exist only within the sphere of interest of law enforcement. At the top levels of government community service and social planning, any reasonable and open-minded study of strategic policing and justice issues must inevitably consider a broad range of matters beyond merely the obvious police issues.

When we seek to understand any significant issue of criminality, it is essential not only that we consider those aspects that relate to the crime as committed, using typical police information sources, but that we also search for an understanding of such aspects as facilitation, motivation, and others of this ilk, that impact on and explain the issue being examined. Without this broader, more comprehensive approach to analysis, it is unlikely that we will be able to develop justice policies that effectively provide the essential matrix covering all the legitimate concerns and responsibilities of the stakeholders. In fact, unless we are prepared to develop such a holistic approach to viewing crime in its total setting, the policies and programs of agencies and governments will inevitably be designed and executed in a piecemeal fashion.

Numerous examples can be given of the unstructured development of enforcement policies and programs that unfortunately ignore the necessary interaction with other stakeholder interests. Conversely, there are useful examples of attempts to undertake a serious, structured, and disciplined approach to develop strategic overviews of the criminal environment from a "total" perspective. Clearly, this second approach is the one that ought to be adopted by governments at all levels, recognizing strategic analysis for the powerful tool that it is.

Such subjects as illegal drugs, immigration, fraud, domestic or gang violence, and corruption are all obvious examples of a genre in which there is a demonstrable need to take a broader view of all the issues likely to be involved. In these cases, strategic intelligence must be given the opportunity to probe beyond what is simply of interest to enforcement organizations: to examine the wider arena of issues and aspects that are both relevant and necessary to any comprehensive understanding of what makes these crimes occur, how they operate, who they involve, and what is their impact. Without this breadth of understanding, how can organizations and governments hope to establish sensible, workable counter-programs?

IMPLEMENTING STRATEGIC INTELLIGENCE PROGRAMS

Accepting that strategic intelligence activity already occurs in some organizations, its enhancement—or introduction, where necessary—needs an organizational commitment to strategic thinking coupled with a methodical approach to strategic intelligence study and analysis. Within the law enforcement community, implementation of strategic intelligence raises two principal issues:

1. selling the concepts and the "need" to executive management levels; and
2. putting in place the resources and mechanisms to carry out the functions.

Decision making is never difficult of itself; it is, however, very hard to do with any semblance of getting the process and the outcomes "right." The law enforcement community does not lack any availability of dynamic decision makers. Professional policing often demands quick response to perceived situations, a matter of understandable pride to its members. But forward planning, in whatever field, demands something more than quick, conditioned response and requires a great deal of care and thought about the objectives and the processes involved.

If the enforcement community is to meet and best the challenges of both the present and the future, it is essential that management executives be given the opportunity to see and understand the need for a more useful approach to strategic thinking and analysis. As a matter of course, most enforcement agencies have for some time involved their senior officers in strategic management training and the development of corporate plans and programs.

Regrettably, what remains lacking, for the most part, is any substantial emphasis on strategic analysis as the key component that links "thinking" and "planning." To counter this, managers and executives need special exposure to the sort of training and development and familiarization opportunities that will convince them of the logic of investing effort in the structured analysis of strategic issues. At the same time, they need to be given direction and encouragement to understand the requirements—and the obligations—they will face in tasking, guiding, managing, and utilizing the strategic intelligence service and its products.

It is equally important to provide specialized training and development programs for strategic intelligence practitioners at all levels. In simple terms, such programs would be aimed at applying existing or known intelligence skills and techniques in a way that suits the special requirements of strategic intelligence. The reality is that strategic intelligence activity is, if anything, even more structured and disciplined than we are used to undertaking in serving tactical or operational needs. The reason is not complicated: Strategic intelligence calls for the examination of issues and application of intelligence practice across a wider canvas, with more imponderables, and the application of greater levels of knowledge, specialization, and judgment.

Meeting these challenges and committing both the managers and clients to realistic expectations and obligations concerning resources both involve a substantial emphasis on what might be called front-end engineering of the strategic intelligence project. This is properly the joint responsibility of practitioners themselves, clients and managers alike, but it is certain that no strategic intelligence project can proceed without first investing in considerable planning (see figure 5.1).

Both strategic intelligence doctrine and the training in its practice emphasize the care and thought essential to the planning and process of strategic intelligence activity. Perhaps it is of more interest to note that the aim throughout is to empower intelligence officers to accept that the breadth of the strategic study will inevitably lead to less precision in forecasting and greater reliance on personal knowledge, expertise, and judgment of the issues at hand. This approach is somewhat at odds with developed tactical intelligence practice and traditional intelligence training, in which intelligence, investigation, evidence, and prosecution are intermingled. Nonetheless, it is a key feature of strategic intelligence that the analysis and conclusions have to be accepted for what they are—imprecise best guesses and expert opinions of what remains, until some future date, inconclusive data and impressions.

CHALLENGES FOR THE EXECUTIVE TO ACCEPT STRATEGIC INTELLIGENCE

The foregoing comments deal with some of the basic issues surrounding the introduction and development of strategic intelligence for law enforcement. The following brief comments outline some of the major issues and dilemmas that many enforcement agencies currently face.

Clearly, the introduction and overlaying of another form of intelligence activity in any agency presents, in some cases, problems associated with the conflict of priorities for scarce resources. This relates to yet another myth that surrounds strategic intelligence—that it is resource-hungry—yet this does not truly reflect the real situation. Wherever intelligence units are established and information collection mechanisms operate, the addition of a strategic intelligence role adds little real cost burden to existing operations beyond the additional staff members needed.

Given the nature of strategic intelligence and the long-term investment of study and involvement of particular topics—which would themselves be the priorities set by each agency—even the human resource implications can be minimal compared with the operational and tactical intelligence environment.

Where strategic intelligence really is "hungry" is in its desire for information that includes, but is by no means limited to, all that data normally collected by traditional intelligence units. Strategic intelligence will always need to look beyond and outside of the agency perimeter, tapping into a wide variety of sources, most of them free of charge (libraries, other government departments or enforcement groups, public databases, and academic study centers, for example).

Two final notes about challenge are important. First, although it may be a somewhat bizarre reflection of the realities of the enforcement community, one cannot escape observing that intelligence "power" increases in concert with the high visibility of strategic intelligence activity. So too does the propensity

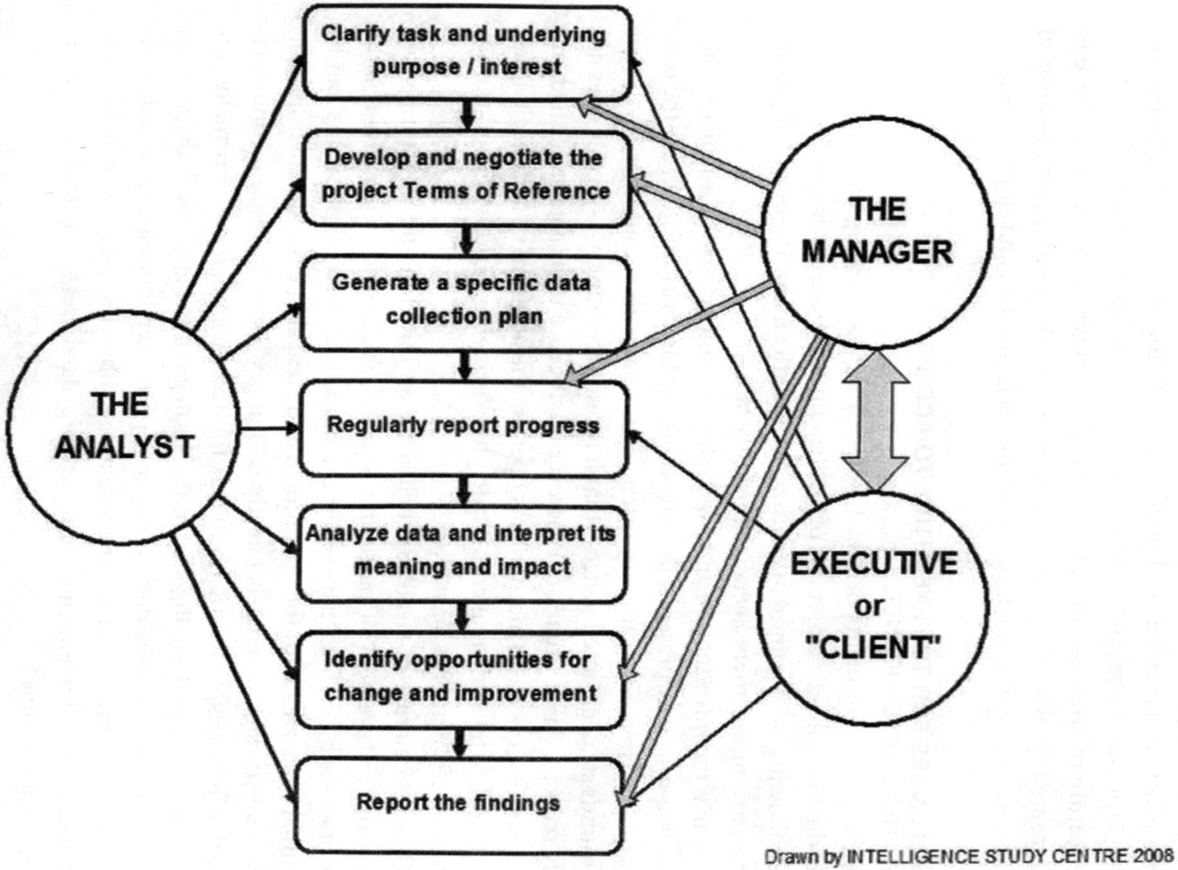

FIGURE 5.1
Interaction between Analyst, Manager, and Client

for competition between different agencies and power groups, an environment that can lead to tension, instead of one demonstrating genuine cooperation. Changing this all-too-common pattern has been difficult, and one assumes it will remain thus.

Second, in a climate of continuing "rationalist" management, there are increasing demands from political and auditing interests for law enforcement to conform with performance measurement mechanisms unsuited to their unique needs. Intelligence activity is not excluded from this, and yet little real work has been done on conceptualizing performance measurement mechanisms that are relevant and appropriate to the nature of intelligence tasks. Clearly this is a priority if we are to properly gauge the efficacy of strategic and other intelligence work. Unless some appropriate regimen is developed, intelligence will continue to be saddled with the expectation that all intelligence lead directly to arrest—with predictable consequences if we are unable to show that such a nexus exists.

CONCLUSION

From a practitioner's standpoint, the development, adaptation, and introduction of strategic intelligence into the law enforcement environment is the most exciting development of recent years. Realistically, the battle between increasing crime and diminishing enforcement resources creates, as one unfortunate outcome, a feeling of frustration that overtakes any but the most cursory review of what exists and threatens in the "now." There is just not enough time or mental energy to sit back and think through issues at a macro level.

It is therefore natural for individuals and agencies to focus on their own specific areas of interest and responsibility, and to strive for efficiency in that arena. What is missing, however understandably, is the realization that no agency "owns" a discrete area of responsibility free from concerns about or impact implication on other areas.

For many years, coordination, communication, and cooperation concepts have been the mainstay of management seeking to minimize the interface difficulties between areas of responsibility. While this package of approaches remains vital, a greater commitment to active, fulsome evaluation and exploration of issues is paramount if the community is to get the protection it deserves, and indeed imagines it already receives.

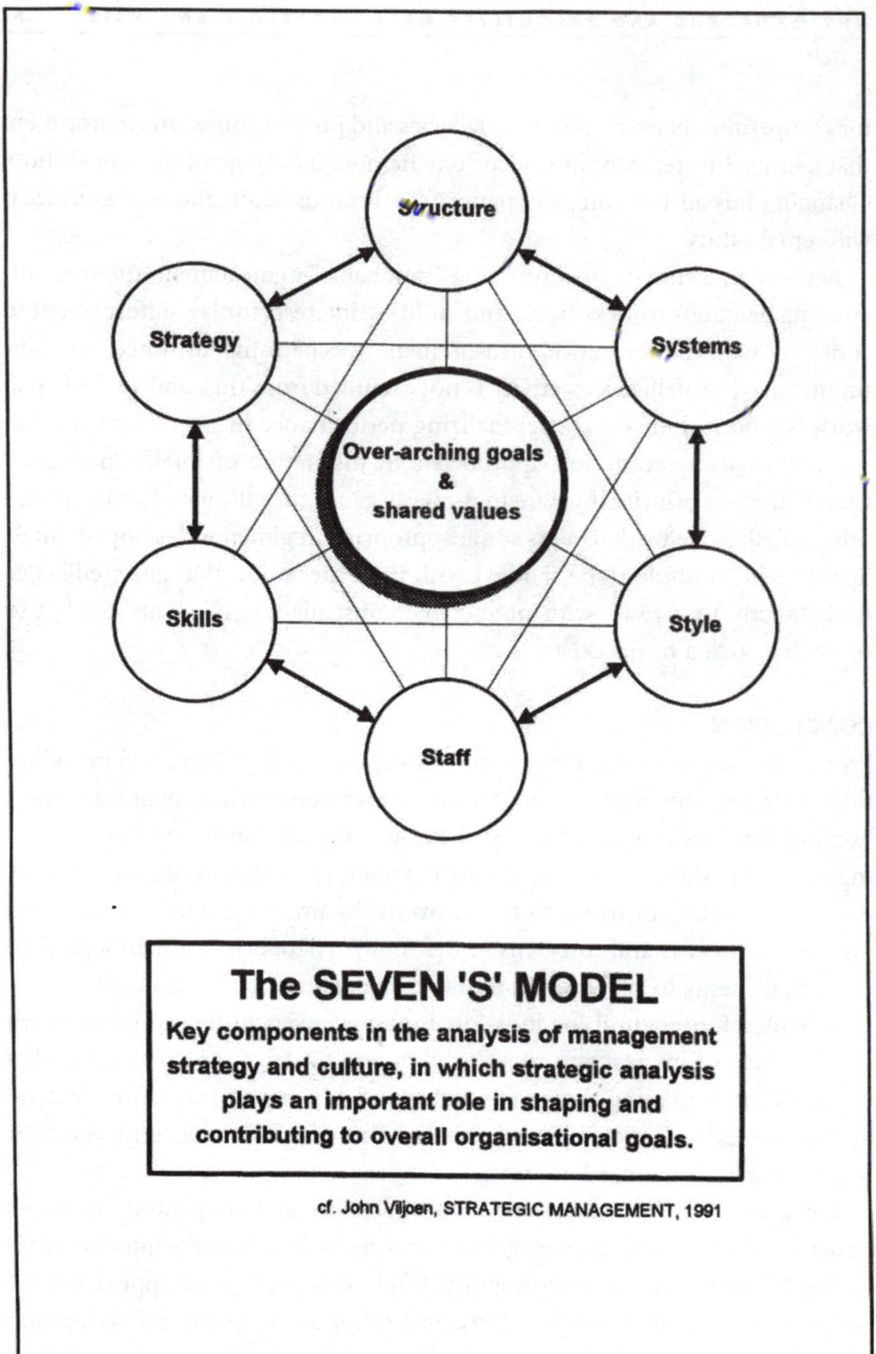

FIGURE 5.2
Seven S Model

Certainly there are challenges and probably trying times ahead, but one thing is certain: Now that the enforcement community understands the need for better, more informed analysis and planning, strategic intelligence is a fixed feature on the agenda. The modern police force executive can cope with change only by having access to a strategic intelligence, research, and forecasting capability.

6

Management Models and Behavior: Impact on Intelligence

INTELLIGENCE AS THE SERVANT OF THE EXECUTIVE

This chapter approaches the topic from the perspective of analysis and its role in any management environment. The obverse side of the picture is also presented: management style and its interaction with intelligence. As intelligence practitioners, it must seem obvious that real intelligence serves a variety of masters. Intelligence is indeed a service; it is not a self-serving entity it is own right. It should not, in the best of worlds, have any self-sustaining life of its own, and as such, it can never serve its own interests, for no such interests legitimately exist. And yet many of us would, in fact, be able to observe from personal experience that this dictum seems often to be breached. So what is the reality of intelligence and what is it actually meant to be?

From a conceptual point of view, intelligence as a practice exists to illuminate the obscure, to forecast what is yet to come, to explain the "iceberg" of truth beneath the "tip" of what can be seen. The uses to which this craft can be put are unbounded: History is replete with examples of famous and infamous actions that have taken place as the direct—and sometimes indirect—result of the views arrived at through an intelligence-based understanding of people's motives, intentions, and capacity. The fortunes and misfortunes of peoples, races, cultures, and empires has often turned on what, in retrospect, can be seen to have been either "good" or "bad" intelligence.

We should be prepared to admit, then, that any pretensions one might have about what might be called the "purity of purpose" of intelligence are hardly borne out by historical, or even current, fact. Intelligence is a weapon: it is a tool just like any other. It can be used for good, not-so-good, or even downright evil purposes. It can be used competently or with little apparent skill. It can be applied to worthy causes, just as it can be underutilized and even wasted.

The essential truth about intelligence, whether one uses it as a weapon or as a tool, is that it, in a sense, remains "neutral." It exists to be used, and the values we might place on the efficiency, the purpose, and the outcomes of its use are, in fact, those values imparted by the user. They are not intrinsic to the intelligence product itself. It is people who desire the service of intelligence: People operate the processes and people determine the outcomes. Finally, these same people act on the product, interpreting it in the context of their priorities and agendas. So when we observe that "intelligence often seems to serve its own ends," we mean not the practice or the craft or the underlying philosophy of intelligence, but merely those people who are involved in conducting, acting upon, or manipulating intelligence.

HISTORICAL PERSPECTIVE ON MANAGEMENT STYLE

In the popular sense, *management* is a catchall term used to denote and describe the process of visualizing, planning, and leading an enterprise or activity. The nexus between the management idea and role and function of intelligence is that there will always exist in organizations an identifiable body or group to which the intelligence specialists provide a service. This is a group one might refer to commonly as the *clients*, but equally may think of as *consumers* or *customers* of the intelligence service. Whatever the term used, this client represents that body of people in organizational positions of power who are logically the ultimate users of the intelligence output.

Depending upon one's affiliation, the notion of "client" might encompass a sovereign, a government, or a political grouping within government. The client—he, she, or they—might be a leadership group within industry or the civil service. The important feature is that those who have responsibility for determining the direction and decision making of organizations are, inevitably and logically, those who are the consumers of an intelligence service.

In examining some of the features, mores, and values of various historical management models, it is easy to see how differing management approaches might impact upon the role and functioning of analysis services within organizations. The sweeping generalizations that follow are, of course, founded in fact. However, there are exceptions to these sometimes harsh or provocative observations as a result of the good sense and patience evidenced among the ranks of managers. The aim here is merely to highlight some of the standards so that we might examine historical difficulties against a setting of present practice and experience.

Some—perhaps many—readers will have firsthand knowledge of management practice throughout the middle part of this century, in which management could best be described as "patriarchal." The key features of this approach revolved around a style that was absolutist in upholding managers' power over the individual; in all things, the person was subordinated to the organization. Though always cited as being for one's good, the fact is that patriarchal styles of management inevitably meant that one group of involved persons "gained" in terms of power and influence, and other, larger groups lost their capacity for input and involvement except in pursuit of loyalty and only under close direction. This is not to say that this patriarchal style was, however, always necessarily bad. Clearly it suited those for whom following was better than leading, and a strong perception of paternalistic goodwill went a long way toward minimizing any latent dissatisfaction. Indeed, the style was evidence of the continuing "old order" of natural division of classes of worker and was congruent with general social patterns up to the middle part of the twentieth century.

What effect did the patriarchal style of management have on the issue we are discussing here? Was decision making dependent upon the sort of analytical input that we know intelligence could provide? This management culture, once operating, tended to be self-perpetuating in that it generated an institutionalized acceptance of rather submissive "order taking" among the work force. Power groups exercised control over all aspects of the working—and sometimes the social—lives of others.

In this climate, whole generations of workers generally came to tend toward conformist behavior, trusting their futures and careers to others and providing obedience and loyal support to a nurturing management structure. At the same time, this supportive workforce was actively prevented, more by circumstances than by order, from playing to its full potential in providing intellectual, innovative, and imaginative input to work processes.

Management power, exercised in this way consistently without input or feedback, tended to view decision making as necessarily operating as the sole right of those in management positions. Such a practice was often devoid of balanced input and became one in which strength of will and determination to succeed were valued more highly than any other features of managerial activity. This sort of approach bred confidence to a level that often outstripped reality.

Managers who operated alone, perhaps with the best of intentions, came progressively to believe in the value of their own experience and training and, hence, their own judgment. The solitude of life at the top of an organizational unit, and the lack of other sources of qualitative input, created a strong potential for "closed-loop" management. This fed upon itself, with little expectation of the availability of other advice and no inclination to seek it.

In these circumstances, analysis and research had little chance of competing successfully for attention. Perhaps a rule of thumb might have been articulated thus: If managers have to operate under stress and without substantial availability of real support and advice, then those managers will, in time, come to believe that they do not need any such support or advice. However, this was about to change.

CONTEMPORARY MANAGEMENT APPROACHES

Management styles have changed dramatically over the past several decades: changes in management and industrial relations that allegedly mirror changed societal beliefs about the value and rights of the individual. The "new-wave management" theories of the 1970s and 1980s publicly emphasized a dramatic opening for worker participation in planning and decision making. This move evolved as a strategy to satisfy the principal goal of harnessing goodwill and talent from the workforce within a contributive framework. The concept of participative management, with its attendant workforce involvement—or at least the expectation of having it—in all matters affecting the future of workers, was a significant extension beyond the historical involvement of unions and workplace representatives. In the past, such involvement was more likely in matters relating to safety and conditions of employment than to the business future of an enterprise.

The rhetoric of this shift in management style encouraged worker expectations of a life in which business decision making would become an exercise in genuine participation, in which the quality of decisions and management plans would thus be better for all concerned. This would mean an end to the decisions of patriarchs and absolutists governed by a "this is for your own good" syndrome.

THE PRESENT SITUATION

Rather surprisingly, in some respects modern management practice is little different from older styles. One might well ask how this could be, if the governing theories seem to be so different.

Perhaps the answer lies not in any subterfuge about the theories themselves, but in the particular stresses and strains that modern living and economic conditions impose upon organizational behavior. We should not be surprised at this, since we only have to look at the difference between industrial theory and practice relevant to the industrial revolution to understand just how persuasive was Robbie Burns's observation about "best laid plans."[1]

In fact, in many ways modern management practice—as opposed to theory—is just as patriarchal as its predecessor, at least in terms of the "power syndrome" though not in the context of familial concern for the workforce. It is true that what has evolved in these recent decades is a participative approach to management practice that has set in place industrial mechanisms to guarantee the involvement of all levels of staff in discussing issues that face managers. The term *involvement* is used here because there are no guarantees that opinions will be heeded or that staff requirements will be met; the guarantee is merely that each voice may be heard even though not necessarily considered.

The reasons are obvious. Competitive pressure, even in the public sector, to perform to standards set by others has taken its toll of the implementation of what began as sound management vision. As senior executives and managers at all levels are placed on notice that performance is paramount, it is no wonder that all aspects of management practice are examined against notional standards of what "good performance" might look like. In far too many organizations the criteria for judgment have slipped from a basis of quality toward quantifiable measures.

In such a climate, decision making is seen as a process that can be evaluated in the following way: Was it quick? Were all the right moves taken? Were the right people informed about outcomes and impact? Was no one else's decision making adversely affected or delayed? Questions of this ilk quickly become questions about lists, checks, and balances, with ticks in the box, due-by dates, and backlog figures as attractive measures.

The hidden outcome in such circumstances is that there has been little to distinguish how so-called modern managers exercise their responsibilities in any way better than the historical models. Decision making can become subject to the pressures of time and decisiveness (the need to appear to be "dynamic"), with quality being a last-run issue. This does not mean that wrong decisions are rewarded; rather, dynamic decision making creates an image of success, enthusiasm, and vibrancy that ambitious managers (and "survivors") value highly.

BLENDING ANALYTICAL SUPPORT AND MANAGEMENT THINKING

Not only are there pressures of this sort—the tension between quality and quantity or process and outcome—but one should consider the added impact of stress arising from rationalization moves, restriction, constraint, and increasing competition among and within organizations. This pressure creates an environment in which conforming to standards of urgency and dynamism, set by upper-level corporate executives, is valued above other, more qualitative measures. In essence, my observation is that while managerial theory may have changed, there remains little evidence of managers yet committed to "thinking smarter" rather than continuing to work even harder. Yet, at the same time, management training has become an object of particular emphasis, with a focus on concepts such as strategic thinking and planning, the development of visions, and corporate plans. While it is clearly important to many that their organizations follow the rhetoric of intelligent, responsive, and forward-looking management concepts, there is too little in practice that translates this into real commitment to careful and structured thinking.

There is enough evidence to suggest that many managers remain, to an unhappy degree, intellectually isolated from those able to support them, victims of corporate urgency to "act." The pivotal argument here is that all the pressure previously described actually creates a tense and busy management environment in

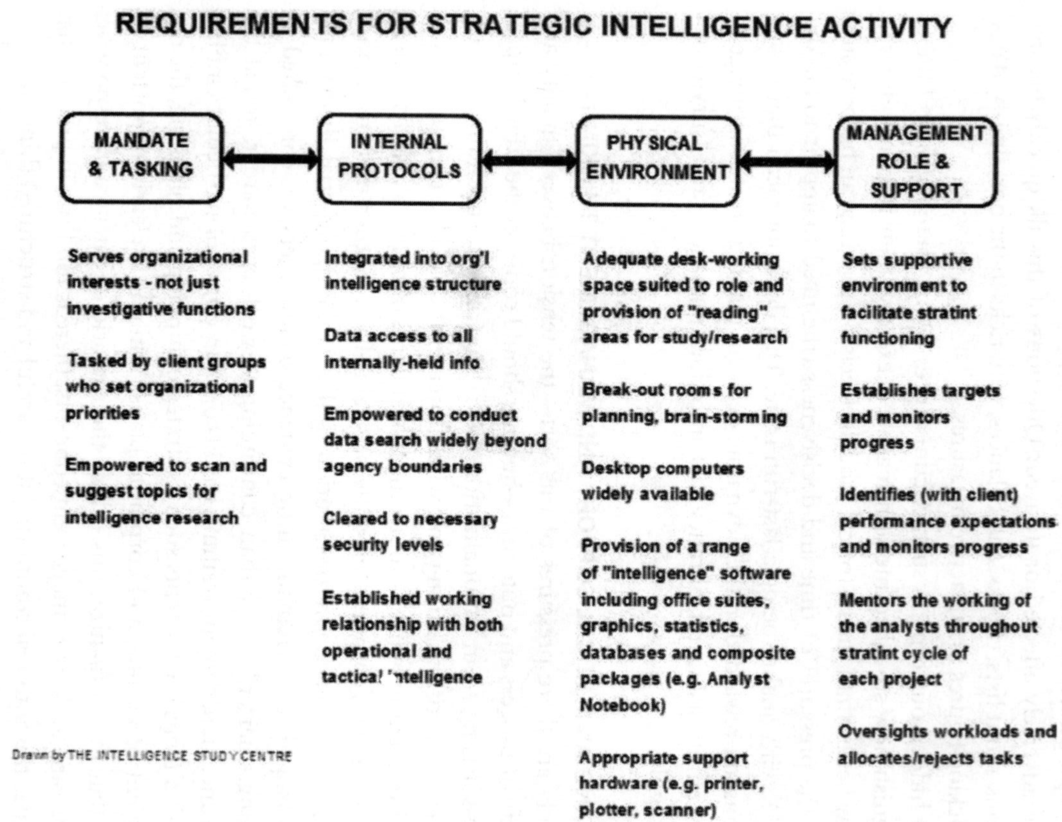

FIGURE 6.1
Requirements for Strategic Intelligence Activity

which a sensible response would point to the need for analysis and research in decision making. The all-too-common alternative is almost inexplicable: one that assumes analysis is a bothersome activity that doesn't actually serve the needs of busy, dynamic executives. Yet clearly there is a role for responsive and reactive carriage of many business activities, in government or elsewhere; careful thought and impact analysis is, however, what is needed in the realm of forward planning. To do otherwise is a ludicrous proposition.

If one accepts the foregoing as an explanation of how things currently work, what is it that we need to do differently? To return to the theme of this chapter, clearly a package of "tools" to assist managers in their work exists: included among these is the availability of analytical research and interpretation skills and methodologies. A key stumbling block, though, is the possibility that managers and executives will either misunderstand or trivialize the importance of analysis: yet, apart from luck, surely good decisions are driven by careful consideration.

To put this into context, we should also remember that current theories clearly identify "analysis" as an essential step between the thinking, or visioning, phase and the plan development phase of managerial activity. What seems to have happened, though, is that the analysis step is generally truncated and glossed over, in terms of both time and quality, and indeed little is ever actually taught about this part of the process of management practice. The analysis process—and this includes the planned collection, research, and interpretation of information—is relatively simple to establish in any organization. It is not hugely costly or resource-expensive to run, nor does it need an inordinate amount of time to complete projects to provide input to management. All these are, after all, issues of application and implementation, and do not constitute a logical barrier to putting the analysis system in place, whatever the organization.

What is at issue is not "how" or "where" or "when" to introduce the analysis links into the management chain. The challenge for many, now, is simply "why not?"

The answer is both simple and obvious. The development of major policies and programs and the determination of operational priorities and plans all demand and indeed deserve our best efforts. It is true that there are pressures that can lead to the sacrifice of detailed consideration of issues in the name of urgency and expediency. Yet these same pressures are the very ones that we should accept as being the mandate for acting not only decisively, but intelligently: acting to maximize our potential and thus, at the same time, avoiding "average" as a level of attainment. Were we to accept this approach—inserting good analysis into the decision-making routines—then what are the implications for management, and how should we deal with them? There are several obligations in following such a course of action.

First, all the participants would have to structure opportunities for pause and careful consideration of key issues. This would permit the widest possible examination of all the relevant features of a problem or opportunity. This would have to be done in a way consistent with time-critical requirements, but not truncated or otherwise put at risk by tradition, form, bias, or any other imposed behavioral limitation.

Second, executives would need to commit themselves to working with analysts and researchers to clarify the issues and priorities involved. In addition, they would need to describe the framework of the context in which the ultimate decisions will have to be made. They would need to provide active and real support and mandate for the analysis and research process to take place effectively. They must empower those involved, giving them clear authority and an expectation that their assessments, answers, and recommendations must be as objective as can be achieved, and certainly free from organizational prejudice.

There are, of course, further implications that relate to the responsibilities of managers once they have the results and advice from the analysis, research effort, and input. First and foremost is the challenge for management to consider fairly the "neutral" assessment of issues, free of any flavor of conformism or self-interest. This is a challenge that is not always easy to meet, since managers themselves can be expected to already hold views on these same issues. While the analysts and researchers have to maintain their objectivity as best they can, this same challenge has to be met by the decision makers in weighing up the advice and reaching conclusions on outcomes and priorities.

On a more positive note, one pleasing outcome will be the enhancement to staff morale and self-worth that derives from becoming meaningfully involved in shaping the organization's direction. This will have the additional benefit of tending to improve the overall quality of advice as experience grows, but, more particularly, as they are seen to be trusted in their assisting and advising roles.

There are, on the other hand, some inhibitors to putting in place this sort of commitment to analytical advice. First, the present trend for an isolationist and conformist approach to management style and operation, often seeking only advice that supports views that are already safely held, can lead to a continuing sense of complacency about how well management is currently performing. It is all too easy to accept that power, the mantle of responsibility, and intense levels of activity are synonymous with infallibility. Yet one must wonder: If there is that high a degree of frenetic involvement in just getting on with managing, where does the time, skill, and energy come from that will allow the manager to gather, sift, and analyze the information necessary to make such intelligent decisions? Ego and self-reliance are part of the emotional and intellectual conflict between dynamism, conformity, and survival, on the one hand, and acceptance of one's needs and recognition of imperfection, on the other.

Finally, in this discussion on implications there is the question of costs of establishing and operating an effective analytical and research apparatus within an organization. The good news is that there exists both a relevant body of knowledge and the availability of skills; indeed, the skills and techniques can be learned relatively easily. Human resources are relatively inexpensive, and analysts with varying types and degrees of experience are available, needing principally encouragement to utilize their talents, enthusiasm, and intelligence. A prime cost is, of course, the need for management levels to meet the challenge of mandating the analytical function and encouraging it to operate effectively. This is easier said than done, for it requires corporate executives to accept that they cannot function alone in decision making. For those managers and organizations that either do not have or use the analytical support activity suggested here—or use it only sparingly or prejudicially—there is the challenge of showing courage in choosing to think fully and carefully about issues, courage in being seen to pause when the organizational environment seems to call for dynamic action.

Not only are these pressures real and ever present, but there are those organizational and cultural features that often perpetuate and institutionalize thought processes and idea generation to "fit in" with current belief systems. This is the stuff of "safe" management—in the sense of decision making in a style that stays in tune with established peer practice and current organizational thinking. Yet what could be better than doing well, using all the tools at hand, rather than mirroring what one thinks are the acceptable ideas and practice?

NOTE

1. "The best-laid schemes o' mice an' men/Gang aft a-gley," from the poem "To a Mouse, On Turning Her up in Her Nest with the Plow" (1785), by Robert Burns.

7

Management and Self-Management of Strategic Projects and Processes

One of the continuing issues of debate in intelligence work is that surrounding the question of management. From a practitioner's perspective, these questions revolve around the quality and style of management and the knowledge and understanding shown by their own managers and supervisors. Practitioners in intelligence, and perhaps more so in strategic work, regard themselves as doing something really quite special.

Managers in the intelligence field often find themselves trying to use traditional management styles that are heavy on "rules" and less accommodating in terms of understanding and flexibility. It is frequently observed that many managers expect intelligence staff to generate their product on demand and with a high level of certainty, without understanding that intelligence—and analysis particularly—are mental pursuits that are not so easily controlled. Nor is intelligence about certainty. The broader the view required and the further forward in time a prediction is placed, the greater may be the analyst's level of uncertainty.

If there is one common criticism that managers and intelligence staff could level at one another, it is focused mainly on their lack of understanding of differing perspectives and urgencies. Intelligence officers believe that their managers need to have a special understanding of the intelligence role in order to get the best out of it. Managers, for their part, often state that they find intelligence staff to be so preoccupied with their own worlds that they fail to understand their obligation to provide the service that their clients demand.

This chapter looks at the management issues involved and discusses the ways in which all participants to the strategic intelligence process might act to achieve success in their task.

THE ROLE OF INTELLIGENCE MANAGEMENT

It is important to understand that there are really no particular, special, or unique requirements for strategic intelligence management that set it apart from other management applications. What is needed, above all else, is good, supportive, intelligent applications of established, sound management principles.

The nature of strategic intelligence work demands a highly detailed, orderly, and intellectually disciplined approach to all phases of the intelligence cycle, commensurate with meeting the requirements and expectations of its clients and consumers. Although it can be argued that this approach should be the norm for all intelligence work, the fact is that the concentration of thought and effort are hallmarks of strategic intelligence. Thus there is, at least superficially, a noticeable difference between strategic research activity and the more usual operational and tactical intelligence functioning. It is, however, arguable that all intelligence activity requires application of the same commitment to detailed and careful implementation of the steps of the intelligence cycle, and thus deserves—and perhaps demands—skillful management.

ISSUES AND PRINCIPLES

If it is to be fully effective, strategic intelligence has to be based on the acceptance of several clearly identifiable management practices.

- No matter what sort of client expectations it is dealing with and responding to, strategic intelligence remains a "total" service committed to providing comprehensive assessments and predictions. All management action impacting upon the intelligence service should reinforce the complementary—not competitive or conflicting—nature of this relationship, thus reminding clients of the links between their need for decision making and the strategic analysis support they can draw upon.

- Sharing of information, views, skills, and products—among those involved in any intelligence activity in the organization—is pivotal to success, and managers must actively promote this.
- The client must be educated and helped to understand and expect the constant level of imprecision evident in any strategic intelligence product developed. This is logically the case, given that the broader view of issues sought of strategic analysis will invariably place greater reliance upon judgment than on methodologies and approaches more suited to techniques designed to suit measurable data.
- As a consequence of the negotiation climate that must be created and sustained between intelligence officers and clients, there will be an absolutely clear agreement concerning the objectives set for any assessment project.
- At the same time, it is essential that managers, practitioners, and clients negotiate and agree—before commencement of work—on an appropriate mechanism for later review and performance/efficiency measurement of the project and its outcomes.
- There must be client/management commitment to the high levels of input and effort, faith and trust, needed to feed the strategic intelligence activity.
- Close and continuing relationships must be established at the outset of intelligence projects, among clients, intelligence managers, and intelligence analysts, to facilitate the negotiation, ongoing monitoring, and review of the work being undertaken.
- Managers must make clear and conscious choices concerning a range of important staff-related issues, giving appropriate consideration to the impact of these decisions for clients, staff, and management:
  1. the arguments for and against encouraging specialization within subject interest areas applicable to the organization;
  2. choosing an appropriate balance of staff selection criteria that considers the issues of qualifications, experience, organizational knowledge, career tracking, cross-pollination of skills, and multi-skilling;
  3. training and development requirements for staff and management levels alike; and
  4. career development strategies and opportunities within and beyond intelligence.

MANAGING STRATEGIC INTELLIGENCE PROJECTS

Chapter 10 deals in detail with the topic of "project planning." However, some general notes within the setting of this chapter are appropriate. While the use of good management practice throughout the strategic intelligence process should be accepted and expected as the norm, there are, in fact, quite special requirements necessary for setting up a "management plan" for individual strategic projects.

Some intelligence tasks hardly warrant being called "projects." They may be routine, uncomplicated to the point of being simple, and intelligence staff and clients alike may become so practiced in carrying these tasks out that no particular or special requirements are generated. On the other hand, as strategic intelligence increasingly produces results and insights that, from the perspective of the client, are of particular benefit, it is likely that intelligence staff will be asked to undertake progressively more complicated or creative strategic projects.

These tasks will inevitably require more effort and careful input to the process to ensure that each has a high degree of potential for success. If this is what is needed, then intelligence staff will need to develop a comprehensive plan to achieve success and avoid confusion. The plan must cover all the various parts of the process. It should identify the "extra" requirements that might be expected, such as the wider collection of data and the additional potential for useful sources, particularly those outside the norm of routine contact.

An essential prerequisite for the project plan is the definition of the strategic intelligence problem. This is necessary to ensure that the client's original statement of tasking is enhanced through background research undertaken by the intelligence officer and discussed with the client, and that a negotiated restatement of all of the component parts of the problem is agreed between both parties, making sure that no nuances or issues are left undescribed.

The strategic project management plan will outline all the component parts of the intelligence process, identify special needs, identify the number and type of resources required, propose reporting targets and times, and outline the type of assessment product, even to the extent of notes on topic coverage. The purpose is twofold:

- The intelligence officer needs to have a "blueprint" of the stages to be covered in the project. These must be drafted or otherwise communicated in sufficient detail to allow it to be used not so much as a one-time passive record, but as a practical tool that can be updated or modified according to changing circumstances.

- Perhaps more importantly, the strategic plan represents the endorsed arrangement between client and producer, ideally locking both into a useful commitment to achieve the required outcomes.

Various means can be used to outline the project plan. Several computer software packages are available to chart events and timelines and to break down activities to allow for budgeting for each subroutine. These software packages, in fact, have their foundation in industrial applications suited to engineering and production line activity (see chapter 10).

What is important is that for every separate project of any complexity or challenge at all, a structured project plan must be thought out, drawn up, and negotiated and agreed among practitioners, managers, and clients. Anything less than this approach will likely result in a situation in which the lack of structure and agreement inhibits effective implementation of the strategic intelligence project.

STRATEGIC ANALYSTS AND SELF-MANAGEMENT

Aside from the responsibility of intelligence managers to look after the well-being and environmental health of their staff, there is a particularly strong need for strategic intelligence practitioners to apply rigorous standards of self-management of their own. This is true regardless of whether those officers are functioning in individual or team roles.

Apart from the benefits involved in maintaining strong levels of control at a personal level over their use of time and other resources, one of the principal dimensions of an intelligence officer's character should be the combination of emotional balance, integrity, and intellectual honesty in all work-related pursuits. Ultimately, these are both the goals and the responsibility of any committed intelligence officer, and although they can be established and maintained within a well-managed work environment, it remains a question of inner strength for the intelligence officer to find and retain.

In addition, and quite apart from maintaining this level of personal qualities, intelligence officers must establish a similar degree of control over the work processes and activities in which they may be involved in everyday intelligence tasks and routines. To this end, there is again a personal level of responsibility involved in ensuring that the following desirable outcomes are achieved:

- maintaining progress toward established project goals and in accordance with the work plans; and
- ensuring that these objectives, plans, and processes are subjected to critical and ongoing personal—as well as unit—review to keep the aims of the intelligence project work in proper perspective, establishing the capacity and opportunity to apply correction wherever necessary.

> The application of good management practice is essential to bring out the full potential and best qualities of an analyst.

CONCLUSION

Those involved in strategic intelligence often consider it to be remarkably rewarding. It may not be unusual for practitioners to be regarded as dedicated to the point of being single-minded about their work. This takes energy, personal honesty, and persistence—all desirable qualities of an intelligence officer. None of these qualities matters if the intelligence analyst is undisciplined, lacks a sense or orderliness, and fails to plan the assigned research.

IV

PROCESSES AND TECHNIQUES

8

Developing Concepts: Understanding the Topic

PROCESSES AND TECHNIQUES FOR STRATEGIC INTELLIGENCE

In this part of the book, the focus is on imparting a sense of process to the whole realm of strategic research and intelligence activity.

In the opinion of some intelligence officers and researchers, the idea of a "process" per se is something of an anathema to their assumptions about the intellectual freedom to undertake serious research. Yet the author has always found that one of the prevailing features of strategic intelligence has been the difficulty the analyst faces in knowing where and how to start a project, let alone how to plan and continue it to best effect.

It is my belief that no serious or comprehensive research can be started without a plan. Equally, how could one expect to take the research task to completion without a routine that, if followed, will provide one with every expectation of success? The point to be made here is that strategic intelligence, like every other type of research, follows familiar and time-honored protocols, routines, and processes that actively assist the conduct of the project. This is in direct contrast with any view that says freedom to think and then act is all that is needed.

Some sort of robust, disciplined, and orderly process is key to the success of the venture. There is no question in my mind that such a process, however defined to meet specific environments and work needs, is precisely what researchers actually do.

In both this and the following chapters, the processes defined and the way in which I recommend they be used have been proven over years of strategic intelligence project work, both within and beyond government enforcement and compliance pursuits. Readers will find that although the emphasis is clearly on adopting the processes and following them without shortcuts, there is an equal emphasis on the continuing challenge to be flexible in the way in which each process is to be used. Moreover, the synergy to be gained from creatively applying the whole process regime is a positive benefit to the analyst, ensuring that strategic project tasks can be dealt with efficiently and effectively.

On the negative side, where strategic analysis goes wrong, it is often found to be that analysts refuse to accept the inherent discipline of following the sort of routine established here. Sadly, some analysts assume that it is all right to carry out some sections of the process—for example, defining the problem properly—but too time-consuming to be bothered with the detailed thinking involved in developing indicators as an aid to collection planning. In these circumstances, it is not the process routine that is at fault; instead, it is lazy and undisciplined thinking that is the root cause of failure or, at the very least, underachievement in the task.

Since the processes themselves are easy to follow, there is every reason to do so, and I strongly recommend that the reader approach this part with this message in mind. Certainly, many hundreds of my students of this training doctrine have discovered the benefits of doing so.

One view often advanced as a fundamental difference between so-called basic intelligence techniques and strategic analysis is that the former is merely processing while the latter represents creative thinking as the key to facilitating research. This is an interesting line of argument, because it helps emphasize just how cloudy our thinking is when it comes to defining intelligence at all, let alone differentiating among the various types, levels, and applications. The idea of defining intelligence authoritatively is one that certainly attracts a wide range of individuals and organizations. Some clearly seem to be trying to provide clarity in the void of established doctrine in the application of intelligence to enforcement particularly. On the other hand, there are those who appear to act in a way that suggests that perhaps they see merit in using the intelligence definition and doctrine generation function as a way of gaining, strengthening, or asserting some moral and intellectual "high ground." Whatever the motivation, none has yet succeeded in defining the concepts, protocols, and rules in the form of a universally respected and acceptable "doctrine" for intelligence in the enforcement community.

I am attracted to the simple idea that intelligence should not be considered just in terms of the amalgam of all the usual wordy process phrases. Rather, it might be better thought of as the activity of generating insight and interpretation of data in a way relevant to one's interests and needs. By this way, we see clearly through the processes to the ultimate goal, but the processes themselves are essential to achieving that goal.

As to the line of argument about the differences between basic and strategic intelligence, there are many inherent flaws, but two stand out as the most obvious. First, it is untenable to suggest that so-called basic—that is, tactical and/or operational—intelligence and analysis activities require solely the processing of information, devoid of any creative thought, to arrive somewhat "automatically" at an answer. This is the chain of reasoning that might lead to the seductive, but incorrect, suggestion that computerized processing software equates to analysis.

Second, and the real focus of this introductory section, no strategic research project could begin, survive, or successfully conclude without reliance on a disciplined and formalized process-facilitated approach to identifying and exploring the phenomenon or problem. Certainly, strategic thinking involves creativity and imagination, and courage, too, to go beyond the boundaries of more "traditional" intelligence activity that serves urgent operational and tactical needs. An abundance of creativity by itself, though, is no substitute for honest hard work. This is simply an essential complement to the processes.

The focus of all the chapters in this part, therefore, is on laying out a sequence of processes. All of them need to be followed, since to omit any will unbalance the whole chain of activity. Moreover, each process in the entire chain must be approached in a rigorous way if the end result is to stand the best chance of achieving success for the analyst.

CONCEPTUAL FRAMEWORKS

Strategic intelligence clearly differs in many ways from what the analyst may have been used to dealing with in handling tactical or operational intelligence processes. Yet, for all the differences, there is a constancy of underlying similarity in the fundamental concepts.

One element that sets strategic research apart from other forms of intelligence is the very nature of the problem itself. Often, an analyst is given a task that deals with topics that are "unusual" in the sense that they have not been encountered before by the analyst or even the intelligence unit itself. It may be that the issue being raised has never actually been seen to be problematic before. Perhaps it was problematic in the past but not relevant for that analyst's unit or jurisdiction. It may even be that the subject is just so unexpected and "new" that the analyst is totally unfamiliar with what it actually is. On the other hand, the topic may be an issue that is familiar in concept—for example, drugs or fraud—but not in terms of the level and breadth of research now required—a common enough phenomenon that demonstrates the move up the intelligence chain from tactical and operational activity (serving line managers) to strategic study and forecasting levels (serving corporate executives and department heads).

An interesting dilemma now occurs. All the analyst's prior training and experience in intelligence and investigation might generally suggest that the only way through this minefield of uncertainty, unfamiliarity, and inexperience is to simply get on with the task, gathering data and "learning on the way." In addition, this is likely to be the preferred option when dealing with normal workaday pressures from clients and managers to act quickly. When given the strategic assignment, almost the first challenge that the strategic analyst will face is simply this:

> How can I do this assignment unless I first understand the broad background to the topic?

However, it is no easy matter for the analyst to start an intelligence probe into a subject that is unfamiliar. You should not even assume, just because you may have worked with the topic at an operational level, that you have yet developed a thorough understanding of just how it all works. Often, operational or field experience is so focused on specific issues and targets that you just do not have enough time to get to familiarize yourself with the full range of its many aspects. Yet to instantly start to gather data about a topic one does not yet comprehend, even at a basic level, is to run the considerable risk of wasting time by collecting information without a well thought-out plan. It is establishing some baseline ideas about the topic—a simplified version of the familiar formula of who, what, when, where, why, and how—that is essential as a means of correcting the lack of topic familiarity of the analyst.

In essence, the task immediately facing the analyst is one of gaining a fundamental understanding of all the elements and component parts of the strategic

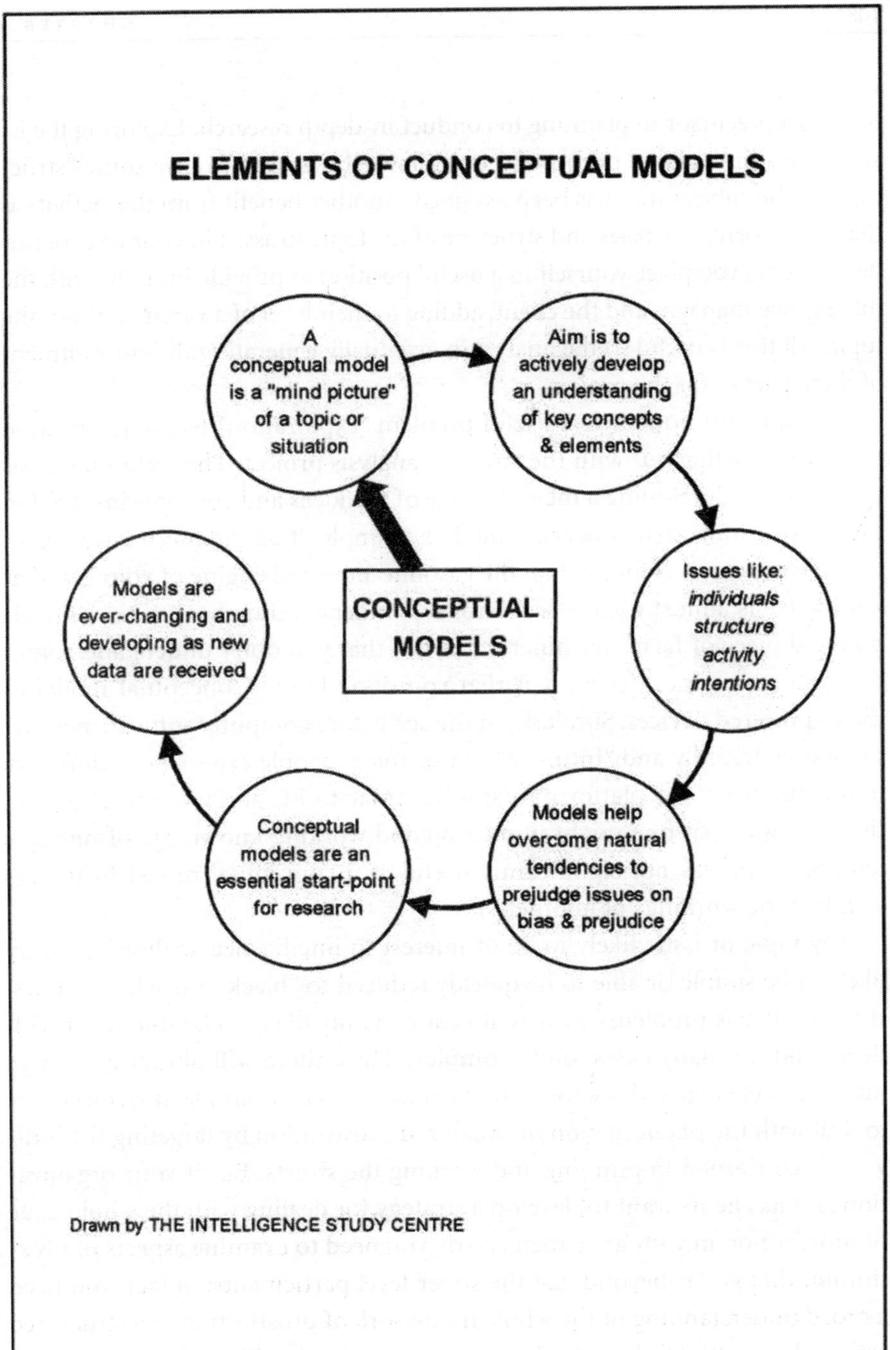

FIGURE 8.1
Conceptual Model Features

topic as a precursor to planning to conduct in-depth research. Exploring the issue in this limited but purposeful way allows the analyst to give some "structure" to the subject that has been assigned. Another benefit from this activity is that in exploring the basis and structure of the topic to assist in your level of understanding, you place yourself in a useful position to provide input to both the intelligence manager and the client, adding to their level of awareness about the topic. All this is useful to the analyst in eventually generating the commitment of these parties for the project.

A simple but nonetheless useful problem "exploration" technique is often the key to starting out with the strategic analysis project. The technique basically involves developing a mental image of the ideas and concepts involved in the issue or topic that concerns you. For example, if all the mechanical experience you possess is focused on the gasoline-powered engine of your car, that knowledge is almost useless as a basis for understanding how to fix a diesel-powered piece of farm machinery. It is not that you don't understand something about engines per se; it is that you don't have a conceptual model of diesel-powered devices. Similarly, in the age before computer software became more user-friendly and "intuitive" to use, many people experienced difficulty in moving from one platform to another (Mac to PC and vice versa). Again, the issue was that one might possess a good working knowledge of one system, but that was not significantly useful as a conceptual model in understanding the workings of another.

Any topic or issue likely to be of interest to intelligence analysts is hardly likely to be simple or able to be quickly reduced to "black-and-white" values. If the matter is problematic, it is almost certainly likely to be one filled with detail and, in many cases, quite complex. Thus, there will always be a large number of elements of the topic to understand. As an example, it is important to deal with the phenomenon of organized prostitution by targeting the individuals concerned in pimping and working the streets. But if your organization and its clients want to develop a strategy for dealing with the whole issue of prostitution in your area, then clearly you need to examine aspects of prostitution that go far beyond just the street-level participants; in fact, you need a broad understanding of the whole framework of prostitution as a structured criminal activity. All those traditional questions of intelligence and investigation—the who, what, when, where, why, and how questions—need to be asked and answered. As the strategic analyst responsible for handling such an assignment, you need a feeling for the "big picture" before you can start deciding what data to gather and how to put it together.

When we talk about developing a big picture, the phrase we use is "establishing a conceptual model (or framework)." This is a way of describing the characteristics and features of the area or topic under intelligence interest. Regardless of the type of intelligence product required by a client, placing the intelligence problem in its appropriate context is pivotal to the future development of the intelligence process, and it is this conceptual focus that facilitates all further activity.

In strategic intelligence, assigned topics usually possess considerable breadth and detail. Since this goes well beyond the normal experience of operational analysts, there is a need to establish a focus on the contextual setting of the topic for its strategic meanings. It becomes particularly important to find and describe the relationship between the features of the intelligence problem and the broader conceptual understanding of the whole area of strategic interest.

> A conceptual model is the mental image you develop about a phenomenon that explains it in terms such as what it is, how it works, who is involved in it, and why it exists.

IDENTIFYING THE FEATURES OF A STRATEGIC TOPIC

The strategic analyst needs to gain an awareness of the wide range of features of the central topic issue as soon as possible, even before a project plan has been developed. The reason for this is obvious: No detailed problem or task definition can take place until you gain a working level of understanding about the very nature of the topic.

For any topic, it is possible to develop and use a list of features—these could be termed *descriptors*—that will serve as a starting point in gathering information to gain familiarity with the topic detail. A standard checklist for this will include some or all of the issues listed below. But while this checklist is always a useful starting point, it is not to be taken as the only solution, and the analyst must not exclude other aspects of the subject that seem to be relevant.

- Organizational structures and features
- Geographic location issues
- Political conditions or features
- Sociological issues
- Cultural aspects
- Economic conditions and their impact
- Industrial and commercial considerations
- Legislation and penalty systems

This checklist is for example only and certainly not meant to be exhaustive in coverage of all the relevant issues. As topics change, so should the list of information the analyst might want to gather to understand at least some of the basic issues involved. Some of these categories will not necessarily suit the particular topic given, but others will. In any case, it is important to remember that this is not the collection plan for the entire project. It is a first step in every sense of the term. The key is that to be effective, conceptual modeling does require some collection of basic background data to give an outline of what is involved.

HOW TO DEVELOP THE CONCEPTUAL MODEL

In order to design the appropriate conceptual framework to suit the subject of strategic intelligence interest, the analyst must know—or must acquire knowledge and understanding—about those political, social, cultural, organizational, economic, and geographic features and structures that we have discussed already.

- The first step, before addressing the specific intelligence problem, is to assemble and study available information relating to the general problem area. This type of preliminary study provides the backdrop to further consideration and development of the framework.
- The second step is to examine the specific intelligence problem, not just to acquire generalized background knowledge but to focus on what happens and why. One way of thinking about this is to place the criminal activity under the microscope, so to speak, and examine it in terms of cause and effect. What you are looking for is a feeling for the motivation and impact of all activities undertaken as part of the topic.

The following example of conceptual modeling demonstrates this approach.

EXAMPLE OF DEVELOPING A CONCEPTUAL FRAMEWORK: THE GARMENT INDUSTRY

Of course, you can always learn about the specifics of this or any business; all you have to do is to gather every piece of detail to fill in the picture. Typical questions might include those below.

- What sort of people does your business, and others like it, employ?
- What do they do?
- Is it profitable?
- What are the business's prospects?

Gathering this sort of data gives you only the bare minimum of what you need if you are to come to a considered view about whether or not to stay with this business. What you *really* require is a larger understanding of the field in which this business fits and some feeling for how it all works.

In short, you need to develop a conceptual model of the garment industry and the particular market niche that your business relates to. Right now, you should be thinking along the following lines:

- How is the clothing retail trade structured for the types of garments your business specializes in?
- Is the trade typically one of "tied" houses, or is it a freely distributed market? That is, are your products sold on the basis of contractual agreement for distribution to specific chains of stores, or may sales be made to any and all buyers?
- How are contracts organized—short- or long-term, high- or low-volume range, COD or consignment?
- Are key staff (designers, cutters) tenured, contracted, or casual?
- How are supplier contracts formulated, and are supplies of materials and accessories held in stock or called up when needed?
- What are the key financial features of these businesses? Is the cash in/out activity constantly in motion or subject to fluctuation, seasonal or otherwise? What are the business's assets typically

considered to be: equipment, stock, supplies, or staff talent, or some combination thereof?

These and many questions like them help you understand how the trade works—a true conceptual model. Once you understand how things normally occur, *then* you can get on with the more detailed and specific planning and data collection to suit the project.

If you look again at the garment factory example and are involved in trying to understand the whole concept of garment design, manufacture, and distribution, some very relevant questions would include:

- What happens?
- Why did that happen?
- What happens next?
- What are the outcomes?

Start at any point in the chain of activity and work forward (think of this as "downstream") or backward ("upstream") to make sure that you cover absolutely all the events that are related to the basic question. By constantly asking yourself "Why did that happen?" and then proceeding to a range of "So what?" impact questions, you will eventually have a firm grasp of the whole network of action within this topic.

In all this, the analyst seeks to develop a conceptual model or framework of the topic, one that explains the structure and features of issues that surround what has become the intelligence problem. Sometimes this framework of understanding merely serves as a mental model for your personal use in the later steps of the strategic intelligence process. However, in generating this level of understanding, it may well be more useful to develop some more formalized diagrammatic representation of the features of the problem area, identifying and charting the relationships and interaction involved. Even preparing simplified flowcharts may aid you in the further steps yet to come.

The most important thing now is to take time and think about how to acquire enough broad understanding of the topic to enable you to begin the detailed planning necessary to complete the assignment. As a strategic analyst, if you begin working without a conceptual understanding of the strategic problem, then you will be committing yourself to a course of action that may well be incomplete and could be seriously misdirected.

CONCLUSION

At the start of any new strategic assessment project, the single objective of the strategic analyst is to gather useful background that will help in shaping the project. You need to list likely subject headings that will help to explore the full meaning of the topic you have been tasked to assess. Then you will need to gather the appropriate information and read and assess it. This step in developing a conceptual framework suited to each intelligence problem is as essential to the conduct of strategic intelligence studies as it is to the development of other types of intelligence. In its own way, it is just as important in starting off an investigation.

What is particularly important to the strategic analyst is that this step be carried out in a planned and orderly fashion, knowing that you have a clear understanding of exactly what you want of this phase and how you can go about getting it.

It is certainly possible to begin any intelligence process, regardless of the problem posed, without a full understanding of the issue and its ramifications. In the name of urgency, analysts are commonly encouraged to get on with their work without undue delay. But the inevitable result of doing so without proper preparation is that the lack of prior understanding will inhibit the process. Worse still, it will threaten the integrity of the outcome, since time and effort will not have been optimized and may instead have been wasted.

However, no useful redefinition or restatement of the component parts of the strategic assignment can take place until some level of background understanding has been reached in this way.

The purpose of approaching strategic—and other forms of—intelligence problem solving by first defining the environment that surrounds the problem is directly aimed at providing focus to the subsequent intelligence effort.

A sound conceptual understanding of the problem will lead to more efficiency in the various activities of the intelligence cycle, increasing the potential for greater effectiveness in the outcome. One final observation is worth mentioning: The more you learn about the topic, for all the reasons outlined in this chapter, the more effectively you will be able to discuss and negotiate the project with your client.

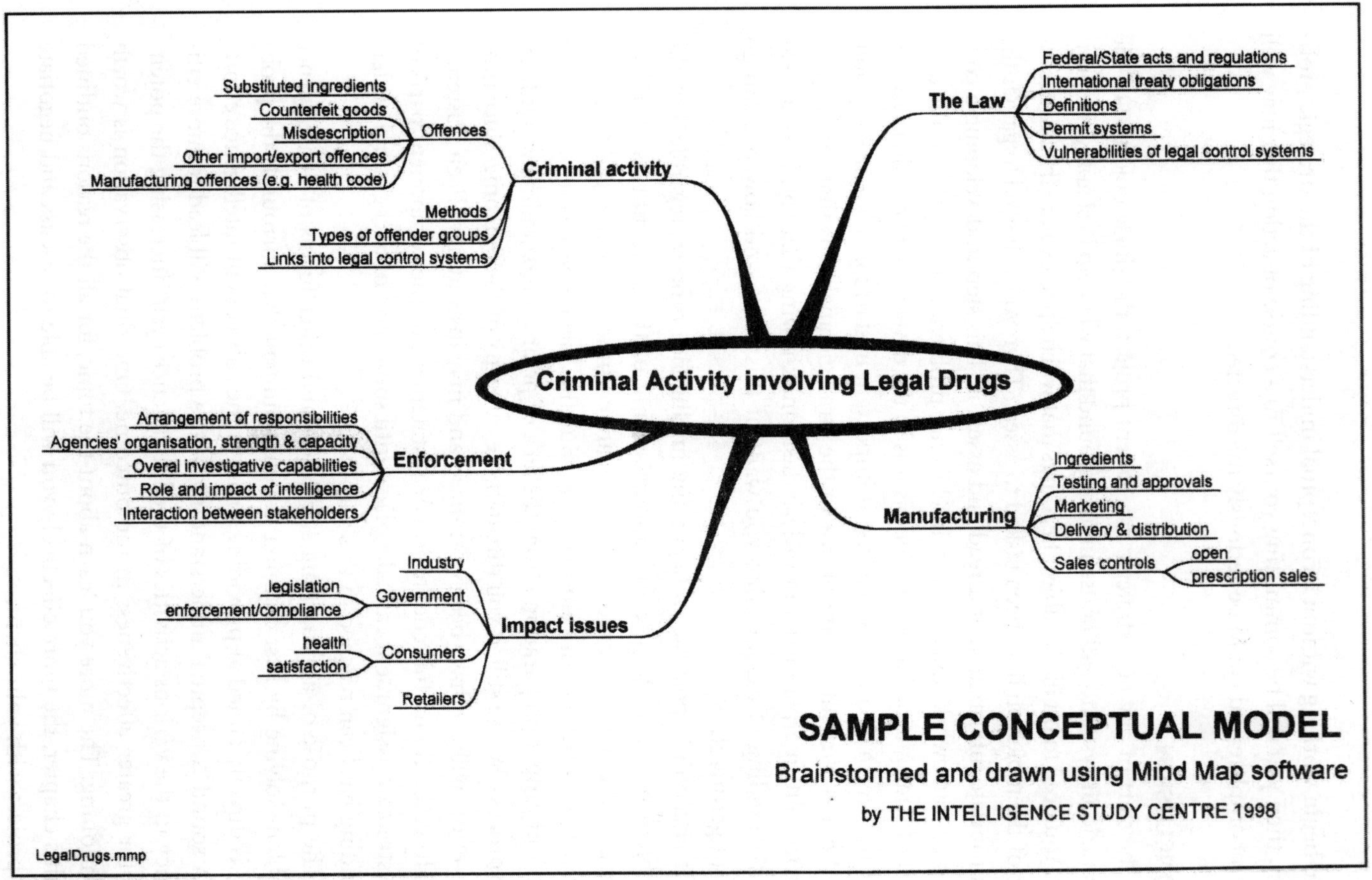

FIGURE 8.2
Sample Conceptual Model Mind Map

9

Defining the Task: Prescribing the Boundaries of the Project

Assume that the strategic topic has been assigned. By now you will have done some basic research into it, as outlined in the previous chapter. You will have developed an understanding of the way in which the subject is structured, what and who is involved—in short, a conceptual framework or model for this topic. Now you can move into the detailed planning that will help you conduct the strategic analysis project.

With this basic understanding already in place, you need to reexamine the wording of the task that has been assigned to you. Often, the case directive can be a single, simple sentence that requires you to "examine" or "assess" such-and-such a topic. You may find that this type of directive is more confusing than it is helpful. After all, in order to plan and conduct the analysis project to achieve a satisfactory outcome for you and your managers and clients, you need to know a lot more basic information about what is intended. There are many key issues here and, for instance, you need to understand:

- Precisely what is wanted, and who wants it?
- How is it going to be used?
- How much breadth and detail should your intelligence investigation and research contain?

- What issues should you focus upon; which ones might be given less priority, or even none?
- What other criteria and project parameters exist that will affect what you do to carry out this assignment?

It is absolutely essential to delve into these issues before you get busy on the project. In fact, in these circumstances, just getting on with doing something is not as important as planning it properly first. The purpose of this chapter is to present the techniques every analyst must use to prepare the groundwork of the strategic project. This involves examining the task from every angle and describing it afresh so that there is no doubt in your mind—or those of your managers and clients—that you know exactly what is to be attempted in the strategic assignment.

Unfortunately, strategic assignments rarely start with a complete and clear directive. More often than not, the intelligence task is defined in perhaps one or two sentences that merely provide an overview of the client's interests in the topic. This is not unexpected, for it is a form of managerial or corporate shorthand that merely sketches in the essentials of the subject. From your perspective, however, you will not be able to plan and conduct the intelligence assignment unless you have a vision of its component parts. Of course, there is a need to know the client's perspective in terms of the reason for the organization's interest and the potential uses that will be made of your analytical product. For example, these might be to inform policy making or to provide a backdrop for operational planning.

The analytic effort to solve the strategic intelligence assignment must logically begin with a clear definition of the problem in all its parts. No matter how important the client's perceptions, they are never likely to be wholly comprehensive in terms of understanding the issues involved. All too often, managers and clients tend to put a spin on the way in which a potential strategic study topic is articulated, a spin that embodies their expectations, most urgent priorities, resource problems, and frustrations. Understandably, this is because of the operating focus of the agency or organization concerned, and is not meant as a criticism. However, it is not the whole story, and the fact is that the task will always turn out be not one single issue, but a collection of a wide range of individual problems for which data must be gathered and assessed. Only by taking an approach that allows exploration of the phenomenon as a whole can the analyst piece together all the relevant components into a single interpretive view.[1] This approach, not one that follows preordained thinking, will more likely result in properly addressing the original request.

Strategic topics vary immensely in terms of complexity. Some elements of a topic may be very simple and specific ones for which there may well be factual answers. For example, in examining the threat posed by fraud involving credit card misuse, one element of the research will be into the mechanisms and safety features of credit card operations conducted and controlled by banks.[2] Other elements may be highly complex, and even apparently indeterminate, and in these instances comprehensive definition and exploration of the key parts of the topic are essential if the intelligence effort is to become effective.

To forestall any potential difficulties caused by a lack of clarity in the wording of the assignment, the analyst has first to turn to the task of defining, restating, and redrafting the intelligence assignment. While the analyst will do most of the work involved in achieving this, the manager and the client must also be involved so that they can endorse the prescription that is developed. The added benefit to them is that this preparatory phase results in discussions and negotiations that bring heightened awareness of the topic and the issues involved.

The end result of this activity is that those involved will reach a shared understanding of what is going to be done in all its aspects. The outcome can best be confirmed by the development of an agreed project directive that you will draft, based on your examination and dissection of the strategic task.

ASSESSING THE SCOPE OF THE ASSIGNMENT

What's Wrong with the Task?

Many strategic intelligence assignments are worded in such a way that the task statement is not very helpful in terms of understanding exactly what is wanted. As an example, consider this task and you can probably recognize what is lacking in its current wording:

> Provide an assessment on illegal drugs in your state/province/territory.

Some simple difficulties and uncertainties immediately become obvious. While the list below is not exhaustive, it does illustrate the types of issues that you need some guidance on.

- What time period is to be covered?
- Are all illegal drugs included, or are there preferential priorities for one type or category over another?
- How does the client want the problem described—in terms of size, financial impact, numbers and types of players (criminals), extent of involvement of victims, and so on?
- Is the focus on criminality, or on the wider issues of drug problems, such as motivation, victims, education, and the like?
- Is the purpose to handle the illegality through enforcement action, or is the client interested in the broader strategies of education and treatment?
- Are legislation and enforcement powers to be considered?
- Is the impact of illegal drugs to be measured or otherwise commented upon?
- Is the client interested in how government counter-action (including enforcement) is coping with the problem?
- . . . and so on.

As the analyst, you need to know all these things before you can proceed with project planning and implementation. You also need to reach a point where not only do *you* know what is required, but your manager and the client have been encouraged to endorse your complete list too.

Solving the Dilemma

What is lacking in the example given above is that there is no precision about the assignment. Nor is this lack likely to be resolved unless the analyst takes a personal hand in making it happen. You can, of course, simply go back to your manager or the client and ask a few questions for clarification. This will help answer your immediate concerns, but it definitely won't address all the issues that need to be sorted out. Why? Because you have yet to consider the whole problem and the subject area carefully. The original strategic task statement needs to be revisited to develop new viewpoints, some multiple interpretations, and many new perspectives. The analyst needs to reexamine the problem from a range of viewpoints to ensure that, whatever its final shape, the problem statement focuses right on the central, key features of the issue and yet avoids being caught up in addressing peripheral aspects of it.

Consider this further example:

How bad will the illegal drug problem be in your state/province/territory in five years' time?

How can the analyst hope to deal with the question posed in this form? It is an intriguing challenge, of course, but it nevertheless lacks clarity, specificity, and precision. However, since the issues involved are both real and complex, it is possible for you to examine the problem area from its several perspectives and pose a range of questions and issues that could be explored to address the overall requirement. This approach demands intellectual rigor that, while it draws on the combined wisdom and experience of those in the organization, nevertheless avoids being distracted or pointed in specific directions. You have to take the task statement and subject it to critical appraisal to achieve several key outcomes. The three steps in this process are:

1. examine the task and list all the important dimensions to it—much as we did in the example of drugs—be careful to consider the less direct and obvious issues, and include them where they seem relevant;
2. look at these aspects of the strategic problem from different angles, and in so doing open your mind up to various ways of gathering and eventually analyzing the data, making notes as you go; and
3. consolidate your list of topics and ideas, and draft them in a format that gives you a clear direction for conducting the assignment—this will become the Terms of Reference once it is endorsed by your manager and the client.

Breaking Down the Problem into its Components

Strategic intelligence problems are not just simple, single ideas. They represent a collection of interlocking concepts, ideas, issues, and features. So this step of breaking a so-called strategic problem down into its component bits might be time-consuming, but it is conceptually quite uncomplicated and even relatively easy to do. You need to do this manually or visually (e.g., on a whiteboard)—or both—to get the best out of the process. Moreover, it is the sort of activity that, while you can do it by yourself, it is better done using others as a sounding board for brainstorming at some stage in the process. Start with the original statement and complete the following steps.

Developing Key Ideas

Write down the key ideas in that statement, including anything that has been added in discussion with your manager or the client when you were assigned this task. For the drugs example at the end of this chapter, you will probably resolve that there are just two key ideas: illegal drugs and State X.

Expanding the Ideas

Take each term, examine it, and dissect it for meaning. You will have to rely upon the knowledge of the topic you gained during your study to establish a suitable mental or conceptual model, and of course you will draw upon your own personal level of experience of this topic. For example, you might use the checklist system developed earlier in this book in chapter 8, and apply each category of information to the central topic, as follows.

Now ask yourself what other elements are involved in the problem. Look to the original statement and consider whether or not there are likely to be more key ideas available and relevant than merely those already recognized in it. There is an established mode of thinking about these issues that will work for you. Assuming the strategic subject is one concerning crime, you might well use what has become a relatively standard set of issues that always can be examined. The list of questions that follows will help you to take the preliminary work you have already done and extend your consideration of matters that ought to be examined. This list, too, is not exhaustive, but merely an indicator of the sorts of questions that you should be asking yourself if the topic is to be properly examined.

- What crime is being committed?
- Who is involved in its commission, in organizing, facilitating, and funding it?
- How is this criminal "organization" structured?
- Who are the victims?
- What motivates the crime?
- What direct outcomes are there, for the criminals as well as for the victims?
- What are the indirect outcomes?
- What is being done about the crime, and with what impact?
- What more might be done about the crime?

Brainstorming as a "Tool" for Problem Definition

In the discussion so far, the role of the analyst has been described as if he or she were acting alone. This may turn out to be necessary in view of various resource constraints. Indeed, in some organizations the "cultural" environment may preclude an analyst from being able to invite participation from others. However, the important fact to remember is that all the thinking essential to developing a comprehensive list of potential features of a strategic subject can be done more efficiently and effectively in the company of others. Properly structured brainstorming sessions can and do provide a forum for imaginative insight and creative thinking far in excess of what an individual analyst may achieve.

It is often said that brainstorming is an activity that "knows no rules." This is incorrect and, in the context of intelligence business, unworkable. At a minimum, the analyst arranging to host a brainstorming session needs to have in mind the following guidelines and rules:

- Identify the issue clearly. This may be simply a statement of the task as originally given by the manager or client.
- Set the objective—for example, "to brain-storm topic X in order to develop a project directive for strategic research."
- Select some people who can—and are prepared to—devote the time to thinking seriously about the issue. Keep the number relatively small so that the group can remain focused and avoid disruptive factionalism—three to five is a workable number.
- Schedule the time for discussion, identify the limit, and advise those involved.
- Arrange the resources necessary—a suitable quiet, comfortable room with whiteboard/flipcharts and other visualization tools.
- Determine who will be in control. This means simply that someone ensures that the rules are followed and that discussion remains ultimately focused on the objective.
- Keep notes and develop mind maps and board drawings/charts/lists, so that they can be referred to after the brainstorming session if need be.

> Brainstorming is a technique that involves grouping people together to encourage them to freely generate ideas about a given issue.

The intended outcome from the brainstorming discussion is a listing of every single point that could possibly be relevant to the strategic study. Massaging this mass of detail and ideas into the form of a Terms of Reference, or project directive, is covered in the following section.

Collating, Clustering, and Formatting All the Elements

Follow the type of "what if?" and "so what?" thinking suggested in the list given on page 120 . For each point, force yourself to list a series of keywords or phrases to cover the ideas that you are generating. You will start to see that every time you list an idea on paper or the board, you can start to show the subissues that come off it. Alternatively, as some ideas are generated, it quickly becomes clear that they are subsets of a more overarching "group description." This clustering approach is designed to bring together all of the myriad ideas generated by the analyst within and beyond the brainstorming and synthesize them into logical sets.

For example, once you think about the idea of "victims," then you could categorize them by user groups—children, runaways, young singles, addicts (as opposed to "social" or occasional users), and so on. There are other indirect victims, too, and you might consider the impact of drug crime on families and work situations.

The result of this activity will be that you develop something that could look like an organization chart or a family tree, with key points at the top, progressively leading to more and more detailed lists as the diagram moves downward. There are many formats that can be used successfully for showing this. For example, Mind Maps™ and associated computer software,[3] organization charts, and text lists with main and subheadings all can be used to good effect. While each is intended to show clearly the issues and subissues that are to be involved in the research, some are particularly useful as briefing aids. Whatever the format, what you end up with is a complete picture of all the elements of this strategic task. Moreover, as you go through this process, you will achieve additional benefits both for the present and for later on during the project:

- You will automatically be mentally cross-checking between key point lists every time you think of another idea, making sure that there is nothing left to chance nor anything overlapping between ideas.
- You will inevitably start thinking: *How can I gather the information I need for this point?*

Why a Terms of Reference (or Project Directive)?

At some stage, however, the analyst must produce a text document that clearly identifies what is to be studied, for whom, and why. This is what becomes, ultimately, the Terms of Reference that forms part of both the working file and the final strategic report.

As the analyst "in control" of the strategic project, by following the above process carefully and creatively, you will end up with a full list of all the issues that could—and perhaps should—be examined under the original assignment. However, if you present this to the manager or client in its current form, it is not necessarily going to be welcomed. At this stage, what has been produced is likely to be a very comprehensive set of tables, lists, and diagrams, though not yet in an orderly form. This is hardly suitable as the basis for serious discussion and agreement at manager/client level. What is needed instead is some form of "presentation document" that, at a minimum, should meet two criteria:

- it presents issues in such a way that they come across as being comprehensive, thoughtful and persuasive; and
- it covers the essential features of the task without being long or wordy.

The objective of problem definition and restatement is to illuminate the problem and, by so doing, inform and educate your colleagues. It should not be your intention to overwhelm the process with detail. Perhaps the most important requirement of all is that the document has to be developed in such a way as to provide you with the basis for a meaningful plan. After all, it is in effect a charter for the strategic assessment activity that is to follow.

DEVELOPING THE TERMS OF REFERENCE[4]

As explained earlier in this chapter, agreement on the complete outline of the strategic assessment is possible only through a process of good preliminary analysis of the issues involved. This must be followed by a negotiation of the study project design and reasoning behind it. The negotiation is ideally between the analyst, the manager, and the client. There are three key reasons for doing this:

- to explain your views on what the project should contain and to give them the consolidated results of your thinking;

- to listen to their statements about their areas of interest or concern, the motivation for assigning the task, and any explanatory comments on aspects such as priorities, no-go areas for intelligence investigation, and related matters; and
- to seek endorsement and agreement among all three parties as the basis for moving on to implementing the project itself.

The analyst needs to explain to the manager and the client just how comprehensive the assessment could be and, in fact, ought to be from a wholly logical point of view. Their responsibility, in return, is to explain clearly what is at issue and come to an accord about just how far the project should go, in which directions and with what limitations, and why.

What Makes a Project Directive?

The project directive is a simply document outlining the Terms of Reference for a strategic intelligence project. It has two major components, and may include a third, as outlined in the following paragraphs. These are the *aim*, *scope*, and *general comments*. An example is provided at the end of this chapter.

1. The Aim

The aim is a clear but brief statement that commences the project directive encapsulating the whole essence of the strategic assignment. The principal features of an aim statement are:

- It is generally limited to a single sentence. If clarity demands it, the aim can be longer, but brevity is important.
- It succinctly describes the topic or subject.
- It identifies the client/commander.
- It indicates the purpose of the assessment: policy development, program change, resource deployment, or operational priority setting.

2. The Scope

The scope is a concise collection of individual statements, each of which covers a single key feature of the strategic project. The analyst's objective is to cover all these broad categories and, for each one, include a summarized coverage of the subissues that were identified through the redefinition and brainstorming process.

- The "clustering" together of individual questions about a single key point of the topic makes it easy to cover all the important features of an intelligence probe within this single, brief document. As a guide, illegal markets for any commodity often have a range of common features that could be considered as key issues:
  1. Objectives
  2. Organization
  3. Financing
  4. Transport
  5. Profits
  6. Recruitment
- The point of listing the issues in this way is to ensure that the draft project directive can be seen by the client to represent a comprehensive coverage of the topic. There is no need for the analyst to go into any detail about the extent of data collection in this document, providing considerable flexibility to address issues in the depth required.
- For example, in considering the trade in illegal immigrants, a typical key point cluster statement (one of several in the scope) might be as follows:
  1. Motivation and organization of potential "illegals," including:
     a. particular socioeconomic or ethnic groupings;
     b. perceived benefits of leaving the home country;
     c. perceived benefits of migrating to the target country;
     d. activities of recruiters and local organizers in the home country; and
     e. use of familial links to the target country.

3. General Comments

For some topics, it may be appropriate to write a general statement that will describe your intended approach to the assignment. Some examples of what you might feel the need to include are:

- whether the assessment will focus exclusively on strategic issues, or whether it might also include or at least make reference to operational ones;

- the authority given for information gathering and the extent of that activity within and outside of government circles;
- whether the project should explore policy and strategy options and make recommendations;
- whether there are security implications in the study and how they might be dealt with; and
- how broadly the findings might be disseminated.

ADDITIONAL ASPECTS OF THE PROBLEM DEFINITION PHASE

The key to redefining the original problem rests with the analyst's ability to brainstorm through what has been asked. In doing this, you aim toward achieving a redefinition that gives recognition and meaning to all the component parts of the problem.

Although by now you will have some knowledge about how to produce a list of component issues that go to make up a strategic topic, there are still some difficulties ahead in the process. The point of breaking down the strategic topic into its individual parts is so that you—and others—can plan how to go about dealing with the challenge that each of them poses. At this stage, you have yet to determine what data you will want for the project and how to get it. After that will come the task of collating, then analyzing the information, as you try to find the most appropriate and justifiable interpretation that you can put upon it all for your client.

Problem "Types" and Their Differences

It is useful to understand that there are, in fact, several "types" of problem-solving challenges yet to be faced. These are not caused by the nature of the topic or subject matter itself. Rather, it is more likely to be from the type of data that must be collected to solve the particular issue or subfeature that you are looking at which creates the difficulties facing you.

For example, consider the case of a question that merely requires a measurement, a single piece of information, or even a set of easily obtained facts to answer. The number of arrests, the amounts of drugs held by each arrestee, and so on, are all questions that rely simply on factual data for their answer. There might be some interpretation necessary, but it is the factual data that holds the key.

> **Problems vary in complexity, caused by the level of exactitude or vagueness that is inherent in the question itself.**

At the other end of the scale, there are questions that are loaded with indecision and imprecision. If one were to ask how society would react to the legalization of heroin, for example, there are many possible theories. Unless you are in a position to conduct a specific experiment to model this situation, your conclusion has to be based on analysis of possibilities and of sets of alternatives generated using guesswork, analogy, or even "what if?" surveys to gauge the outcomes.

Once the list of key points and their subissues for the strategic topic has been produced, you will recognize that you are dealing with a wide range of very different types of questions. This variation in question types can be labeled, for the sake of convenience. While you do not need to understand all the detail involved in addressing each question type, you should at least be aware that there are five major distinct *types*, as set out in the list below. Each demands a different, appropriate problem-solving analytic approach since the balance between certainty, on the one hand, and inspired, creative interpretation, on the other, is different in each case.

The problem types most often encountered are commonly termed

- simplistic;
- deterministic;
- moderately random;
- severely random; or
- indeterminate.

The difference among these problem types is directly related to the amount of interpretation needed to answer the questions. Factual data may solve some problems easily and completely. However, in many cases, the analyst can only gather qualitative and impressionistic information that, in turn, needs considerable interpretation.

Future Impact of Problem Definition on the Research Process

The logical future outcome from satisfactory completion of this step is the development of a project work plan. This too is a formal document set and covers the following components:

- the extent of the study to be undertaken and the specific objectives (the Terms of Reference discussed earlier in this chapter);
- the client's expectations in terms of the depth of subject coverage and the level of detail required;
- time-critical targets and other milestones during the life of the project, reporting requirements, and the arrangements for continuing further contact between client and the analyst;
- client wishes with regard to the making of recommendations by the intelligence staff involved in the project;
- project administration details, including resource availability, timing, and special data access requirements; and
- arrangements to measure performance and effectiveness of the project upon its completion.

CONCLUSION

The primary objective of this step in the strategic intelligence process has been to produce a clear restatement of the original intelligence problem, turning it into a detailed subset of issues. Strategic problem definition does, however, have further benefits. The process itself causes you to think about what you will need to gather in terms of data and from where you might collect it. Moreover, this process sets you up mentally to start the project-planning phase—because by now you will start to understand the likely extent of the task facing you in terms of gathering, collating, and analyzing the information you need.

Problem definition is not a difficult activity. It does require intellectual discipline, though, to ensure that you consider all the potentially useful aspects of a topic. What is unacceptable is for you to assume some shortcuts in this phase. If you merely focus on the things you and your agency have usually done in these cases, you will find that the whole business of carrying out strategic analysis is limited by the amount of imagination you showed at the very start of the project. Nor is it necessarily appropriate to merely accept the manager's or the client's view of the topic at the outset. This is not to say that their views will be wrong, but it is important that you examine and expand the horizons of the topic, at least for discussion purposes, before a final decision is made on the parameters, limits, or constraints that might be put upon it.

The main point of this phase is to gain an understanding of the whole issue and suggest a suitable framework of intelligence examination before deciding upon the model to be followed. The problem definition phase demands a mixture of intellectual professionalism, coupled with creative thinking, to arrive at a balanced and workable outline for a strategic intelligence probe.

The ability to think creatively about the originally defined problem, free from your own and your organization's biases, is the key to being able to successfully break that problem down into its component parts. Having done so, it is far easier to build it up again in a more comprehensive fashion to suit the real needs of the client. The skills involved in strategic problem definition can be learned, and it is up to you to invest the effort necessary to break through the limitations of routine, predictable thinking. There is an added advantage in doing so, too. As you develop the problem restatement and negotiate it with your client and manager, you will be providing them with valuable added insight into the topic. In addition, this whole process of exploration and discussion will help commit them to endorsing the project and its aims.

SAMPLE PROJECT DIRECTIVE: STRATEGIC ASSESSMENT—ILLEGAL DRUGS

AIM

To produce a strategic intelligence assessment of the national drug problem in all its aspects, which will provide high-level policymakers with a basis for deciding upon future law enforcement strategies, priorities, resource deployments, organizational requirements, and training needs.

SCOPE

- Define and describe the nature and extent of drug-related crime.
- Describe the conditions which allow or promote the relevant criminal activity, for example:
    a. the nature of demand for illegal drugs
    b. community attitudes
    c. enforcement strategies and powers
    d. international trends and influences
    e. drug market structures
    f. opportunities for facilitation of crime
    g. funding of criminal activities and disposal of profits
    h. government agency cohesion and effectiveness
- Describe the reaction of criminal organizations and individuals to drug market influences and to law enforcement efforts.
- Provide a prediction of emerging patterns and types of drug-related crime.
- Describe the existing programs, strategies, and capacity of government agencies and law enforcement to meet the current and perceived illegal drug threat.
- Identify information gaps that need to be filled in order to support the development of similar assessments in the future.

GENERAL COMMENTS

- It will feature a national, strategic perspective rather than a tactical one.
- It will examine current and alternative national policies and strategies.
- Data collection will extend, as required, beyond official government sources and include the private sector, nongovernment agencies, and open-source information.

- It will define a conceptual approach that will act as a model for a program of comprehensive, integrated assessments of the general criminal environment.

This example was that actually used for the first major strategic intelligence assessment undertaken in 1990 by the Australian government for the Attorney-General's Department, by the author's team.

Example: Strategic Assessment on Illegal Drugs in State X

Initial Key Point Headings

Illegal Drugs	=	four major categories:	
		marijuana (grass/hashish/oil)	
		cocaine (coke/crack)	
		heroin	
		chemical drugs (list main types)	
	=	supply	(external/internal to State)
	=	distribution	(wholesale/retail/street/schools)
	=	manufacture	(include reprocessing/repackaging)
	=	financing	(bankrolling/money flow/laundering)
	=	arrests	(by drug type/amount/agency/ location/date)
	=	prosecutions	(cross-match to arrests/sentence)
State X	=	location	(cross-match to arrests/distribution/ manufacture/drug type)
	=	supply	(origin of supply/by drug types/ crossing points/MOs)

NOTES

1. Phenomenon research has been in use successfully by the Dutch Criminal Intelligence Service for many years as a form of background strategic study of various issues.

2. Since such information is largely factual, in theory, the relevant data can be gathered, described, and interpreted relatively simply. In fact, in a competitive

environment such as banking, such information is confidential and generally made available only to those who work within the organization. This can leave "outside" investigations hampered by their need to respect the commercial privacy of corporate operations.

3. Computerized "brainstorming" or idea generation and management tools are available and work well in the intelligence environment. Such software as Mind Manager™ can produce graphic outlines of the thinking that goes into problem definition, exporting them to working documents, and making them available on intranets and the Internet. Some examples appear elsewhere in this book.

4. The terms *Terms of Reference* and *project directive* may be used interchangeably in strategic intelligence practice.

10

Strategic Project Work Plans

It should be clear by now that your approach as an analyst must be a carefully structured one, to prepare yourself for the work yet to come. A strategic intelligence assignment certainly needs detailed planning. One of the limitations in doing so right at the very beginning, however, is that you don't exactly know what it is that you're planning for. The previous steps, of developing a mental model of the topic—your conceptual framework—and of examining and redefining the strategic topic, were essential prerequisites for what follows in the strategic intelligence process.

Developing a project work plan entails several important steps that are pivotal to the future success of the project. Obviously, you will be considering what data you need to gather and where you will get it. Just as importantly, you need to consider just how the project will have to be arranged and structured to facilitate the collection, collation, and analysis of the information in an orderly and disciplined way. All this can be planned now, before going any further. The plan will cover all the sequential steps in the process, the timing and interaction among them, and the essential administrative issues of resourcing (people, equipment, and funds). The plan will become a useful tool for briefing your seniors and colleagues, for monitoring progress, and for expediting change as circumstances shift throughout the project.

The steps you have so far taken in the strategic intelligence process, coupled now with the development of a work plan, all contribute to what can be thought of as the front-end engineering of the project, a collection of processes that, together, set you up to achieve success in what follows.

A strategic intelligence assessment project comprises many components that have to be brought together efficiently if you are to produce a desirable outcome that is effective in its impact on managers and clients. Handling a strategic intelligence project, whether alone or with others, always involves a balancing act. You will have to deal with matters of resourcing, trying to meet time-critical targets, and maintaining a climate of objectivity—inasmuch as you can manage to do so—throughout the analytical phase. At the end, you must try to piece together the myriad elements of analysis and interpretation that will provide an impartial, considered assessment report for the client. Some analysts try to "manage" this process informally and, by calling upon their experience in intelligence, convince themselves that they have everything under control. It is more likely, however, that any worthwhile strategic assessment will comprise so many elements that you simply cannot rely on anything but good, solid planning and management of the whole activity. If you have commitment to producing good work, then you must recognize that this involves care and attention to detail.

By developing an orderly approach to planning, the analyst gains the benefit of having a tangible, flexible tool to manage and monitor the progress of the strategic intelligence project. This chapter explains what is needed in terms of structured, disciplined planning of a strategic intelligence and research project. It outlines the steps that must be taken and discusses how you should consider allocating time and resources throughout the project. Finally, it outlines and suggests several ways of presenting a project plan to suit both your workplace environment and the expectations of your managers and potential clients. Finally, we discuss the benefits to you in taking the time to develop your plan in a graphic, flexible form—one that aids you in briefing and negotiating with your managers and clients.

STRUCTURING A STRATEGIC PROJECT WORK PLAN

By far the easiest means of developing the layout of a project work plan is to draw up a timeline that plots all the phases of the strategic intelligence process against your expectations of their timing. This is relatively easy to do at this stage of the project, since by now you have already gained general knowledge of the topic through your conceptual modeling and have developed a wealth of detailed insight through the process of redefining the strategic task and producing the project directive. However, no timeline is capable of holding all the information you need for your plan, and therefore this chapter discusses the notes that you will need to generate and cross-reference to the chart, backed up by notes on specific issues.

There are several key elements that must be brought together to include in your strategic assessment work plan. The aim is to take account of all the main steps between starting the project and completing it to the satisfaction of your managers and clients. The full sequence of thirteen steps, shown in figure 2.4 in chapter 2, is listed below in sequential order. However, it is not always necessary for a particular process step to be completed before the next one can start.

Elements of the Strategic Intelligence Process

- Original *task*
- Developing a *conceptual framework* or model
- *Problem definition* and restatement of all elements of the task
- Development of *Terms of Reference*
- Preparing a *project work plan*
- Planning and implementing *data collection*
- *Collating* and *evaluating* incoming data
- Integration, *analysis*, and interpretation of data
- Generating *hypotheses*
- *Progress Reviews*
- Preparing a *strategic assessment report*
- *Final Review* of the task against the expectations of the Terms of Reference.
- *Distribution* of the report to managers, clients, and other consumers
- Post-action *performance review* of efficiency and effectiveness

Some overlapping of these processes can occur if certain circumstances exist, and not everything has to be done sequentially. The answer lies partly in the fact that if the topic is one you are very familiar with, it will affect how quickly you can move from one phase to the next. For example, take a circumstance in which you know quite a lot about illegal drugs and their markets. If this is the topic of your assignment, then you probably won't find it difficult to apply your knowledge to incoming data (during the collection phase) and start to carry out some evaluation and preliminary analysis not long after the data flow has commenced. In such a case, there is no point in waiting until the entire collection phase has been completed before starting on subsequent steps—in the interests of time and efficiency, waiting is neither necessary nor desirable.

Further, it is neither necessary nor logical to wait for phases such as data collection to be completed before commencing the processes that follow. Data collection can take so long that to wait for it to be completed would delay the research activity unreasonably. Moreover, if the data are read, collated, evaluated, and considered from an analytical point of view as they arrive, the analyst can often identify shortfalls in its quality and quantity and relevance. To do so earlier rather than later allows the analyst to modify the data collection plan in time to rectify any problems.

Planning the Critical Path of a Project

Each one of the phase steps will involve you in carrying out certain tasks. Each, too, may be somewhat dependent upon the task before it. As a general rule, you cannot start a phase without having acquired knowledge in the previous steps. However, just how much knowledge you require is a variable and differs according to several conditions. As we have said, some processes overlap and others do not, and cannot. Trying to design a sensible program that outlines just what to do, and when, can be thought of as *critical path planning.*

In simple terms, critical path planning is the technique of scheduling events separately, at the same time as exploring concurrence and interdependence, in order to arrive at a schedule that (a) encompasses all the necessary steps, (b) meets the ultimate end goal, and (c) saves time wherever possible. While this is a highly individualized technique that must be done for every single project, there are at least some general rules that you can use to your advantage in strategic planning

Original Task

The original task is the assignment or topic given to you by your manager or the client, starting off the entire project.

Conceptual Model

The conceptual model is a step that you must deal with separately, before anything else can flow from it. It overlaps no other step.

Problem Definition

Problem definition and restatement is a task that will open your eyes to the future implications for collection planning and the eventual analysis. The Terms of Reference is the direct outcome of this work.

Project Planning

Project planning is a task that draws upon the knowledge gained before it and is directly relevant to the collection plan that follows.

Collection Planning

Collection planning cannot, indeed must not, start until you know what you are trying to address and achieve. It is absolutely and directly dependent upon the steps that precede it.

Collation and Evaluation

Once data items start arriving, collation and evaluation can proceed concurrently even while further information continues to arrive. Thus collection, collation, and evaluation all occur during the same time frame.

Analysis

Analysis—the integration and interpretation of information—can start very soon after the collection program has commenced. Therefore, analysis overlaps both the collection and the collation/evaluation phases.

Generating Hypotheses

You can start to generate your working hypotheses while analysis is still occurring just as soon as you think there is sufficient reason and justification for doing so. However, it is important to follow three basic rules:

- Wait long enough to collect sufficient analyzed data about specific issues, instead of leaping to any conclusions.

- Decide upon what is "sufficient" in these circumstances, based upon the complexity of the task and the extent of difficulty you perceive in acquiring and assessing data to provide a picture that is broad yet detailed enough to satisfy your interpretation needs.
- Consistently reassess your preliminary ideas and conclusions in the light of other information as it continues to arrive.

Progress Reviews

The progress reviews take the form of interim briefings and should be considered as a category of "should do" activities to simply report on activity to date. What is important is that the analyst, the manager, and the client all keep in contact and remain committed to ensuring that the work being done for the client is still relevant.

End of Project Review

Reporting once completed is, of course, the obligatory requirement.

If necessary, all the parties involved may need to reexamine the original task and its project directive to determine whether these are still relevant. While there are many practical resource reasons (budget, staffing, etc.) that might drive this type of reexamination of the plan, it is often simply that issues have changed, political priorities have shifted, legislation at home or overseas has placed the issue in a new light, or similar events.

Report-Writing Alternatives

When you come to develop your strategic report, you may decide to write this at the end of the final analysis. There is, however, a very useful alternative and that involves you in following three steps throughout the life of the project:

- At the time you write up the project directive, draft the outline of the report you think is likely to be the result of the project—without detail, except for headings and subheadings, since this gives you a planned structure to work to.
- Throughout the analysis phase, and as conclusions about specific issues become clear to you, enter some notes into the framework of the report and start to get a feel for how it will hold together.

- When the analysis is completed to your satisfaction and you have developed your conclusions, return to the report and write in the detail necessary—and allow yourself at this stage to restructure the report if you feel it is necessary.

Presentation and Distribution

Finally, the report needs to be presented to the client to discuss it, explain and justify what has been done, and gain endorsement for distribution of the final product. Several judgment issues occur at this point, and the analyst must be careful to deal with the following matters.

Providing a Verbal Briefing Presentation of the final written report needs to be planned if it is to achieve complete success. The report itself is likely to be comprehensive in its treatment of the topic and will therefore probably be fairly lengthy and quite detailed. Its exploration of issues may well go beyond the original expectations of the client. The report will quite possibly describe issues and interpret circumstances in a way that neither the client nor other readers would necessarily expect. Giving the client and your manager frequent opportunities to be brought up to date via the "progress review" mechanism should ensure that there are not too many surprises in store. Nonetheless, it is not all that common to find a client who is totally prepared to accept any views that run counter to conventional wisdom. In some cases, the types of options drawn or recommendations made by the analyst may cause some concern among those who have not yet been made privy to the logic behind the analysis.

If the report truly represents the best possible canvassing of data, analysis, and interpretation, then the analyst should make strenuous efforts to present the report in its best light.

After all, it represents a considerable input of professional effort, courage, and faith on the part of the analyst, not to mention considerable resource costs to the organization. A highly effective way of going about this phase is to arrange to provide a briefing on the task, the issues, the data collected, the analysis, and the logical interpretations that can be drawn from this process, ending up with the options and recommendations that may be appropriate. This briefing should ideally precede the handing over of the report. The reason for this is that with a lengthy report, it is common to be asked to provide a summary of findings and recommendations as an introductory component of the report. In many cases, experience shows us that readers at the management and executive levels do not necessarily read the report itself but limit their perusal to the summary. No matter how well thought-out the summary, it will always lack the supporting detail of analysis and interpretation about individual highlight points. This is the problem: Recommendations backed up by only scant "summary" detail and the interpretations made by the analyst may well be seen out of context, and decisions may be made about them in ignorance of the underpinning analysis. It is for these reasons that the analyst should provide a verbal briefing, giving the opportunity to recognize client reaction, to address it immediately, and to provide statements of reasoning about the analysis.

While it is always possible to merely complete a report and send it through to the client in, for example, an internal mail system, such a routine never allows the analyst the opportunity to show and explain the value of intelligence work.

To Whom Should It Be Distributed? One other issue that creates continuing difficulty for strategic and other intelligence analysts is the question of the distribution of reports. If an organizational executive, acting as client, has asked for a strategic study of some issue, then there is often an underlying assumption by that client that the report will be the property of that client. Yet during the course of the research, it may become increasingly obvious that the issues affect a wider audience or market than simply the original task giver. It is up to the intelligence analyst to point this out to the client—for example, identifying stakeholders in different organizations, at higher jurisdictional levels, in the public domain, and so on. Clearly, the original client will have a legitimate claim as a stakeholder, but, as the span of research into a topic broadens, it is not uncommon to find a dilemma emerging: Who should this project actually benefit?

The fact is that there are both "clients" and "other consumers" of strategic research product. If the customs organization of a particular country wants to conduct a strategic study of the phenomenon of fraud against tariff regulations, then it is certainly arguable that customs, which administers that legislation, should be recognized as the main client. However, it can easily be recognized that treasury and finance departments would be beneficiaries of the data and the interpretation, as would trade and industry departments and industry associations. The question about distribution centers on this very point: If the strategic assessment vitally affects other stakeholders, does one single client have the moral and/or legal right to limit its distribution?

Stakeholders and "Ownership" Two arguments generally have been offered to explain such behavior. The first is that if the client has in any way contributed resources to the conduct of the strategic assessment, then ownership—it is argued—ought to be vested in that client. The question here is not one of who paid for the work, but rather, what does "ownership" really mean? For those who would use the argument to avoid giving access to the research to others outside of the client organization, such argument fails on legal grounds. Any police force or government department within a jurisdiction must understand that in terms of intellectual property practice, the report belongs to the jurisdiction. That is, if an immigration department argues that its reports cannot be seen by other national government enforcement groups, this ignores the reality that the report belongs to "the Crown" or "the state," not to the individual department.

Nonsharing, Security, and the Need-to-Know Principle A second argument often made is on the grounds that security provisions (data collected, sources involved, and even the matters considered) preclude allowing strategic reports to go beyond the boundaries of individual departments or units. If one looks to the military as an example, then the notion of "sanitizing" reports has been well explored and forms part of continuing practice. Sanitization involves the editing of reports to ensure that they exclude sensitive data. This does not mean that whole sections of a strategic assessment might end up being excised; it simply means that, in practice, the analyst may obscure some data sources and items, but nonetheless actively seeks ways to avoid limiting the issues covered.[1] Unless this protocol is adopted, intelligence assessments at the strategic level will increasingly fail to reach those individuals and agencies that need to take their content into account. This can have serious repercussions involving opportunities missed, programs failing apparently without cause, and even counterproductive actions and operations being mounted by different agencies.

The old intelligence saw that defends secrecy on the basis of the need-to-know principle is hugely misunderstood in modern times, certainly within government enforcement communities. A defense mechanism frequently encountered as an argument for not sharing intelligence—particularly strategic intelligence—is the need-to-know dictum. In mainstream tactical and operational circles, need to know is almost always based on security of information relating to sensitive sources or imminent action; this is understandable. In dealing with strategic research, however, the need-to-know principle is often cited in connection with arguments about who are really the paramount stakeholders. Interdepartmental arguments, tension, competition, and envy all may play a role in creating an environment in which legitimate access can be denied to needy consumers of intelligence assessments. It is this division between clients and consumers that seems, again, not to be well understood within management circles. Finally, it is up to the analyst to argue for the most practical and logical distribution arrangement on behalf of the wider user community. This ought to be done if the intelligence effort is to be seen as intended for the common good, whether it be organizational, corporate, or governmental. Many agencies have real difficulty with this concept, and this can be understood in an age where performance measurement schemes in government and corporate life often tend to create an individualist and competitive society.

The critical path diagram (see figure 10.1) gives some idea of the way in which several functions can be overlapped and critically charted during the strategic intelligence project. All of this detail about what to do, in what order, and with what overlap is outlined simply in the diagram. The time scale is only notional, not real, and as a result you will need to look at every project separately in order to determine exactly how much time you need for each phase. This will vary according to the difficulty or complexity of the task and your degree of familiarity with the topic.

Performance Review

Finally, there is the question of conducting a performance review to consider the project as a whole. The key issues for all parties to consider are as follows:

- to separate performance ideas into efficiency benchmarks and effectiveness concepts;
- to ensure that the analyst, the unit manager/supervisor, and the client all discuss and understand just what expectations the client will have;
- to agree on those performance aspects that mostly concern the client, as opposed to those that are internal to the intelligence unit;
- to identify the means and techniques of performance appraisal, acknowledging and agreeing that measurement, observation, or judgment might each be applicable in certain circumstances;

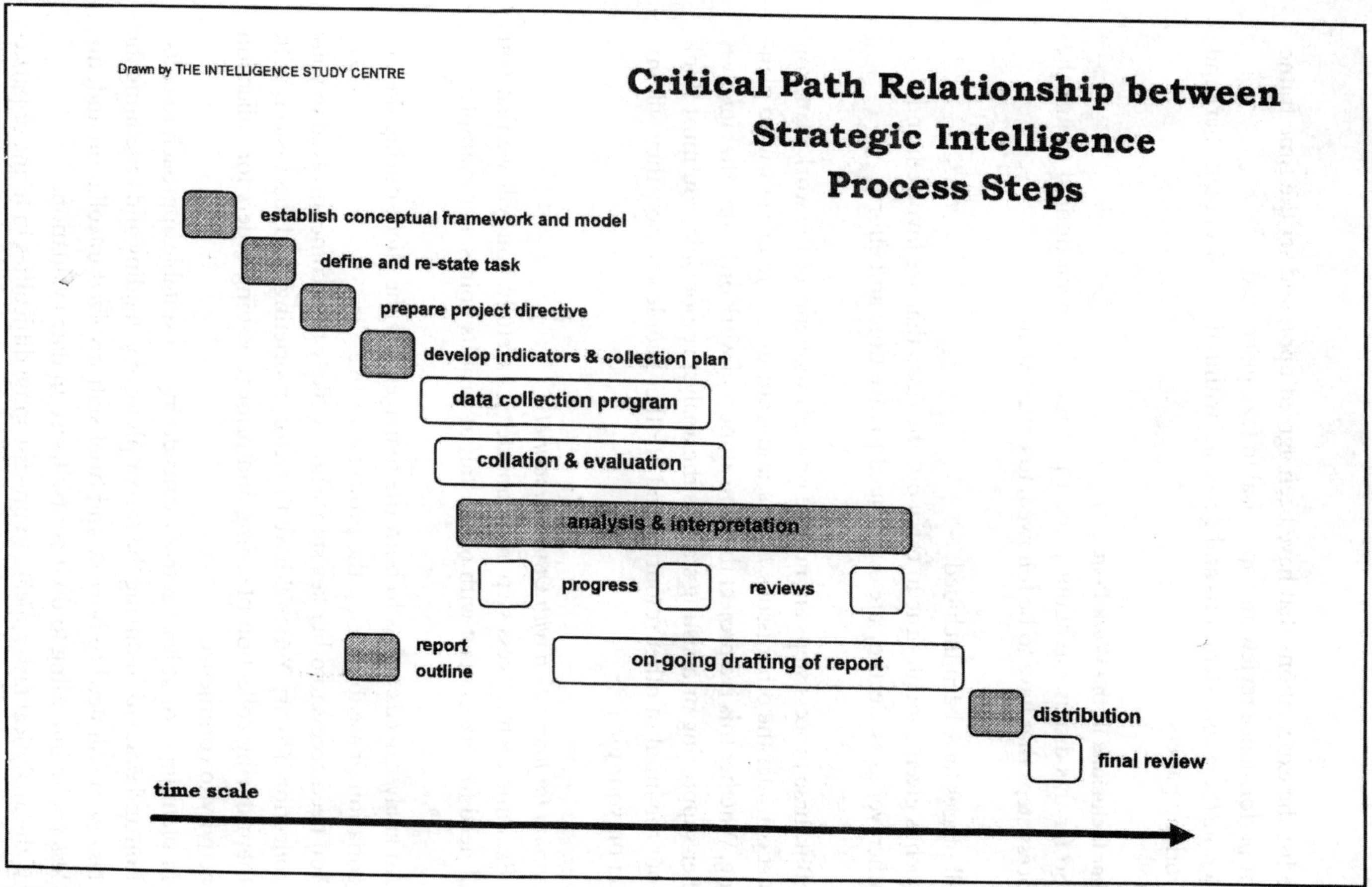

FIGURE 10.1
Critical Path

- to list the expectations that have been agreed upon and set the time frame for performance review and appraisal to take place; and
- to note these considerations and decisions within the project plan chart and working papers.

Other Inclusions in the Work Plan

So far this discussion about project planning has been limited to just the process steps that have to be followed, to ensure that

- all phases have been included;
- each is given enough time to carry out the tasks that are involved; and
- wherever possible, they are overlapped to save time and effort.

But these process steps are not the only components of the work plan. You must consider the other issues, events, and features that require forward planning. Whether this is a project that you alone will work on or one that involves other supporting or assisting staff, as the analyst responsible, you must think about the input of other resources and of other people and how they will impact on your plan.

Planning for Interaction with Other Personnel

Examine each process step and consider it carefully. You will see that you will need to have contact with other staff at various points. For example:

- An analyst needs access to both the manager and the client during the negotiation phase to develop the project directive.
- You need access to other key staff who are likely to become involved in your collection activity. You will have to factor in briefings and discussions with them during collection planning and prior to issuing orders for collection activity to commence.
- In planning—or at least actively considering—a suitable approach to collation and evaluation during the earlier phase of extending and redefining the task, you will need to borrow and brief staff involved in collation and, unless you're intending to do it yourself, also in data evaluation.
- If the analytical task appears to present some difficulties in terms of particular skills that might be needed, you will want access to specialist staff or ex-

perts. For example, if number crunching and statistical modeling are not your strengths, then getting someone else to do statistical analysis of, for example, drug event data may be the best solution.

- Throughout the whole process, what is needed is regular, scheduled access to your manager and/or your client, to give them reports on progress to date.

The Next Step

A good plan takes account of all the foreseeable issues, but an imaginative planner retains the flexibility to deal with emerging issues and changes. Every analyst needs to determine a way to include all the foregoing features of time, money, and human-resource needs in a graphic plan, rather than solely relying on a set of notes. This is beneficial because you will be able to "track" events throughout the project more easily if you have a visual aid. Unless you do so, your "plan" will merely be a list of scheduled activities that, while it discloses the events, does not do so in a way that focuses your attention.

DESIGNING AND PRESENTING WORK PLANS

How to Design and Display the Work Plan

A project work plan must achieve several objectives. It has to provide an easy means of identifying what should happen and when. It may also identify the responsibilities of specific groups or individuals. To be successful, this component of the work plan ideally should be a *visual chart.* The second component *lists* or otherwise records notes, comments, reminders, observations, and explanations of issues relevant to the way in which the analyst is thinking about the project plan. For the sort of in-depth strategic research usually envisioned by analysts, unit managers, and clients, a comprehensive work plan can provide significant benefits for all concerned. The objectives of the work plan will need to meet the following key criteria.

- The base document should be some form of event/timeline that describes the various process steps, in order, showing the amount of time you estimate they will take, plus their start and stop points.
- On such a chart, you should indicate "special events" that involve other people—for example, reporting dates to management, briefings for key personnel, and so on.

- Finally, other key events should be in the form of written notes, particularly those involving important issues of finance and equipment. For example, you may have a time-critical need to access certain computer equipment at a specific time in one or another of the process steps. This should be noted on the planning chart.

This whole approach to developing and using a project plan stresses using some form of easy-to-read graphic chart as the basis for recording and presenting the timeline element of the project-planning data. The strategic intelligence work plan is not just a "snapshot" of totally fixed arrangements; it is also a tool to allow you to respond flexibly to changing circumstances. The reason for recommending strongly the use of a visual timeline chart rests on three simple observations:

- as the analyst, you need the work plan as a visible, accessible tool to which you can refer as often as necessary, and which prompts and reminds you about target dates and important milestones;
- your manager and client will derive benefit from the visual nature of the work plan, because this will aid their understanding of progress and consequences; and
- finally, all of you—including your work colleagues—will gain value from the plan's being a visual aid that allows you to show the impact of changing circumstances on people, on time-critical targets, and on shaping the future activity to still meet the original objectives.

Preparing a Work Plan Manually

The manual method of drawing up a project work plan has a lot of attraction for some analysts. Typical advantages of this approach are seen to include the following features.

- If you lack confidence in dealing with computers, then clearly you might stick with what you know best—your imagination, attention to detail, and a pencil, colored pens or highlighters, or similar implements.
- Manual charts can be simple, yet detailed enough to show the basics of what you want to display.

The alternatives for displaying the project work plan come down to a simple set of variations between manual drawing systems versus computer-assisted graphics. Although many readers may find it strange in this era of easy access to computer technology for many daily tasks, some analysts prefer manual work plan charts. Indeed, in some units they may go to the extent of using preformatted blank sheets for the purpose—for example, using a year planner chart similar to those available from stationers and office supply companies. They have been trained to do things in this way and are quite comfortable with continuing to do so. However, as we increasingly rely on computers to assist us in other work functions in intelligence—for example, in databases—many analysts prefer to find ways to use computers to assist them also in designing the work plan.

Again, as in other areas of intelligence practice, it is not easy to state unreservedly that there is a right or a wrong way to develop and display a project work plan. There are pros and cons that govern the choice, and before deciding to stay with the method you have currently in use—or, alternatively, changing it—you should consider these arguments.

- Drawing charts may not take a lot of time and, depending upon what implements are used, you may be able to note corrections and edit changes easily.
- Hand-drawn charts can be as large or as small as the drawing medium you choose to utilize: paper, cardboard, or whiteboard.

The Computer Alternative

Many analysts have ready access to computers and already use them enthusiastically in other aspects of their intelligence work. For those who are truly comfortable with their use, there is often a natural reaction to want to try to find ways to extend the use of the computer by getting it to draw the chart—or, at the very least, to help you by providing the graphics capability.

1. Computer-Generated Work Plans One choice is to select a computer software package that will actually calculate and "draw" the timeline for you once you have entered the timing, data, and text. There are several such packages available commercially,[2] and the analyst will need to make a choice based on the capacity of the program, its user-friendliness, and its cost. The advantages of a computer-generated work plan include:

- for the computer enthusiast, it is quick and easy to draw;
- although its format is standardized, it is capable of variation (often within considerable limitations) to suit the analyst's preferences and the project's requirements;
- alterations to any step in the process plan can be quickly entered, and the software will automatically calculate and display the time impact on the rest of the work plan;
- as with all computer-assisted products, the work plan can be reproduced in black-and-white, color, or grayscale, as required; and
- it can be printed in almost any size—depending upon available printers—as often and in as many copies as is required.

2. Computer-Assisted Work Plans. Many analysts and intelligence units do not feel the need for expensive project-planning software to do all the work for them, especially when such software is often resource-hungry. Indeed, many of those sorts of packages are rather too large and powerful for what is needed in this phase of the strategic intelligence process. On the other hand, it can be argued that if your organization already uses such software—and many do—then why not take advantage of its availability to help you plan your project, even if you might be underutilizing its capacities?

There is, of course, a compromise available to the analyst. In this option, the analyst conceptualizes the project work plan and then uses computer graphics software to draw it up. Such a work plan often looks very impressive—depending upon how creative is your use of the graphics package—but the key feature in this case is that the computer is assisting your mental processes, not drawing the whole chart for you. In choosing this approach, the analyst will generally accept that the compromise offers several advantages:

- you are not forced into having to rely totally on a computer package with which you may be unfamiliar, one that you consider may be somewhat unresponsive as to presentation design and layout;

- you feel a sense of continuing "control" over the planning phase, because it is you, not the computer, that is conceptualizing and designing the work plan;
- you have a wide range of choice about how to graphically display the charting, using color, layout, typeface, and like aspects to support your creativity and the challenges of providing quality presentation; and
- assuming you are confident in your use of whichever graphics software you select, you know that redoing the work plan chart to change it according to circumstances is a relatively easy and enjoyable activity.

CONCLUSION

Given an intelligence problem to solve, an analyst could start the intelligence cycle without a formalized plan. Many analysts would assert that they don't really need such a tool. Some might cite as their reasoning the view that they have considerable experience in conducting analytical projects, and "know" how to get on with what has to be done. In the environment of tactical and operational intelligence, where the topic or problem may indeed be a very familiar one, it could be argued that this is a necessary and defensible approach. After all, spending time on planning could be considered by some to be wasteful of a scarce resource.

But consider an alternative view: Unless what you are asked to do is truthfully some task that you can carry out "automatically," one that is totally within your competence and knowledge levels, is it realistic to start working unless you know what it is you are to do? If your colleagues, clients, and managers expect the best answers possible, then you have an obligation to do the very best you can.

In the field of strategic research and intelligence, no analyst can afford to assume that he already knows everything there is to know. Nor are assessment projects likely able to be completed without some considerable investment in time and other resources. In this arena, there is simply too much effort involved to risk taking anything but the most careful approach possible. This means committing yourself not only to careful implementation and analysis throughout the project, but also to careful and comprehensive planning at the outset.

We have discussed in this chapter the many ways in which plans can be formulated and presented. These are important factors in selecting what you do in developing your work plan. But the key message remains one of taking utmost care in making sure that your plan contains all the essential elements. At the commencement of a project, the plan will be an invaluable tool for helping you order your ideas and negotiate the project with others. This is particularly true of your relationships with your manager and client, for the plan allows a useful, visible tool to be used throughout your negotiations and discussions with them.

However, the work plan must never become a fixed, inviolate concept. Quite the contrary: If you have taken a lot of care in putting it together and know all of its detail, then you will find that it becomes even easier for you to compensate for necessary changes as events force you to adapt to them. In essence, the key to understanding about project planning lies in the following thoughts:

> The work plan is a flexible and adaptable matrix for future action. No strategic intelligence assessment enterprise should begin without a work plan. No work plan should dictate the progress of an enterprise when events demand change.

NOTES

1. In military practice, data from sensitive sources such as signals intelligence (SIGINT) can result in intelligence forecasts that, to achieve impact, need to be promulgated. It is not uncommon practice for military analysts to seek to reword reports to avoid any mention of such a source, yet retain the essential flavor of the forecast or interpretation of events.

2. Perhaps the best known of these programs for the past decade or so has been Microsoft Project, a highly professional and very powerful tool for general use across the project-planning spectrum. Other excellent packages are available within a wide price range to carry out similar functions.

11

Generating Hypotheses

No feature of the strategic intelligence cycle could be more important or more demanding than the generation of ideas, opinions, and conclusions. This phase can represent the culmination of weeks or months of research by the analyst. Alternatively, the techniques used in critical thinking can be put to good use to help the analyst figure out just how the project should proceed. A hypothesis is often thought of as a theory waiting to be tested, or sometimes an answer that is not yet confirmed. Whatever the definitional phrase used by the intelligence community, the fact is that when you come to that point at which you can develop your hypotheses—ideas, views, or conclusions, whichever word you use—you have reached the epicenter of the strategic study. You have already undergone the learning and thinking process to reach it, and you now have to move beyond it into the arena of checking and testing.

In the field of strategic intelligence, the technique of developing hypotheses is absolutely critical. This is because only in this field are you likely to be called upon to make judgments about the long-term future, about issues in breadth, about matters of inherent complexity and even some vagueness. You will have moved from the close and exciting work of target intelligence, serving tactical or operational aims, into a form of future research. Strategic intelligence demands a high degree of careful but nonetheless speculative thought about what could be happening. Herein lies the challenge of developing a good grasp of techniques to generate suitable, imaginative hypotheses.

This topic is arguably the most critical one in this series of "process" chapters, for it is crucial to everything that follows. As the responsible analyst, you must be prepared to take a great deal of effort and care to develop good, sound theories. Unless you do so, complacency and intuitive, subjective thinking may well flaw your results.

What is a hypothesis? A hypothesis may be thought of as a conclusion or assumption you may reach about anything at all. It doesn't have to be right; it only has to be realistic and reasonable in terms of being able to be right. In other words, a hypothesis is a plausible explanation. The hypothesis doesn't represent the end of your problem-solving activity; it is just a point en route to formulating your final interpretation.

In the context of using these processes, every time you embark on a strategic project you will reach a point, or many such points, at which you suddenly come to believe that such-and-such is possibly—or probably—right. The hypothesis (or theory, or view, or conclusion) that you arrive at is therefore a function of three distinct elements:

1. data;
2. understanding; and
3. speculation.

Hypotheses, then, are the analyst's "best guesses" for the moment, given the state of understanding of the strategic topic and the problems posed. Hypotheses represent preliminary analyses of specific situations or issues, but unless you can obtain further data to reinforce and hopefully confirm your theory, then they remain just that—theories.

Intelligence analysts can develop hypotheses at different times in the life of a strategic project. They can come to you in an almost unplanned, accidental manner, or you can be deliberate in setting out to generate new ideas and theories. You can generate them early in the whole process, as in (1), below, by using the minimal data you have in hand as a result of your conceptual modeling and thinking about the problem definition, to help you focus on particular avenues of data collection. Alternatively, you can follow process (2) through its steps and into analysis, and then start to interpret what you are examining to give you a set of workable hypotheses. These two approach possibilities are shown below:

1. question > thinking > hypotheses/ideas > focused data collection > analysis > etc.
2. question > thinking > data > analysis > hypotheses > testing

The development and subsequent use of hypothetical theories is a legitimate and well-established research tool. The objective is to use your analytical powers to develop suitable working ideas that in turn help you to focus your further research. The only requirements are that you pick hypotheses that could be true, and then follow up with specific data collection and analysis to prove or disprove your theories. The overriding requirement is that you maintain a sense of objectivity throughout this "testing" phase, and not merely seek to reinforce your ideas regardless of what the additional data might be telling you. This chapter describes in some detail just what is involved in generating hypotheses, and some of the mental approaches you might use to help you maintain a sense of reality while nonetheless striving to think creatively.

HYPOTHESES: BASIC CONCEPTS

Definition: What Is a Hypothesis?

Anyone who has ever theorized about the how and why and who of a series of activities and has come to a conclusion or formed an idea about something has developed what is termed a *hypothesis*. What is a hypothesis? It is merely an idea that explains a situation. Until proven, it represents just your best guess of the situation as you see it. In intelligence usage, and in research in all its forms, hypotheses serve a specific and useful function—to prompt the analyst/researcher to explore the hypothesis further, seeking conclusive data that will either refute or confirm the original idea. For a dictionary definition of the term, you might consider the following edited extract from the *Concise Oxford English Dictionary*:

> hypothesis . . . (1) a supposition made as the basis for reasoning, without assumption of its truth, or (2) a supposition used as a starting point for further investigation from known facts.

It is normal for analysts and researchers to go through the collection and analysis processes and finally arrive at a point where it seems crystal clear that such-and-such is the appropriate conclusion. All that remains, then, is for that conclusion to be tested. Until it is, and until you are persuaded that the idea or theory is indeed correct, then all you have is a continuing hypothesis of greater or lesser probability. A hypothesis is only a theory; no matter how plausible it sounds, it needs testing.

Hypotheses don't have to be developed as the culmination of a long chain of analysis; they can also serve as shortcuts in the analytical process by providing a focus for specific data gathering. This will be explained later in this chapter.

The Key Elements of a Hypothesis

Regardless of whether you will ultimately develop your hypotheses after some considerable analysis of the strategic issues, or early on in the chain, the fact is that you need the following conditions to apply before you can develop a hypothesis at all.

- You need a clear idea about the problem or topic you need to comment upon.
- You need a certain amount of data, awareness, or knowledge about that problem or issue.
- You need to analyze that information against the backdrop of knowing what problem you're trying to solve.
- You need to be mentally prepared to interpret your analysis in a way that permits you to speculate or assume things might be so, even though you know that you may not have enough conclusive data at that point.
- You need to consider the sort of indicative data that, if seen or gathered, might help reflect on your hypothesis by suggesting a positive leaning toward or against it.

We might well ask that, if you have developed your own hypothesis about an issue, what is it based upon? The answer is that it is a mix of your assessment of the data consciously and unconsciously available to you, coupled with any emotional and moral beliefs you possess about these issues. Right or wrong, they are *your* hypotheses and the question remains: What would cause you to either change your mind or firm up your beliefs even further? The answer should be obvious: Information and analysis hold the key to conviction.

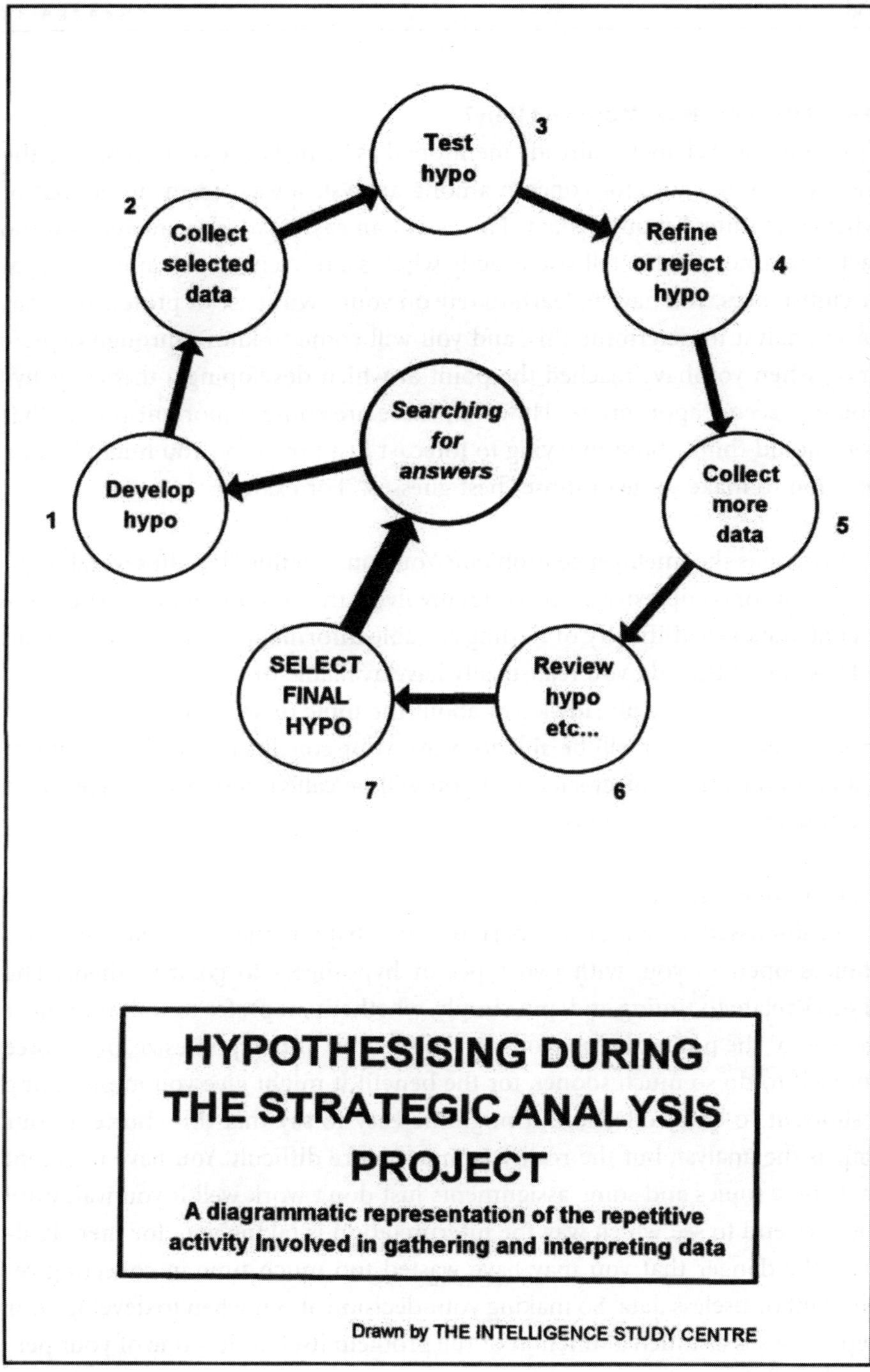

FIGURE 11.1
Hypothesis Circuit

Data Gathering: How Much and Why?

Of the three elements already mentioned as being key to hypothesizing, the most common cause for concern among analysts always seems to be that of what constitutes "enough" data. This is not an easy matter to answer, and the fact is that no one can tell you exactly what is sufficient to suit any analytical circumstances. You have to learn to rely on your own sense of professionalism as an analyst to determine this, and you will come to know, through experience, when you have reached the point at which developing a theory or hypothesis seems appropriate. However, there are some important points that you should think about in trying to forecast just how soon you might be in a position to make some of those "best guesses." For example:

- How big is the intelligence problem? You could define "big" in several ways: in terms of complexity of the issues involved, the amount of data to be gathered, the likely difficulty of finding suitable information sources, and so on.
- How much time do you realistically have available to you?
- How much do you already know about the topic or scenario?
- Is it likely that you will be able to prove your conclusions, or is the subject and level of the project such that you will be called upon to give your best estimates and conclusions?

When to Hypothesize

As discussed in an earlier part of this chapter, there are basically two choices open to you, with two types of hypotheses to go with them. The choices relate to timing and, put simply, whether you prefer to wait until near the end of the project before you start to theorize and hypothesize, or to force yourself to do so much sooner, for the benefit it might give you in providing a shortcut to data collection. It might be easy to say that this choice is your call, as the analyst, but the reality is much more difficult. You have to accept that some topics and some assignments just don't work well if you wait until the very end to see which way the interpretation is taking you, for there is always the danger that you may have wasted too much time in collecting redundant or useless data. So making your decision about when to develop your hypotheses is as much a function of the problem itself as it is one of your personal preferences.

Let's examine this question of choice a little further. You can opt to gather as much data as possible and analyze it, then come to your best hypothesis at the end of the analysis phase. Providing that you have exhausted all reasonable expectations for data gathering, then your theories probably will stand critical examination, for they are, after all, based on exhaustive analysis of extensive information collection activity. These theories become your considered theories and probably become your final conclusions. Your data collection will have been exhaustive and will certainly support these hypotheses, and you personally will know that the results are firmly founded on good process.

The Useful Alternative: "Working Hypotheses"

There is, however, an alternative method of approaching the strategic problem, and the decision to take this route can be made early in the project, for the reasons discussed below. At least two circumstances may occur in which selecting this alternative to the usual process seems to be defensible.

- Some topics are so unfamiliar to you—and quite possibly to others—that you might determine that data collection and sourcing will take an unreasonably long time. This could be because of the complexity of the topic or, as is often the case, the fact that intelligence and operational staff have rarely, if ever, had cause to probe that area. In very recent times, the need to examine the worldwide trade in human body parts was just such a problem.
- The topic may be so large in breadth that while analysis might not be the problem, the sheer volume of data to be collected is so massive that it will overwhelm the whole project. If you are expected to produce answers in a reasonable time frame, then you will be faced with the dilemma of not knowing exactly how much data would be "enough." Whatever the type of challenge facing you—and examining the whole issue of illegal drugs is just such a case—the likelihood is high that you will find the data-gathering plan a daunting task.

Working hypotheses can be developed as a self-help mechanism for developing indicators, but only as needed by the analyst. The working hypothesis is precisely what the phrase suggests—any hypothesis you use to help you conduct the intelligence and analysis activity. These hypotheses are generated and then used deliberately to help you to focus the task and avoid collecting too much and too slowly. The best time to generate these preliminary theories—for that is really what working hypotheses are—is early in the project. This will be around the time that you are finishing off the project plan and getting on to developing the data collection plan. By that time you will already have acquired some working level of knowledge through your conceptual modeling and the extensive re-examination of the original task.

In breaking down the task to prepare and negotiate the project directive, you will have been calling upon your existing knowledge of the topic to help you plan the project thoroughly and sensibly. Is there any reason, then, why you could not already find yourself able to develop some initial theories about the types of answers that you might well encounter? Well, for many analysts, the whole idea of generating ideas at this early stage is simply one of reacting to the whole notion of being premature. We are all schooled in the idea that answers follow analysis—and who could argue with that?

Conversely, there is a body of research experience that demonstrates that, if properly used, early and preliminary analytical thinking will help you to set up some useful analytical goals. The reasoning is that while you are engaged in testing them, the process educates you to see further options and routes for detailed examination.

The outcome of this alternative approach, if used deliberately and carefully, is that you manipulate the intelligence process in such a way as to help you avoid some of the pitfalls involved in massive, universal data collection. That this method of approach works is well demonstrated in research texts, but it must be used carefully and with a close eye to objectivity.

Making the Choice

Every analyst, by training and usually by inclination, gains strength from knowing that the intelligence process is logical and comprehensive, and is thus likely to lead to a good result. Although we easily admit to the idea that intelligence is speculative, the fact is that many analysts don't want to speculate along the way through the process. For them, the concept of "speculation" seems reserved for describing—usually to others—that our answers and forecast can never be conclusive until events prove them right, hence, the use of the word *speculative*. Therefore, the idea of actually speculating within the process itself is not necessarily a comfortable one for every analyst. The fact remains that, as described earlier, many tasks are fraught with uncertainty or overwhelmed by the massive nature of the data involved. One answer, always, is to convince your manager and client that because of these circumstances, the assignment will take months or even longer to complete.

The other approach is to critically examine your abilities, balance them against any misgivings you might naturally have, and look for alternatives. Be assured that the idea of using preliminary working hypotheses to help shape your approach to the project is well tested and, moreover, extraordinarily useful if you can learn to use it to good effect.

TECHNIQUES FOR GENERATING HYPOTHESES

A hypothesis is not just something that comes "out of thin air" without a reason. All analysts should be capable of thinking logically, and it should come as no surprise that the cartoon depiction of someone suddenly developing a lightbulb idea is, in fact, founded in some logical thought process. While you may be unaware of just how your thinking is progressing in this search for ideas, the fact is that you—like every other analyst—will generally use one or more of the following thinking patterns:

- searching for a *theory*;
- using *situational logic*; and
- using *comparison* as the basis for developing your views.

Developing a Unique Theory

A theory is a vital tool for any investigation and can be considered as a generalized conclusion based on the study of many specific cases. In a theory, when a given set of circumstances exists, certain events will follow inevitably, or at least with some substantial degree of probability. By making clear the key elements of a problem, the theory allows the analyst to see recent developments in a broader historical context. Understanding the theory allows the analyst to move beyond the horizons of the data on hand. In the field of law enforcement, we often develop favorite theories about certain types of crime. For example, if we are continually involved in studying different aspects of major organized crime, it becomes easy for us to develop fixed ideas about the elements of how organized crime operates.

If we venture into a new criminal topic and see at least some possibility of those elements appearing, then we naturally tend to the view that this quite possibly "proves" that organized crime is behind the activity. As a result, we may then draw upon our theorized knowledge of how organized crime operates and apply it immediately to how we think this new activity will operate. As a result, we may have ceased gathering any new perceptions of the functioning structure of this new criminal activity in favor of opting to categorize it according to our theories of organized crime.

The key usefulness of a theory is in its general applicability across like cases. Its principal danger lies in its being used indiscriminately, without first checking that it is truly appropriate to the case at hand.

Using Situational Logic

Sometimes, as the analyst, you will become enmeshed in the detail of an assignment project. This may be a new topic for you to consider, representing something quite out of your experience, and even a welcome change from what you are used to. How might you tackle this topic? Even though you may have in the back of your mind that it might relate or compare to something from past experience, you can decide that it is really quite a new challenge. When you focus on the specific elements of the intelligence problem to the extent of tending to ignore any reliance upon broad generalizations or background knowledge, then you are using what is called *situational logic.* While the generalizations—theories—might shed light on such situations, you don't see them as being sufficiently detailed to suit your purpose in this current situation. In fact, you may see this situation as being truly unique, one that might be best understood within the framework of its own separate logic.

The strength of situational logic is in its ability to be used to bring together and consider a large volume of related case-specific data, looking for cause-and-effect relationships to help you understand just what is going on. Whatever reasons you have for favoring the situational approach, you should not ignore the reality that there are two main drawbacks to it.

- It is difficult to do well. For example, it is difficult for the analyst to understand the mental processes and management routines of a criminal organization, because they are unfamiliar activities. Using the same problem arena, the analyst may also be inclined to project too many personal viewpoints into the criminal society, rather than try to understand the logic of the situation as it appears to the criminals involved.

- By concentrating solely on the situation at hand, situational logic fails to exploit the theoretical knowledge derived from the study of related cases in other contexts, at other times, involving other groups.

By looking at related cases, the analyst might get clues about the present problem. An analyst who insists upon regarding the situation as unique might not even think of such insights. In these circumstances, you may have unwittingly set up a personal mental block against relying upon any outside information or views that might help you understand what is going on inside this criminal situation.

As an example, consider the case of a strategic intelligence probe to examine the potential trade in human body parts. Because no true comparisons exist, the analyst may not be easily able to find and draw on any crime phenomenon that operates even remotely like the topic. Since this is a relatively unusual crime, it may not be possible for the analyst to find enough common points to generate any sort of usable theoretical understanding of the phenomenon. Finally, the analyst is left with the knowledge that the only way to study this topic is to examine it in some isolation from other influences. This is what makes the topic one that demands a situational approach.

Situational logic will usually do the most good in cases where it is necessary to assess short-term developments and smaller, self-contained problems. However, a more theoretical approach is appropriate if the requirement is to move further into complex problems with a future dimension. By way of contrast, theoretical analysis is based on presuming that there is little in the world that is truly unique and that for every situation, including the one you are currently faced with, there are probably valid theoretical propositions.

The Relevance of Comparisons

Analysts often try to understand current events by comparing them with previous examples that are chosen for their relevance and the similarity of their features. If the chosen comparative situation is seen to be like the present one, then you can use your understanding of the comparison to fill in gaps in your understanding of the current situation.

- Comparative analysis differs fundamentally from situational logic. The problem situation is defined in the light of appropriate analogies drawn from previous experience and history.
- Comparative analysis also differs from theoretical analysis. Comparisons are drawn with a few, highly relevant cases from history rather than from a very large number of similar cases, as in the case of theoretical analysis.

Reasoning by comparison is a helpful shortcut for an analyst who cannot find either enough data or a suitable theory. Be very careful, however, that if the historical example is particularly vivid, you do not allow it to overwhelm your thinking. This can all too easily happen, and could skew your ability to recognize differences if they exist. The cases may not be truly comparable in all respects, and you will need to draw on the points of commonality as a guide to developing hypotheses, allowing for both the similarities and differences of the cases in comparison. Comparison should not, therefore, be used to form the basis for a hypothesis unless thorough analysis confirms that cases are clearly comparable.

Divergent Analysis as an Approach to Hypothesizing

The technique known as *divergent analysis* is an orderly method of producing hypotheses, outlooks, or ideas. It is easily applicable, regardless of whether or not you choose to rely on theoretical, situational, or comparative logic as your approach. Divergent analysis method involves several sequential steps in its process, and this means that you must try to be at the same time thoughtful and controlled, yet highly creative. While it is not my intention to go into too much detail about using the divergent analysis technique, it is worth looking at the diagram that follows and the relevant notes that go with it. These explain what is involved.

USING HYPOTHESES

The Rationale for Using Hypotheses

There is no doubt that generating and using hypotheses is an absolute must for the intelligence officer. Your manager and client expect that you will provide forecasts, predictions, and estimates about a whole range of issues that are of concern to your organization.

It certainly is possible to hypothesize the "lazy" way, by not exerting yourself beyond the obvious and "convenient" pictures that emerge from data laid

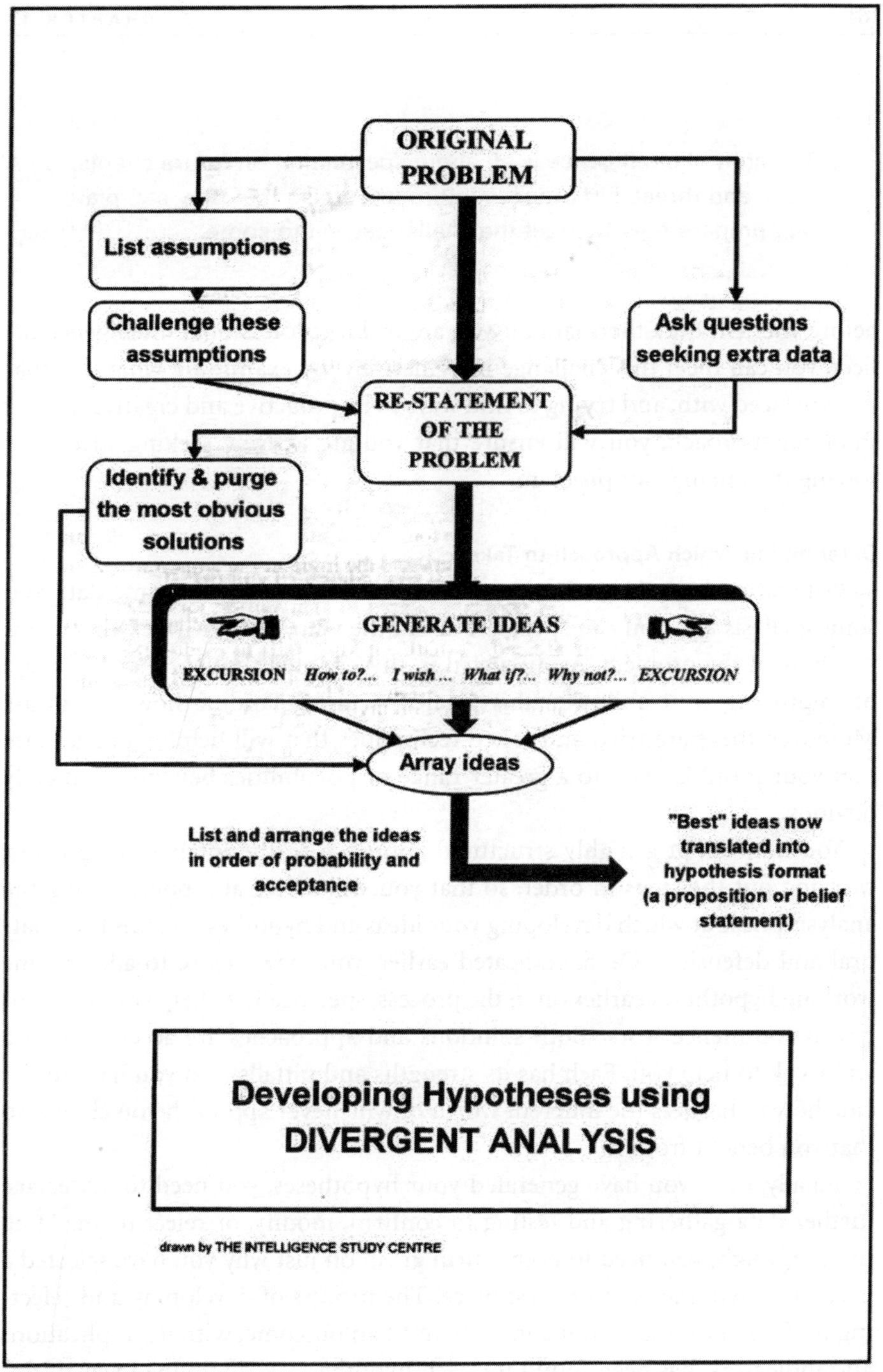

FIGURE 11.2
Divergent Analysis

> The craft of intelligence is all about speculating on future events, risks, and threats, in order to inform others so that they can plan and prepare now to meet the challenges yet to come.

before you. On the other hand, if you are truly a professional intelligence officer, you can meet this challenge imaginatively. By examining what it is that you are faced with, and trying to find ways to be proactive and creative in your thinking approach, you will ensure that you are actively seeking success in solving the intelligence problem.

Determining Which Approach to Take

Generating hypotheses is never difficult. All you need are some data and some analysis and you can speculate about the who, what, where, when, why, and how of the problem. As discussed in this chapter, though, there are ways of improving your ability in this regard by understanding how you think. Moreover, there are tried and tested techniques that will help you make sure that your mind is open to a greater range of possibilities beyond the merely obvious.

You may adopt a highly structured approach to the intelligence process, carrying out the steps in order, so that you will arrive at a point during the analysis phase at which developing your ideas and hypotheses seems both natural and defensible. Or, as indicated earlier, you may choose to adopt some working hypotheses earlier on in the process, specifically to help you find a focus to commence work. Both solutions and approaches are acceptable, and will work to help you. Each has its strengths and pitfalls, and you have to decide how to harness the inherent worth of whichever approach you choose so that you benefit from it.

Finally, once you have generated your hypotheses, you need to undertake further data gathering and testing to confirm, modify, or reject them. At all times, though, you need to keep a firm grasp on just why you have selected a particular hypothesis in the first place. The process of developing and selecting useful hypotheses is not complete until an outcome, with its implications and indicators, has been found for each hypothesis. A disciplined way of doing this is to simply list each hypothesis along with all the reasons that it

DEVELOPING A FORMAT FOR GENERATING AND REVIEWING HYPOTHESES

The purpose of the following procedure is to encourage you to develop and review your hypotheses in a considered, careful way. Anyone can develop ideas, but by doing so and checking the value of each new idea in this way, you will see all the implications of every hypothesis.

This checklist can be used in two ways. First, if you want to generate new ideas as the key to developing a collection plan, this process will result in developing a careful set of indicators for use in that plan. Second, you may have already collected a lot of data, and have arrived at these hypotheses as a result of analysis. In this case, using this process will allow you to review your reasoning, and develop indicators for further collection and testing.

1. List the hypothesis/idea that you have in mind.
2. Think of the reasons why you believe this hypothesis might be true, why you have selected this idea. Write down these reasons.
3. Now consider the hypothesis from the opposite point of view. Consider why you might reject it, and write down these ideas.
4. If this hypothesis were to be true, what results would occur? Write these down so that you can reexamine the relationship between the idea and its outcomes.
5. If the hypothesis were true, and these results occur, can you imagine any further longer-term implications? Write these down.
6. Finally, look at the results of your thinking: You have listed, against each hypothesis, your views concerning the reasons, the immediate or direct results, and the long-term implications. You can now see the hypothesis in its full potential setting.
7. What data should you now look for to test this hypothesis? What data questions need to be asked? Examine all the views that you have listed and develop a list of all the many individual signals or clues that would help you to test the truth of this hypothesis.

should be accepted or rejected. Then, an outcome for each hypothesis is chosen along with a list of the implications or likely results that would occur if that option were chosen. Finally, you list some of the indicators that would be visible if the outcome were chosen. The topic of strategic indicators is dealt with in chapter 12.

There is a useful format for doing this task, easy to complete but full of the potential to give you added insight as to just how and why you find a particular hypothesis useful and persuasive—or not, as the case may be. This is described at the end of this chapter.[1]

CONCLUSION

As a strategic analyst, you cannot escape the inevitability that you will generate hypotheses. You will have to test them and you will be called upon to justify your determination that some are more probable than others. In the world of strategic intelligence, the topics we deal with are often much more complex than those we encounter in operational intelligence. Moreover, we are most often called upon to examine those topics in both detail and breadth, examining everything about all of the issues. Finally, strategic studies require you to project your analysis well into the future. As a consequence, strategic analysis calls for greater levels of judgment and speculation about matters that are unlikely to be proven, at least in the short to medium term. Generating a sensible set of hypotheses, paying careful attention to detail, becomes a very necessary component of the strategic intelligence cycle.

NOTE

1. The following notes describe the steps involved in divergent analysis.

    1. List any initial assumptions you hold about the problem. Now list any of the data collection issues you consider relevant. What information do you need before you can go on, and how does this information feed back and affect your views so far?
    2. Look at the problem again and think about your assumptions. Are they still sustainable? Try challenging them directly, to see how your thinking proceeds. Taking all this into account, try to rethink and restate the problem by examining it from some different viewpoints.

3. Consider the most obvious solutions and ideas that seem to answer the problem. Now set them aside so that they do not block your thinking (this is called *purging*).
4. Now prepare yourself to consider any and every possible idea whatsoever. You need to think about the topic and the problem, and all of the ideas you associate it with, as freely and as creatively as possible. Dream, let your mind wander, think of a personal wish list concerning this topic, "brainstorm"—anything at all to keep you from thinking only about your existing views, which have been purged from this part of the process. Avoid the mental blocks and, if it is useful, do this aloud, with others joining in the process.
5. You will find that as you wander mentally through the landscape of this topic, you will encounter a tendency to drift further and further away from the hard reality of problem solving. This is an important step—an excursion—and you should allow yourself the opportunity to enjoy this and get what you can from it. At a convenient time, perhaps many minutes later, try to relate what you are thinking about at that very moment, to the problem at hand. While you are doing this, your mind is actually perceiving the problem anew from fresh perspectives—all useful in opening up your ideas about it!
6. You are close to finishing this process now. The next thing to do is to list—*array*—all the ideas you came up with: your wishes, views, opinions, whatever. Try to list them in some sort of order that makes sense to you, perhaps simply by listing the most outrageous at one end and the most acceptable at the other.
7. The next-to-last step is to refine your list. Weed out the really strange and radical ideas that just couldn't be acceptable, but make sure that you evaluate them carefully. Don't reject ideas just because they are "new," but because they just won't fit into any logical conception of the problem. This is done in three steps:
   - Select one of the more improbable ideas that you came up with—list the benefits that would occur if the idea became more "probable."
   - List the critical concerns that you have with this idea—don't kill it off, but try to see how to overcome these concerns, what would need to change, etc.
   - Modify the idea to overcome your concerns, and think of any other ways in which they can be minimized or removed.
8. Now bring back the ideas that you had purged earlier on in the process, and fit them into the listing in their order of "acceptability" or "probability." At the acceptable end of your list's spectrum, you now have a larger range of ideas than you originally started with, and each of these hypotheses is at least capable of being true. What happens next is the testing phase, through additional—but very highly focused—data collection, followed by analysis.

12

Developing Indicators for Strategic Topics

Every trained intelligence officer knows that one of the principal challenges for developing an effective intelligence collection plan is to correctly define the exact pieces of information that are necessary for your project. It is possible to develop collection programs that simply list every conceivable piece of data in the hope that some of it, at least, will be useful to you.

Investigators and analysts alike often adopt an approach to the task of data collection that involves merely listing the types of questions that need to be answered. For example, a collection plan might state your needs as being to gather "all data about drug arrests." In fact, this is not a question but just a broad heading. If you are going to task others to provide you with data, you will need something much more specific and detailed. Many issues are themselves so complicated and multifaceted that unless you are specific, you may not get anything like the level and volume of information you need and expect. Moreover, analysts often find themselves taking the worst possible shortcut, one that focuses upon "sources" rather than the "issues" that need to be addressed. (This will be covered in more detail in the next chapter.) Fundamental to the research process is the development of indicators, the perfect key for linking your understanding of what the task involves directly to establishing the specific requirements for data collection.

An indicator is a piece of information that, like the "clues" of detective fiction, provides a signpost to help fill in the gaps in your understanding of what is going on, who is involved, and all the other similar questions. While a clue is often thought of as something observable after an event, an indicator in intelligence parlance can also be considered to be those clues you might seek out before anything actually happens. In this sense, the value of indicators thus lies in this dual capacity: to act as predictors of events yet to come and to substantiate why you have reached a particular hypothesis or conclusion. However, an inherent part of the indicator concept is the fact that you cannot develop a set of indicators unless you have learned a lot about the milieu of the event you intend to examine. Without this learning process, developing sensible indicators becomes immensely difficult. The function of intelligence indicators is to allow you to design collection activity specifically based on a level of knowledge that suggests the types of data to look for. If used carefully to cover all the likely possibilities, indicators provide the intelligence analyst with a means of focusing the data collection phase, saving time and effort, and ultimately aiding the analysis that is to come.

This chapter takes you through the development of indicators for use in strategic projects, and the next chapter deals with the follow-up step of preparing a planned approach to data collection.

WHAT ARE STRATEGIC INDICATORS?

Intelligence indicators are single clues, or sets of them, that point to a specific event or phenomenon. An indicator has two values: One points to past events and acts as an explanation of substantiation of your views about what did occur; the other acts to provide you with signals to look for, focusing on events likely to occur.

Note that this description of the term emphasizes the future tense. The idea behind this, and the value of indicators to you as the analyst, rests in the way in which you can use the indicators to point to possibilities of, say, criminal action and planning. Whatever views you may hold, even at this early stage of the strategic research project, it is incumbent upon you to go about planning the data-gathering regime in a rigorous way to ensure that incoming data will assist in educating, confirming, modifying, or rejecting those views. In this way, indicators save both the analyst and the actual collectors of information time and effort by the way in which they place a high degree of discipline on the data-gathering plan.

There is another potential advantage in undertaking responsibility for putting in the effort to develop indicators and thus shape the collection plan: In utilizing your specialized knowledge to develop the indicators, you reduce any potential for collection staff to impose their own values. This is not to denigrate the value of the on-the-spot knowledge, expertise, and access of the collector. Rather, this input needs to be considered alongside the data in a neutral way to ensure that the collector does not, in fact, "edit" the data being reported. If this occurs without the analyst's awareness, then there is a strong possibility that the data reporting may well be invested with the collector's bias or prejudice in a way that could inhibit the whole strategic project.

A PROCESS FOR DEVELOPING INDICATORS

The process used for developing indicators specifically for collection planning is shown in figure 12.1 and described in the following paragraphs. You will recall that when the analyst first receives a new topic for strategic assessment, there is a period of time necessarily devoted to reading into the subject and preparing a mental model or framework about whatever the topic refers to, whether crime, organization, or trend. This step is formalized not only so that you prepare yourself in a structured way, but so that in doing so you avoid the pitfalls of assuming you already know all you need to about this topic. This is covered in the diagram in the step labeled "develop conceptual model." Under the project-planning step that follows, you prepare yourself to undertake the strategic intelligence project. In both of these steps, you learn about breaking down the original statement of the intelligence task, so that you can consider it in its full depth. The purpose behind this is to create a larger awareness of exactly what is involved potentially in the assessment. You communicate this to your manager and client, arriving at an agreed statement of work that we call the Terms of Reference.

An inevitable result of these activities is that you will have already found yourself considering some of the potential answers and "directions" for the study that might be emerging—even now, before you have started the full data collection phase. This is your preliminary thinking phase, and leads straight into developing the indicators necessary to draft a collection plan.

For example, if you have been asked to work at a strategic level on illegal drug matters, it should occur to you that this problem has many features. Certainly there are more than merely counting the number of drug arrests and examining the data about what was involved, who did it, how much was it worth, and so on. These are interesting features to gather and measure, and would form part of what is known in intelligence and criminology as *crime analysis*. However, they are not the whole answer to a strategic view of the extent and nature of illegal drugs.

At the strategic level, instead, you should be asking yourself what else is involved and worth knowing, beyond the boundaries of data available through police arrest and investigation records. For example, what about criminal organizations, funding, supply, packaging, reprocessing, wholesaling, stockpiling, and like aspects of the criminal trade? You might also seriously start to consider the direct impact of the crime: Does it lead to other crimes? Who are the participants? Who are the victims? What is their motivation? If you then extend your thinking further, you should be prepared to consider questions on the more indirect, or "downstream" impact issues: the impact illegal drug use has on society in general, on families, on health, on work time lost, and so on.

The list of ideas in the example above could go on to become an extremely comprehensive basis for study involving not only law enforcement analysts, but also those from other areas of specialty, working to produce a thorough strategic study of illegal drug-related issues affecting your province, city, or region. With this type of thinking going on, you should come to some views that will help you frame the eventual collection plan. Taking the above example on drugs, to continue along the line of thinking already expressed you might consider the following issues.

If the underlying task is to question the spread of illegal drugs through society, then you might consider as an extension issues such as drugs in all levels of schools—even perhaps in primary schools, where once they may have been considered a negligible threat. What about drugs in hospitals and clinic environments and drugs in prisons? What you ought to be concerned about is whether you can establish that drugs are evident where they were not before and/or whether their incidence is now greater or lesser than it might have been before. At this stage of thinking, you may perceive two options.

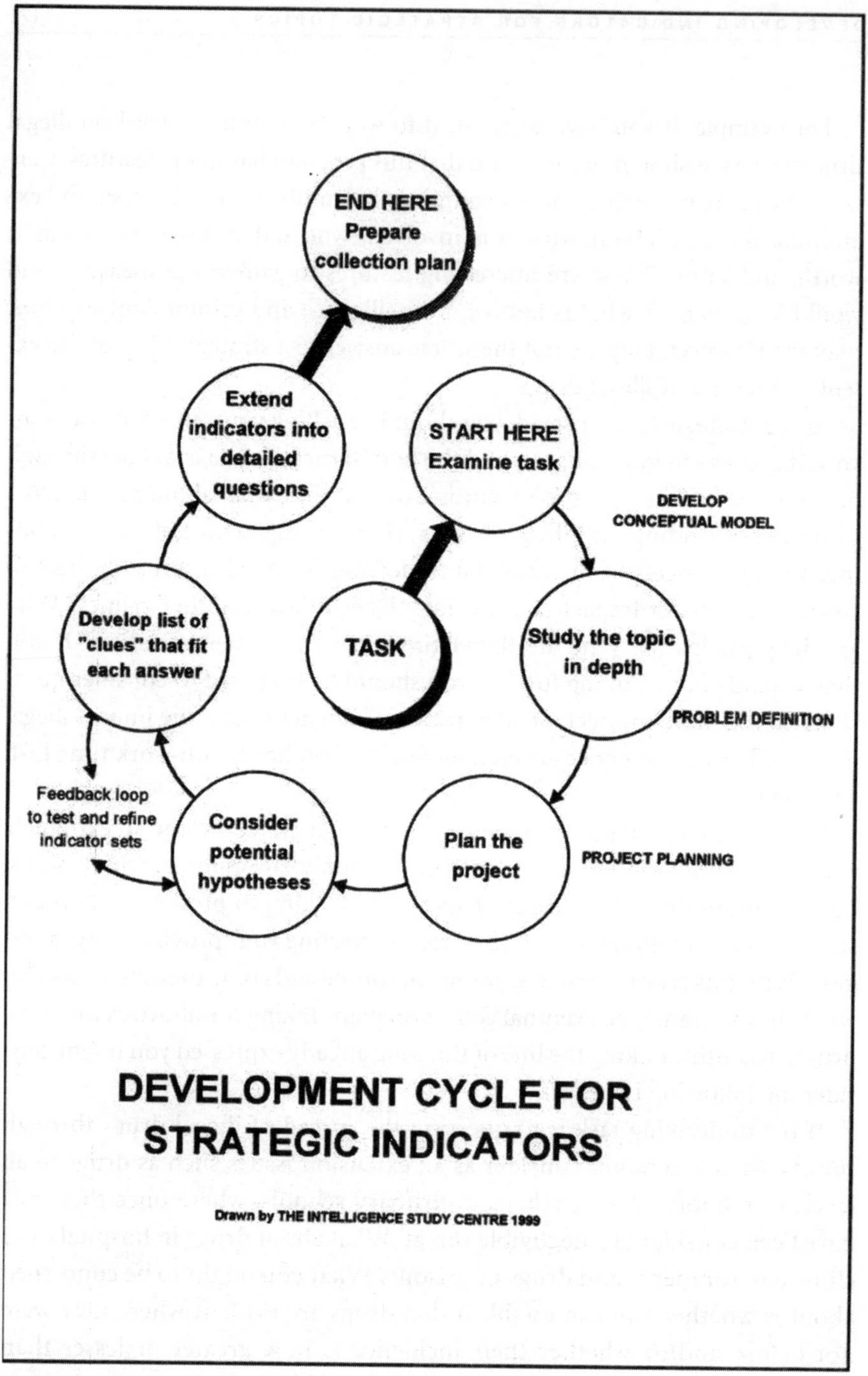

FIGURE 12.1
Development Cycle Indicators

- Develop a collection plan that asks everything of everyone about illegal drugs.
- Pose the following question to yourself: If such-and-such is the case (one of the examples above), what would indicate that this is so? Alternatively, what clues would indicate that this situation does not exist?

In this way, you force yourself to draw on your intimate knowledge of the scenario to determine that if the situation is as you suspect—and this can be a negative as much as it might be a positive—then certain conditions/situations/events will be observable. These are the indicators that you are looking for.

If illegal drugs were in use in primary schools (say, ages five to twelve), then if you could observe them you would expect to see certain things in evidence. Since you cannot physically be present and must ultimately rely upon a "collector," you have to translate your ideas into indicators, which, in turn, translate into quite specific questions. What you do in this case is use your greater knowledge of these affairs to pose absolutely detailed questions for your collectors and gatherers of information. By doing so, you have minimized or even avoided altogether asking people (teachers, for example) to make assumptions about situations that they don't understand as fully as yourself.

Developing indicators not only gives the analyst control over the collection process, but also improves the efficiency of its workings. Additionally, by using indicators you will have reduced the possible range of questions for your collection people down to the optimum set to address your interests. They will not have to waste time interpreting your needs and then working out which questions to ask and what data to collect. How are you, then, to decide which questions to actually ask? The process is simple to grasp. It is absolutely essential that, as a responsible intelligence analyst, you devise your collection plan by first determining what questions and issues need to be answered.

"Children and Drugs" Example

Imagine that you are interested in illegal drugs and their "spread" further into all reaches of society in your own state, province, or territory. Imagine also that you have a list of possible areas that could be infected, where such an impact was not the case previously—primary schools and hospitals are just some of these possibilities. For the sake of argument, let's focus on drugs in schools. Assuming that the proposition about drugs in schools and hospitals were true, in such a case you would have gone through the process outlined below.

1. Ask yourself: If I could observe this situation to be true, what would I actually see? Make this a very detailed set of questions that suit quite specific issues. For example, some of the issues would concern the following:
   - children using drugs
   - children selling or distributing drugs
   - outsiders to the school providing children with the drugs
2. Consider what aspects are observable for each of these issues. If children are using drugs, then you could expect to see or hear about:
   - behavior that is "abnormal" in the context of being under the influence of drugs
   - behavior that is abnormal, relevant to how the drugs are taken
3. For each of these, then, there are again progressively more detailed questions that you would ask observers to comment upon. You might, for example, ask teachers to comment about students that display in-class behavior that shows abnormal levels of inattention, sleepiness, emotional outbursts, and similar symptoms of acting outside of their personal norms. You might similarly ask about behavior outside the classroom in other controlled situations, like PE class, and propose a set of questions designed to elicit comment about behavioral changes in individual students—lack of balance, dangerous actions, and lack of concentration as cases in point.

Focusing on the Detail

The whole point of this process is for you to use your knowledge to develop progressively more detailed question sets. You do not want others making decisions for you about what drug-influenced behavior would look like. That road only invites others with less knowledge to impose their own belief systems and provide you with answers and impressions that have been modified by their own view of things. This is not what you need.

The development of indicators for strategic assessment projects involves a detailed analysis of the features that you are looking for or expect to see. As an analyst, your role is to pose layer upon layer of increasing detail in the questions until you get to the level at which you judge it appropriate to use for tasking your collection "agents," whoever they might be.

The indicator is the direct input entry into the collection plan. It stipulates what you want to know, yet leaves you free to draw conclusions from analysis rather than relying upon others to make those judgments for you. To illustrate the process in another way, it simply looks like a pyramid. Figure 12.2 demonstrates the downward progression from the overall issue to detailed questions that are, in fact, the indicators that you need to use to generate the collection plan.

CONCLUSION

Generating indicators is not difficult to do. If the analyst has paid rigorous attention to developing a familiarity with the features of the topic and has been creative in thinking through the various possible hypotheses, then generating the detail necessary is not intellectually difficult.

The challenge for many analysts comes from a different direction. First, tension and stress to meet time-critical targets, and the culture that drives this in many agencies, create a situation in which the "easy" way out is to fall back upon simple, broad question sets rather than detailed ones. Any analyst looking at the "children and drugs" issue discussed earlier could be driven by time pressure to simply ask collectors to provide "everything known" about child drug use. This leaves the collector to interpret what is wanted and supply information accordingly.

The best practice the analyst can adopt is to take up the challenge of working through the possibilities and developing detailed indicators that can potentially deny or confirm particular thoughts and possibilities. This places the "control" over data-gathering design and collection, at least at an intellectual level, in the hands of the analyst—the sole agent best placed to oversee the entire research project.

Indicator development traditionally falls into the trap of staying aloof and above the real levels of detail necessary for specialized examination of a phenomenon. While there may be many pressures to do so and rely on others to work out what is required, the analyst must simply accept the whole responsibility of running a strategic project. No one else is better placed to do so.

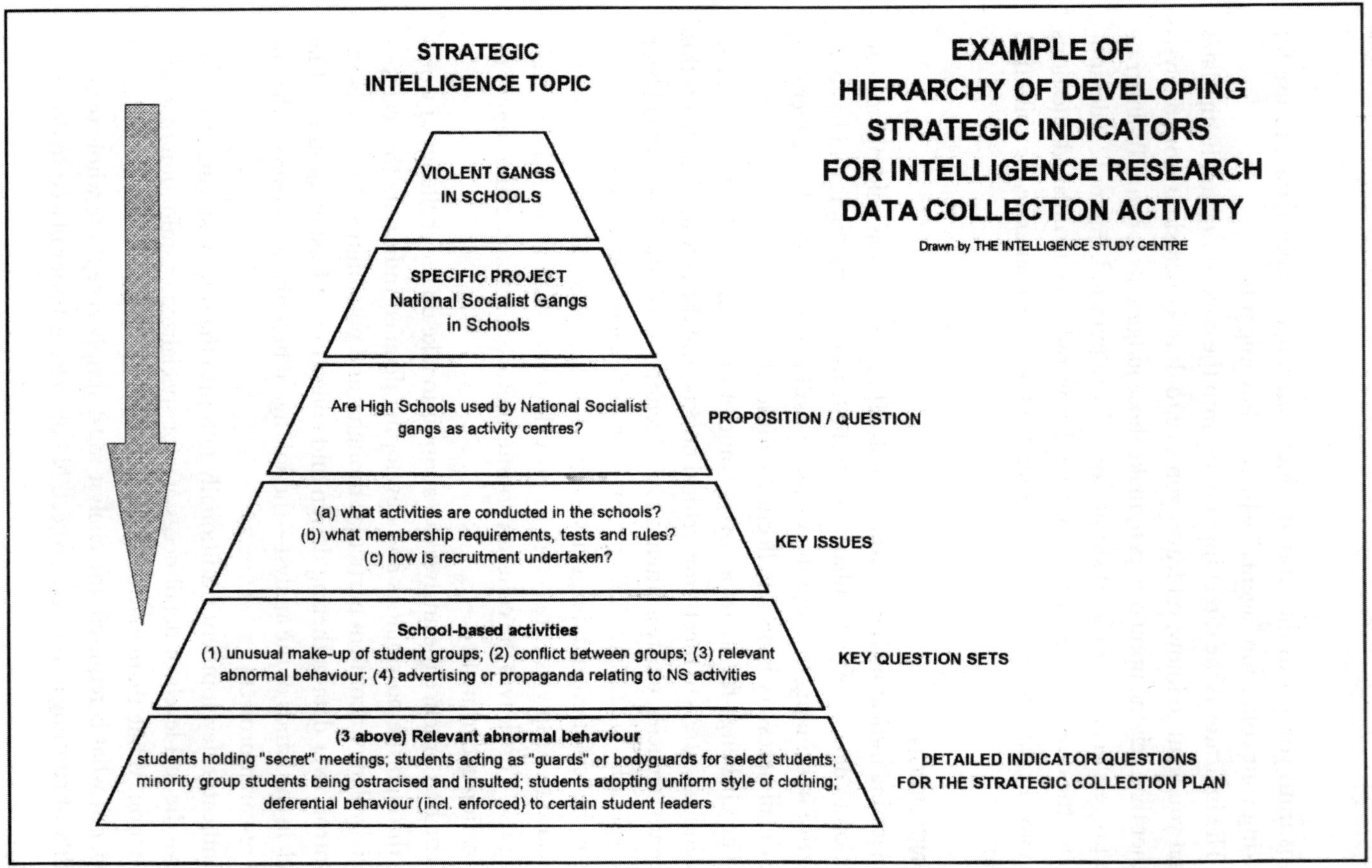

FIGURE 12.2
Indicator Pyramid Example

13

Data Collection Plans for Strategic Projects

Data collection planning is an area of the intelligence process that requires the application of strict disciplines and orderly procedures, without which the analytical conclusions would be less than complete and might in some cases be considered not entirely legitimate.

Much of what is discussed in this chapter takes what should be established doctrine on data collection and planning and adapts it for use in strategic research. However, as discussed in chapter 3 concerning critical observations on current strategic intelligence practice, we find continuing evidence worldwide of standards less than "best practice" with regard to the disciplined and orderly approach necessary for effective collection planning and implementation. Despite the many agencies and intelligence units that demonstrate an adherence to such principles, many more appear to have simply let slide any genuine attempt to think carefully through the whole genre of collection planning. One reason is that much of the "basic" intelligence techniques training available to the intelligence community does not focus in any significant measure on these issues. Partly, this lack is derived from a continued preoccupation with the original Anacapa model of intelligence teaching that did not focus significantly on collection plans. Whatever the reason—and organizational expectations for urgent output is but one—there is scant attention being paid to the importance of developing comprehensive, focused collection plans.

To address what is perceived to be a lack of thorough grounding in the principles and techniques of intelligence collection planning, this chapter covers the following issues:

- the need for information and intelligence;
- availability of sources of information;
- the means of acquiring information; and
- making a plan for information collection.

In addition to the above issues, note that the final section of this chapter focuses on the particular aspects of collection planning that affect or are affected by strategic intelligence projects. However, you should understand that all the principles of good practice apply to all intelligence studies; there is no differentiation between what is applicable to one type and level of study and what is applicable to another. These principles hold good for all intelligence research cases; however, individual case features will, in turn, drive the application of these principles of collection planning.

THE INFORMATION IMPERATIVE

The analyst responsible for a project must gain a general working knowledge of the background of the topic under investigation. This is particularly important in the case of strategic studies and has been explained in considerable detail in chapter 8. That step is the first time the analyst encounters the issue of data gathering.

In general, libraries, official and public databases, academic study centers, and similar sources will provide a wealth of information of this background nature. Even if they do not hold the references in stock, these institutions can readily obtain them. The data held by these sources will be of immense assistance in allowing the analyst to come to an understanding of the type of activity that is the focus of the intelligence study.

A lot of intelligence work carries with it a sense of urgency. However, it is essential that the analyst set aside sufficient time to gaining this background level of understanding of the topic. You should accept that it is the norm of strategic intelligence project work to study the general arena, instead of merely relying on "instinct" to provide a guide through what can be a complex subject environment.

An important element in this whole question of data collection planning is that you must constantly be on guard to avoid what could be thought of as the "official data only" syndrome. This manifests itself in intelligence units where the prevailing culture is one in which trust is vested in official sources only; all others are, to a greater or lesser degree, regarded with uncertainty, concern, or mistrust. If there is one rule to follow concerning your thinking on data-gathering and collection plans, it must be that the questions themselves drive consideration of potential sources to use, as emphasized in chapter 12.

SOURCES OF INFORMATION

It is a popularly expressed notion that the world has, for the past several years, been going through an information explosion. The advent of the Internet has dramatically changed the scene for those involved in analysis. The availability of increasingly sophisticated computers has become commonplace.

Open Source, Open Mind?

More and more data is becoming easily available. This is the age of open source information, after all. A growing amount of information about an increasing range of topics is becoming more easily accessible to anyone with the energy to look for it. In addition to the growing volume of print media information, there an enormous volume of data is now made available through Internet and the array of computer bulletin boards, library catalogs, databases, and so on. This phenomenon is by no means limited to electronic information systems, since it is obvious to all analysts and researchers that there is a rapidly growing amount and diversity of printed information being generated. The key necessities are "official access clearance" and, in the case of the Internet, computer competence. To access those hard-copy, noncomputer sources, establishing and maintaining personal contact and rapport with information source staff is a useful strategy for the analyst to follow.

Yet, for all the increase in access to this plethora of information, intelligence officers and analysts are often limited by the conventions and practices of their organizations as well as by the protocols of government service. Real issues of time and resources, both human and financial, understandably have an effect on just how far the analyst can go in the quest for data. If you are not particularly well versed in computer use, or if you simply choose to avoid the opportunities by staying with familiar, tested sources, then you will have closed your mind to the possibilities that new sources might bring to dealing with the intelligence problem. At the same time, you cannot afford to become so involved in a widening search for new data that you become enmeshed in "surfing the Net" to the extent that the project suffers in terms of timely outcomes.

If you are careful about the way you approach using these computer opportunities, it is unlikely that you will encounter serious difficulties in determining what types of sources to access for information. In fact, it is relatively easy to determine what ought to be done, and you might only strike some difficulty—if any at all—when it comes to actually getting the information. Computerized directories are large and complex, and their access networks often so slow as to make your task one that needs time and patience as well as

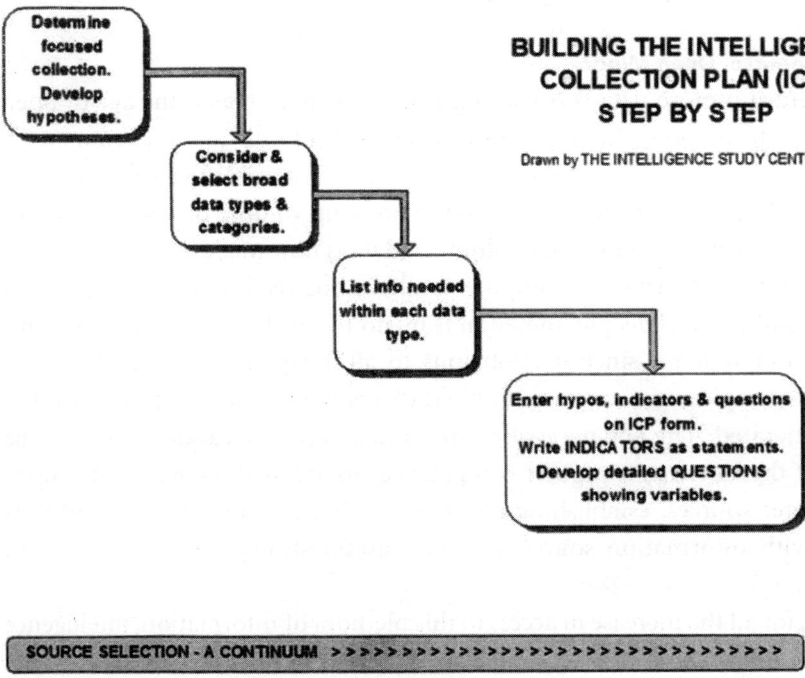

FIGURE 13.1
Collection Planning Progressive Development

skill. Using search engines is not necessarily a skill that every analyst would find easy to master, and the question remains whether or not the analyst should actually do the searching or leave it to a specialist.[1] The challenge for the strategic analyst is to select data that is relevant, useful, and sufficient from the widening universe of information readily available through computerized access networks. You simply cannot ignore this growing resource, but you must, at all costs, remain both selective and objective. The Internet represents both a potential treasure trove of information that is particularly appropriate for the background study and conceptual modeling phases of your work. But it can take a great deal of time and effort to search for it, and you should quickly acquire the necessary skills to do so efficiently and effectively.

Paramount in the consideration of the collection process should be your knowledge that what you are doing ought to be rigorously planned and, in some senses, fixed for all the benefits that that gives you. Yet, to remain relevant and useful, the whole process of collection must end up producing an information collection plan that remains flexible and adaptable, able to change to meet unforeseen events. Flexibility has to account for changes in management/client focus on the original issue, but these are not the only stimuli to change. The best-laid plans to gather data can suffer if it is discovered that the type, format, coverage, and reliability of such data are not what the analyst expected and needed.

For example, consider the case of a strategic study of the potential cocaine problem in what has historically not been a cocaine-using region. In attempting to measure the extent of and potential for cocaine usage, intelligence units will traditionally canvass enforcement records as a first "port of call." Such data will cover what is known within the offense-reporting context as well as any information leads gathered in the course of investigations and informant operations. To extend beyond these fairly limited horizons, the analyst may well decide that sourcing data from user groups for other drugs (heroin, marijuana, etc.) will illuminate different dimensions of the overall drug problem in a way that can help this cocaine assignment. It will generate an understanding of the processes by which users might migrate from one drug to another or to multidrug use, how they raise the funds necessary to make their buys, how often and in what quantities they access the drugs, and any other variables, such as price and perceived purity. By gathering these sorts of data from users, the analyst can begin to understand the need to further explore such issues as user motivation in order to be able to pattern models of drug use. These can then be used as a springboard for assessing how cocaine use might mirror—or, alternatively, differ from—usage behavior for the other, more common drugs. From this, the analyst can work toward identifying the model indicators that point to any pattern changes that would accompany the entry of cocaine into this particular regional market.

Gathering such data inevitably means accepting the realization that it is essential to go beyond the confines of law enforcement sources. This is because those sources will not necessarily focus as much on these features of drug purchasing, supply, and motivation as is needed to address the requirements of a strategic study and forecast of the problems.

Data Quality

There is also a dilemma associated with data quality. The mere presence and availability of information in what, in comparison with the past, might be overwhelming proportions does not in any way suggest that the data is any more accurate, reliable, or complete. The challenge for you is to decide what you need, where it could possibly be acquired, and of what quality it is likely to be. As a consequence, you have the challenge of trying to select the optimum amount of the most potentially useful and reliable data from the huge amount available.

While the Internet might be regarded as a treasure trove of information, you need to become very skilful in understanding its intricacies, strengths, and weaknesses if you are to use it to its fullest potential. You have to decide whether or not to stay with tried and tested routines for data collection, or to make use of the growing information technology in this area. Every data source has something to offer, and it is your role as analyst to sort out what is useful and what is not. No matter how much data is being added to computer sources every day, your reality has to be that until it is tested, it remains just unproved data that, like everything else, has to be validated.

No simple, perfect solution exists for identifying useful sources suited to enforcement or any other form of analysis. Every single case usually displays something unique or different from what you might expect, even in another similar case. You always have to consider carefully exactly what might be gained from a particular source, no matter how useful that source may have been in similar cases in the past. Remember that the potential usefulness of any source remains just that—assumed usefulness—until something significant occurs to make you change your mind. What is recommended is that unit analysts record their observations about how particular sources fare in individual cases and consolidate such information for general agency use.

Deciding How Much Data is Sufficient and What is Relevant

In addition to deciding what type of information to gather and from what sources, you also have to find sufficient personal discipline to determine just how much data is enough. Knowledge by itself, gained from reading large volumes of data, may be relatively useless without a sense of purpose about the specific intelligence task at hand. Only by understanding the task and evaluating what is currently known about the topic or target will you be able to focus on specific sources for particular information. There is little point in assessing mountains of information and analyzing all sorts of interesting intelligence out of it, no matter how satisfying this might be, if no part of the organization needs or wants it.

This is an important principle of collection practice: gather what is relevant. Given the usually high level of interest you might develop in a particular study, this might seem to be a small detail. But you must keep the objectives of the organization very firmly in mind when collecting and evaluating information, so that you can determine its relevance to an eventual intelligence product that is of value to the user. This is certainly not the time to go on "fishing expeditions" out of personal interest.

The foregoing statement should be a useful reminder of the direction of the analyst's real task. If the unit's strategic intelligence work is to effectively support and advise management, it is pivotal that the analyst understand how intelligence is placed in terms of supporting and inputting to organizational decision making. The analyst is there to support management by informing their level of awareness about critical issues.

> An intelligence unit does not itself direct operations. It provides the insightful interpretation needed to satisfy the manager's organizational responsibilities.

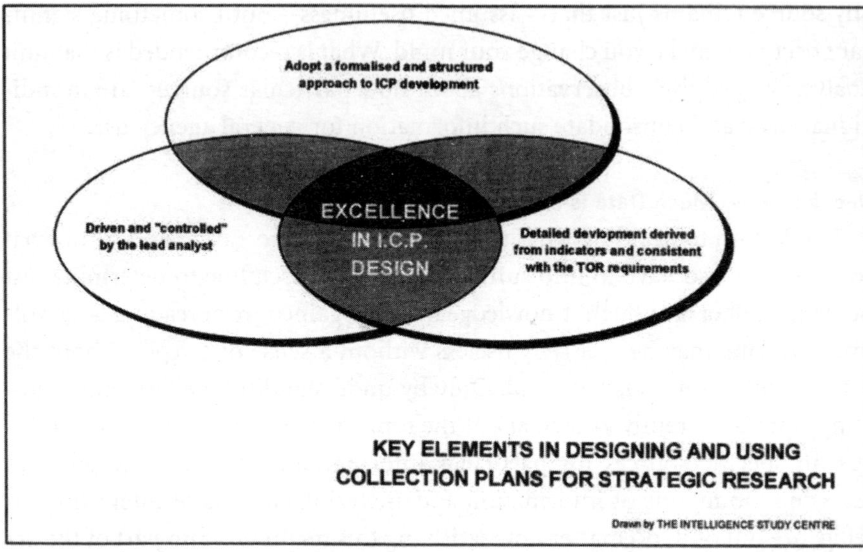

FIGURE 13.2
Intelligence Collection Plan Venn Diagram

PLANNING THE COLLECTION ACTIVITY

In earlier chapters, we discussed that once you have examined the strategic intelligence topic and determined the scope of investigation and research, you can proceed with planning the overall project. Part of that activity now comes to fruition in the sense that you need to become much more specific about detail. An analyst needs a collection plan to enable the orderly and precise collection of the relevant information. Obviously, your collection plan will provide the intelligence officer or collector, if this latter is a different person, with an organized and definitive outline of the data requirements for the project.

Specifically, your strategic intelligence collection plan (ICP) should cover the following aspects. Indeed, all collection plans should perform this function regardless of whether they are intended for tactical, operational, or strategic use.

- It should provide for the focused data collection methodology.
- It should aim to minimize time spent collecting irrelevant data.
- It should define the amount of data to be collected.
- It will help those involved in data collection to understand the purpose to which the data will be put and the form in which it will be most useful.

A second major feature of the collection plan is that, by its very nature, it facilitates the analysis process simply because it provides for a systematic procedure for the collection of information relevant to the task. This is important because it can help minimize lost or wasted time requesting irrelevant data, and ultimately assists you in developing inferences and coming to conclusions that, in turn, are likely to have a higher probability of being correct.

Who Uses and Benefits from the ICP?

Most of the focus of this chapter tends to suggest that the collection plan is the analyst's tool. It is meant to provide for a disciplined and orderly approach to deciding which data appear to be relevant to the strategic research topic. This provides the analyst with an opportunity to continue to control the development of the project to meet its agreed aims. It is important, though, that readers understand that the analyst has to interact with several different parties if data gathering is to be effective. In no particular order of preference, this list of other involved parties will include:

1. The intelligence unit manager. This person needs assurance that the project is proceeding to address the topic comprehensively. Such assurance is gained by being briefed on the direction and thoroughness of the collection plan.
2. The client. This person will similarly require, at the outset as well as in regular update briefings, similar assurance as that for the unit manager, though not in the same level of detail.
3. Intelligence colleagues. Those staff who were involved in brainstorming sessions earlier in the project, to clarify the aims and scope so that a suitable project directive can be developed, now form a useful group against which the collection plan design can be checked and input offered.
4. Collection staff. While it may not be normal practice to disclose the collection plan to all collection staff and data resource persons, there is merit in allowing them enough of a glimpse of the whole plan to provide them with a heightened level of understanding. The default position of the analyst should be to apprise this disparate group—organizational as well as "outside" persons—of the issues unless there are strong reasons involving data security and confidentiality not to do so.

Development of the ICP

An intelligence collection plan is just what the term implies: a formally defined approach to describing the information needed and the means of acquiring it.

The first step in planning collection is to establish what it is you need to know. This is achieved by conducting an "audit" of the situation in which all of the information requirements are defined. The next step is to list the known intelligence and information holdings. Finally, and very simply, you can list the intelligence gaps and deficiencies, listing these using the sort of "indicator" systemology outlined in the preceding chapter. In developing this list of the elements of information that are deficient, you should try to place them in an order of priorities for collection. Once you have done this, then you can draw up a formal collection plan. This needs to be formal in the sense that it is deliberate and particular to both the needs for information and the sources chosen. These are activities that involve not only structured thought about the issues involved, but considerable research into current information holdings.

Components of the ICP

The completed collection plan must be a visible document, underlining your certainty and confidence in its drafting at the time of its inception. To achieve this, you should commit it to writing. The collection plan will provide a list and explanation (where necessary) of the following items:

- the broad information categories in which you have an interest;
- specific data items you want to collect (from your development of indicators);
- all agencies that have capacity to provide it, to make sure that in making a selection you consider the strengths and weaknesses, overlaps, and even contradictions among the various sources that could provide you with the data;
- the agency you have selected as the source for each data item;
- the time frame in which you want the information, and when you asked for it, complete with contact details and references to faxes, letters, and the like; and
- comments about the format in which you expect the data to be provided.

It is important to understand that this sort of collection plan works best when it is done in detail and with the necessary amount of careful thought.

Yet, although we have stressed that doing this in visual form provides evidence of your confidence as the analyst/drafter, the plan must nonetheless remain flexible enough to cope with changing circumstances.

Options for Drawing up the ICP

Drafting of the plan can be done on paper, and many agencies have preprinted forms for this purpose. It is becoming increasingly common, though, for agencies to format their standardized collection plan approach in a computerized format and several approaches are possible.

- In its simplest form, the ICP can be drawn using a template in any word-processing program. This provides a user-friendly option but has the drawback that elongation of the template for later viewing—horizontally (sources, etc.) and vertically (indicators, questions)—is difficult.
- Using a spreadsheet program allows the development of a formatted database file that immediately has the capability of overcoming the difficulties mentioned above regarding extensions. In addition, spreadsheet programs have quite remarkable capabilities for moving cells—information packages—around and highlighting with color or greyscale, and generally provide a heightened flexibility in layout and presentation. Given that the ICP is both a working document and yet one that others must be able to read easily and interpret clearly, this is a strong advantage of the spreadsheet system. An example of its use is shown in the following ICP document.[2]
- An additional option is to make use of the many computerized database programs available. The advantage of using a formatted database file is that, even if the software is not a "relational" database, you can arrange the collection plan items as fields of data, and then search, cross-match, and effect interactive changes easily and efficiently when the need arises. There is no doubt that these are usually much more powerful than required by the demands of an ICP, and they are certainly flexible and adaptable in usage. If there is a drawback to using database programs, it is in the area of user-friendliness. Without doubt, many analysts find that the spreadsheet approach or even the word table format are much easier to use.
- The analyst's objective is, of course, to arrive at a point in the planning where the "thinking" part of the development manifests its outcomes as a formalized, structured document. You will then have something that provides a

Collection Plan

Case Ref: **THE IMPACT OF INFECTIOUS AND RE-EMERGING DISEASES ON SOUTH AFRICA'S NATIONAL SECURITY**

Compiled by Marcel Reutner for
THE INTELLIGENCE STUDY CENTRE, 2008

			Sources												
		Hypotheses & Information Requirements	Internet	Broader Media (Newspa	Defence	Foreign Affairs	SME's	Intelligence Agencies	Dept of Health	Virology Institute	Dpet of Land affairs	Dept of transport	Dept of Home Affairs	When Required	Comments
h1		Infectious and re-emerging diseases within the region within the context of sustainable development will impact significantly on South Africa's national security policy.members.												**2008/02/12 to 2008/04/07**	
i	1.1	The traditional concept of security should also include human security.													
	1.1.1	How can the traditional concept of security be defined?	X	/	X	/	/	/							
	1.1.2	How can human security be defined?	X	/	/	/	/	X							
	1.1.3	What commonalities are there (if any) between the traditional concept of security and human security?	X	X	/										
	1.1.4	What aspects would be included in the definition of human security?	X	X	/			/							
	1.1.5	Where does the existence of disease (or the non-existence thereof) feature within the concept of security?	X		/			/	X						
	1.1.6	Will human security impact significantly on the formulation of a national security policy	X		X		/	X	/						
	1.1.7	How will human security within the region impact on South Africa's national security policy?	X		X		/	X	/						
	1.1.8	Can a commonality or link be defined between human security and sustainable development? (x access to markets; x freedom of association; x security)	/	/			X	X							

FIGURE 13.3
Sample ICP Form

detailed, written listing of what is wanted, from whom, when, and in what format. In addition, the plan will need to identify priorities and allow for fall-back or reserve sources of information in the event of failure of some sources to deliver what is expected or requested of them.

Flexible Planning and Design of the ICP

In the move to develop collection plan forms to suitable organizational needs, it has become increasingly notable that some of the key features are often lost; their rationale has been forgotten as the technique has evolved. There are basically two reasons for this. One is that it is largely attributable to changes in corporate memory about the reason for the design in the first place. In addition, as technology becomes more available and supportive of the intelligence process, changes are often made to make formatting more suitable for presentation. This is a case of making change "simply because we can." As training in and the practice of intelligence develop, the doctrine undergoes change, ostensibly in the name of improvement but not always with that result. One serious flaw in much of intelligence practice remains, as it has been for many years, that the driving force is not the question-directed ICP, but one that is source driven. While this is often the most acceptable approach in terms of the analyst's comfort zone and the unit's routines and culture, it hampers the search for all the relevant data from all the relevant, potential sources.

The wider the range of sources analysts consider as providers of the data essential to the strategic intelligence project, the greater the flexibility provided to meet changing circumstances. True, there are many arguments that can be mounted against the analyst's desire to widen the scan for data. Some of these reasons will focus on resource and time constraints, and they may well be not only relevant but difficult to counter. Another issue frequently raised concerns security and sensitivity, citing the need to gather data only from "trusted sources." If changes need to be made for whatever reason, then the intelligence unit/agency should try to stick as closely as possible to the terms and fields of data spelled out earlier in this paper. There may well be room for improvement upon old ideas, but it is important to remember that in providing better presentation, one should not lose any of the essential components from the original recipe.

In summary, the collection plan is an extremely useful and practical working tool because:

- it is applicable throughout the early parts of the intelligence process;
- it is also used as a referral point throughout the collation and analysis phases, whenever the interpretation activity stumbles through questionable information or suffers from a newly perceived deficiency of some types of data;
- the very nature of the plan itself, given both the detail involved and the requirement for its application repeatedly throughout the process, requires that it be set down in readable form, suitable for correction, modification, and recording; and
- while it can be entered into a suitable computer format or drawn up on a wall chart, chalkboard or whiteboard, or even large-size formatted paper, what is most important is that the entries are concise and clear, and the logic behind them obvious.

STRATEGIC RESEARCH AND ITS IMPACT ON INTELLIGENCE COLLECTION PLANNING

The principles of collection planning apply no matter what form of intelligence is involved. Strategic intelligence is no exception, and it makes few, if any, separate or special demands on issues of principle—but it certainly does have an impact on the application in practice. While the nature of the problem issues involved in the strategic intelligence probe will always differ substantially from tactical intelligence interests, the fact is that developing a suitable intelligence collection plan calls for the same care and attention to detail in deciding what to ask, of whom, and when. What are the key differences to collection planning that strategic intelligence imposes? The list is small but important.

- Strategic topics often are imprecise, vague, or largely unexplored, and this means that the project will be somewhat lacking in the sense of definition and familiarity that are the hallmarks of traditional operational intelligence.
- The depth and breadth of the data-gathering function is much more extensive than in other forms of intelligence, meaning that strategic collection is likely to be both diverse and large.
- The range of sources you need to identify and access is, again, much broader than the norm.

The analyst must appreciate that the requirements of strategic intelligence do make themselves felt in determining just how to translate the concepts of indicative information—the "indicators" of the previous sections—into specific data items that can be described, sought, and collected. Why is this a difficulty? A common misconception held by many intelligence staff and their managers is that some strategic intelligence topic material is quite insubstantial when compared with the hard-edged data usually required for operational purposes. The idea of probing the motivation of criminals, for example, is not one easily measured by simply asking basic questions and expecting to get definitive answers.

The nature of strategic intelligence demands a very high degree of attention to detail in developing indicators and translating these into specific questions for the collection plan. In chapter 11, I introduced the concept that the hypothesis is one means of focusing the collection activity. In simple terms, it suggests that if you are able to develop a view—a hypothesis—early in the process, you will be in a position to start identifying the indicators that should be observable. On the other hand, it may be that you are simply unable to arrive at useful working hypotheses because you lack knowledge about the topic. Indeed, in this circumstance, if you were to try to do so without at least some logical foundation of information, you would run the risk of getting nothing useful from it. There's a greater risk, however, in trying to force yourself to generate ideas when none come naturally: that is, you might become a victim of your own bias and prejudice, caused by your lack of balance in viewing what is an unfamiliar problem.

There are ways around these thinking difficulties, though, and they can be learned by studying thinking concepts and blocks to creative thinking and reading articles and books by such authors as Edward de Bono.[3] In essence, you will know when it feels right to feel confidence in stating some views about the topic you are dealing with. The hypotheses should not be developed until and unless you feel that you have sufficient information and awareness to justify doing so. One sensible approach to strategic intelligence theorizing that works well in practice is for the analyst to ignore the potential for developing hypotheses at this early stage. You could concentrate for the time being on listing basic information requirements about the measurable, routine data related to the topic. Use the familiarity of this activity to provide yourself with an opportunity to take time out, at the same time exposing yourself to a learning experience, since everything you gather will help you understand the topic better. It is likely that you will not feel confident about progressing toward generating hypotheses until you have gathered a sufficient amount of the routine data mentioned above. Once generated, though, these hypotheses will become another springboard for making additions to the collection plan.

Ultimately, it is likely that it will be the length and comprehensiveness of the strategic intelligence collection plan that sets it apart from other collection activities. In many cases, too, it will be obvious that a greater proportion of the data being collected may well be "soft" data: anecdotal, descriptive, and qualitative information that is acceptable precisely because it provides a sense of purpose or inferred meaning to a given situation. By way of contrast, in tactical intelligence, this will be the exception rather than the rule.

Finally, the strategic intelligence collection plan often shows its differences by drawing on a wider range of agencies external to your intelligence unit. Certainly, this extends into the world of computerized information (using the Internet and the like), as discussed earlier in this chapter, and may even go to involving community organizations beyond the normal range of contact of the law enforcement and intelligence communities. It is this feature of strategic intelligence that sets it fundamentally apart from operational activity, demanding that you go outside familiar territory to gather everything and anything that can help you address the strategic problem. There are special challenges in opening up the collection activity, if only because the universe of information is far more extensive than you might think. Nonetheless, you must learn to be selective on the grounds of reliability, believability, comparison, and sufficiency.

CONCLUSION

If there are new "tricks" to be learned about collection planning and implementation insofar as strategic intelligence is concerned, it is simply that the analyst must be prepared to gather more and different data, well beyond the confines of operational intelligence.

The strategic intelligence process described in this book emphasizes that the analyst needs to thoroughly prepare to undertake the deep research necessary for understanding these matters of substance. The collection of data has to be approached in a way that reflects the needs of this serious research. You must not be bound by any expectations that traditional sources will supply everything you need to know. Indeed, your principal challenge is to get yourself ready to decide just what it is that you must learn if you are to answer the strategic problem.

Information can—and arguably must—be sought from any person, source, or organization that has it. Strategic research cases are not bound by tradition so much as limited by how imaginatively you can design your planned approach to collecting and subsequently analyzing all the information that is necessary to providing you with an understanding of the topic.

The process for carrying out a strategic intelligence study is a systematic application of interrelated steps, without which the intelligence cannot be produced. The collection phase is an essential component of the whole process. Although a lot more attention is traditionally paid to the analysis function, the truth is that well-planned and executed collection activity is absolutely fundamental to achieving success in the whole intelligence task. Without it, the rest of the intelligence cycle will fail and organizational objectives will be threatened. More to the point, energetic collection is not enough by itself. What you need is a commitment to carry out detailed prior planning that helps you get the collection service that your analysis deserves and the client wants.

Energetic and enthusiastic collection of data is not enough to guarantee success in carrying out the intelligence study. What is needed is proper prior planning to develop a collection plan that is both comprehensive and soundly based.

NOTES

1. Some agencies have experimented with both options and have, as a result, made a conscious choice to follow the pathway of recruiting and/or training certain staff to handle Internet/Open Source Information (OSI) searching on behalf of the analyst. Certainly this is the case in several large national agencies have data resource specialist personnel to service the data collection plan needs of their strategic and other analysts.

2. I gratefully acknowledge the input from analysts of H. M. Revenue and Customs (UK), who, in 1997, designed this particular example of a spreadsheet ICP.

3. Edward de Bono has published many books on thinking concepts, and these are readily available in the management and business sections in bookshops everywhere. Two that represent enjoyable and informative reading are *de Bono's Thinking Course* and *Serious Creativity*. Other noted authors of this genre are Tony Buzan (of MindMap™ fame) and Michael LeBoeuf. Moreover, there are software packages that assist with the mind-mapping and creative-thinking processes.

14

Collation and Evaluation of Data

Both collation and evaluation are process steps that are well known to intelligence officers involved in analysis at operational and tactical level. As long as intelligence has existed as a recognized practice, these steps have formed the logical link between collecting data and being prepared to analyze it. The latter simply cannot occur until and unless the collected information has been brought together in appropriate sets and then considered for its reliability, relevance, and believability value. Collation is a combination of mechanical tasks—recording and sorting—driven by logical planning. Evaluation is an exercise in judgment about the reliability of the data source and the data quality and content, in terms of validity and credibility.

In sum, collation and evaluation are simple concepts that are readily accepted as part of intelligence standard operating procedures. In reality, while it is common to have established, visible protocols for dealing with both functions, many individual analysts and information collectors find the processes time-consuming and frustrating. In these circumstances, it is small wonder that the steps are sometimes carried out with minimal enthusiasm and lack of attention to detail. Having a system in place is no guarantee of using it appropriately; in many cases, it can readily be observed that the whole process of handling data collation and evaluation is in danger of being trivialized or even ignored.

The point of this chapter is to reinforce the traditional "doctrinal" view that data items are no good to you unless and until you can assemble them in an order that suits your inquiry. Nor can you hope to consider the value of data items in the context of the intelligence inquiry unless they are understood in terms of their reliability and validity. Trying to analyze the true value and underlying picture suggested by several pieces of untested, unevaluated, and therefore potentially unreliable and unbelievable data is likely to be fraught with difficulty. Some intelligence officers excuse their lack of attention to these steps on the grounds that collation and evaluation are difficult to do properly, or they are too time-consuming, or they are no longer relevant given the current state of technology. These arguments might seem superficially persuasive, but they do not stand up against the following logical dictum: The quality of the analysis and speculation is dependent as much on good data as it is on high-quality analysis and creative thinking. Each is critical to the outcome of the assignment, and to make this work, not only should the data be good but the ability to find and retrieve it is fundamental to success.

Certainly collation is much easier to arrange with the increasing sophistication of computer aids. But evaluation remains essentially a human task calling for judgment skills and topic knowledge. Whatever the changes and improvements that have overtaken parts of the traditional intelligence processes, the collation and evaluation processes are just as relevant for strategic research as they always have been in their application in other forms of intelligence practice.

Collating Data

Collation is a simple but time-consuming activity that needs to be carried out carefully. Because of its simplicity, many assume that collation requires little or no planning, and that regular, routine registry procedures will cope with whatever has to be done. While this might work in many instances, collation of data for strategic assessment takes on some added complexities.

As the intelligence analyst in charge of the strategic project, you need to consider what additional challenges are likely to arise during the collation phase, and you can do this while you are planning the entire project. In short, if you can see the need for care and attention to detail in preparing the strategic collection plan, then you can certainly start to project some of the problems that you will encounter when it comes to collating the information.

Special types and categories of data must be accorded equally special handling on arrival at your center of analytical operations to ensure that adequate referencing and cross-checking takes place to assist in later retrieval.

The special nature of the strategic project inevitably also means that there is likely to be a large volume of incoming information that covers a wide range of issues, and this will include data that is neither "hard" nor quantifiable. In this context, *hard* tends to mean tangible and reliable, and it is this latter question of reliability that forms the discussion in the second part of this chapter.

Evaluating Information

The evaluation of data is a key component of both investigation and intelligence. Evaluation concerns determining the reliability of the source of the data, and the notion of *believability* (the term is *validity* in the intelligence trade) of the data itself. These two separate ideas—one about the source and the other about the information item itself—coalesce to form the component of evaluation. The purpose of evaluation is to provide you with a considered view of the overall net worth of any piece of data.

Strategic topics are often complex because they look far into the future and scan the topic environment much more broadly than is the norm in intelligence work. The nature, volume, and often unfamiliarity of the information available to you means that you will have to work to overcome the additional difficulties posed in the collation and evaluation phases of the strategic process. This chapter deals with both of these process steps and provides some useful guidelines for your thinking and planning.

COLLATION PRINCIPLES AND PRACTICE

In this section, it is assumed that as a trained intelligence officer and analyst, you already have a working knowledge of collation processes. The section focuses on the following material:

- a review of the various *collation systems* normally available to intelligence staff;
- a brief listing of the *principles* that should be observed in collation practice; and
- the special nature and *impact of strategic intelligence* projects upon collation activity.

Collation Systems

To be successful, the collation step requires orderly systems to cope with the functions of receiving and accounting for the information, sorting it into sensible category sets and dispersing it to its various internal destinations. The reason for this is obvious: The intelligence analyst needs a quick and responsive means of gaining access to any single piece or set of information from the data bank that has been established for the strategic intelligence project. If your unit has only limited arrangements in place for collecting, receiving, sorting, and recording incoming data, then you will have difficulty meeting your data-searching requirements. A lack of effective controls over the project data can directly and severely limit the overall outcomes of the intelligence process. In such circumstances, any deficiency may even cause the intelligence activity itself to fail to deliver what the client expects.

Every registry in any organization has routines to handle incoming hard-copy information. Moreover, the registry will also be responsible for dealing with outgoing information, and often the principal challenge for a registry is to keep the process flowing, despite a high volume of material. In the case of intelligence organizations, registries do exist for these same purposes, but there is a separate need to establish specific protocols for the handling of data relevant to individual intelligence probes. The analyst's role is to determine what, if any, are the special handling requirements for data concerning the assessment project and to plan for the most efficient and effective means possible.

There are several distinctly different types of data recording and retrieval systems available, from the simple and somewhat old-fashioned to the computer-aided and sophisticated. These can be broadly categorized as follows:

- Manual systems: cards, files, index lists, and the like
- Micrographic format: using microfiche or microfilm to "photograph" hard-copy data that would otherwise be kept in a manual system
- Automated, computer-driven data systems: recording extracted information in text, numeric, or graphic format, and including digitized forms of hard data scanned into the computer system (a variation of micrographic systems)

One might think that almost all organizations would be using computerized systems by this stage of the century. The fact is that many agencies either use informal deskside methods according to each analyst's preferences or chose systems that provide only the barest of detail that ultimately are insufficient for the intelligence analyst's needs. These differences are evident not only between agencies within the same country, but even more so between countries with vastly different levels of development and distribution of sophisticated electronic equipment. Of the above systems, the first two present information in a visual form that is not enhanced in any way. Thus, they are fixed in terms of the form and content of what can be retrieved. In the case of computerized data, automated systems provide a sharply enhanced ability to search for and display specific data in a variety of ways.

In selecting the "right" collation solution to suit yourself and your organizational needs, you will have to bear in mind a few key points such as the following:

- The pivotal argument for selecting the collation systems has to focus solely on the concept of flexible accessibility. Unless you can guarantee this, you will in effect be driven by the system, rather than using it according to your own creativity.
- Some systems are regarded as being user-friendly in terms of input—manual systems, for example, are thought of this way—even though they may be time-consuming. However, these same systems may be extraordinarily difficult to access in any way but according to their original structure.
- Some tightly disciplined systems—manual or computerized—that are reliant upon fixed headings, keywords, or the like will be very responsive to retrieval so long as it follows the same lines. If you think of new ideas or keywords and wish to access data using those terms, then a fixed system will not cope well.
- Many computer enthusiasts claim that the best answer lies in using systems that are based on relational databases—that is, programs that need no extensive lists of prerequisite keywords or phrases to make them work in either input or access mode. Many such programs, although powerful, are often painstakingly slow to respond to multiple queries. You can deal with this potential problem by being careful to ensure that the system you use for your project is capable of both effectively storing and providing the data on demand.
- Suitable alternatives to large-scale relational databases have been found by other organizations, simply by using a text search-and-retrieval tool that

runs across their existing information storage files, including all their word-processing records.

Information Management and Control

There are several essential steps in the collation activity that, when followed, will provide appropriate levels of control and management over the information being received. Insofar as you are involved as the analyst, the following four points are particularly important.

- You and your organization need a formal mechanism to be established to receive, sort, record, and then evaluate each piece of incoming data. Your role in this is to provide guidance from the perspective of your knowledge of the data and the analysis that will be involved in the strategic intelligence project.
- Because this task calls for a careful and orderly approach to the work involved, it is perhaps best done by dedicated staff. However, the work can be rotated through the various members of the intelligence unit. In some cases, you as the analyst may have to do this task yourself.
- The incoming data must be sorted into specific categories that relate to the structural elements of the intelligence problem. These are the key headings under which you originally considered all aspects of the task (in the problem definition section earlier in chapter 9) so that you could then develop a project directive. Unless you refer back to this list of fundamental headings and use it as part of the collation system, you will be unable to set up routines that ensure the system is easy to operate for input and retrieval.
- Part of the collation process is to sift the incoming data and evaulate it, sorting out in a priority order the data that are both relevant and urgent from the remaining information. Inevitably, there may be a temptation to scrap some data that appear irrelevant or unreliable. This is not the function of the person undertaking the collation role—it is properly the responsibility of you, as analyst, because you will have a broader view of the issues involved. If your role covers all these responsibilities, then of course you do have to do everything necessary throughout this part of the process.

Careful collation allows for preliminary examination and preferential sorting to aid the further, more detailed analysis. If the collation phase is conducted with care and thought, the personnel involved are provided with a unique opportunity to examine and assess incoming data in a preliminary manner before the more detailed analysis begins. At this collation point, it is already possible to discern any drift away from the expectations established in the intelligence collection plan. For example, it is certainly possible even now to determine whether certain sorts of data are slow to arrive or if there is a dearth of those items compared with the expected levels of return. In some circumstances, it is also possible to note that the data arriving are qualitatively deficient when compared against what was expected. If you note these events now, during collation, then you have an early and crucial opportunity to review the collection plan by type of information or by source, wherever the problem appears to be. Your intention should be to modify the plan in order to provide the intelligence unit with a better level of information-gathering service.

In contrast, you may find that the incoming information, far from being deficient and therefore disappointing, is surprisingly helpful. In such cases, it is not uncommon to find that the incoming data suggest to you that you should follow up new leads and avenues of gathering further information on topics you previously have not considered. As with so much of the entire strategic intelligence process, you may find that events are helping you to further and better modify and extend your original collection plan.

The Demands of Strategic Intelligence on Collation

In their application to the field of strategic intelligence, the principles of collation covered in this section need no variation; they hold good throughout the whole arena of intelligence activity.

When you undertake a strategic assessment, however, you will become involved in collecting and analyzing a greater mix of both quantitative, or hard, data and qualitative—descriptive and anecdotal—information. In addition, the breadth of scope of the strategic assessment will itself give rise to a range of data categories and subcategories that will often outstrip the experience of more usual, tactical intelligence activity. For these reasons—the range of features and the breadth of data collection of all sorts and quality—the collation system you have available to you must be set up carefully and comprehensively. This allows for the widest possible flexibility and adaptability in the way in which the data, on arrival, are sorted for later retrieval. It is thus the scope of the collation matrix, not the principles themselves, that needs modification for use in strategic assessment activity, as summarized below.

Handling Data Variety and Volume

There is a special need for you, as the analyst, to be careful in preparing the collation regime so that you take into account both the variety and volume of data that can be gathered. Experience shows that in the case of strategic studies, you may find it difficult to cope with the fact that much of the data will contain references to a wide range of subtopics relevant to the study. It is essential that you decide how to handle this problem and establish some simple rules to follow. In doing this, you will deal with the possibility that individual reference documents will need to be cross-referenced under multiple category headings within your collation system. In such a case, you cannot afford to file and archive a document according to its *most likely* future need. It is better practice for you to ensure that those documents that have a wider-than-expected range of application and relevance are recorded against each and every separate heading or keyword, to suit whatever system is in force.

Flexibility in Varying the Collation System

Another basic question facing the analyst concerns the flexibility of the collation system. What happens, then, if the arriving data cannot easily be sorted according to your original ideas about collation headings? In these circumstances, you must consider the need to adapt to the new focus or dimension suggested by the data itself. The answer is simple: If the arriving data appears useful and enlightening, then it is the collation system that has to adapt to take account of unexpected opportunities and changes to suit the data. This will be of direct benefit to the analysis phase yet to come.

Using Computerized Systems

Some readers may by now have wondered why this chapter focuses so much on the principles and practice of collation as if it all had to be done manually. There are, after all, many hundreds of different computer-based systems that will easily search and locate the databases accessible to the analyst. The answer is that if the analyst comes to depend totally upon computerized search engines to gather and sort data, then other opportunities to discover useful, relevant information may be lost.

By the 1990s, free text retrieval systems were commonplace, and they continue to be further developed. Such systems, loaded onto database gateways, provide the analyst with easy access to a world of data that goes well beyond what was imagined by the intelligence community just a few decades ago. There can be no doubt that the availability of more and more data stored electronically, plus the computer "smart tools" to access and retrieve it, provide benefits to the analyst. There are two issues here, though, that impact upon this apparently simple data-searching capability and that need to be considered by the analyst.

Data Volume and Access Issues

Data generally available on the Internet is there because individuals and agencies want it available in the public domain. From the perspective of the analyst, there may be a wealth of data concerning a particular intelligence problem, but it should always be remembered that the data has been posted to the Internet because the authoring agency/individual wants it there. Thus, while coverage may be comprehensive and quantity sometimes almost overwhelming, from a qualitative point of view the analyst still needs to treat it as requiring evaluation as to reliability and validity. In addition, readers familiar with using the Internet will quickly realize that the key to effective access rests in developing skills in using various search engines. Not all are user-friendly and fully responsive to the logic and language used by the analyst, and it is the latter who has to adapt to the search engine, not vice versa.

The Internet is only one gateway source of data and, for many analysts, it may not always be relevant or even readily accessible. However, analysts' access to the Internet often varies according to agency preferences and protocols. There are various reasons for this—some budgetary and some concerning perceived security risk—but the end result is the same: analysts in those units are inhibited by their lack of direct access to yet another major source pathway.

Much of the data relevant to intelligence inquiries are located on "official" databases. These vary widely in construction and, leaving aside the question of access, the analyst is faced with search engines that are usually specific to a particular database. They may be free text systems, or they may focus upon specific fields of data that are comparable with the intent and structure of that database. Again, it is the analyst's responsibility to learn the particular search protocols and use them competently. Alternatively, some intelligence units have dedicated staff, in recognition of these very difficulties, to carry out data searches. This system works well providing that the link between the requesting analyst and the searcher is one in which communication is absolutely clear. At the same time, the analyst must learn to structure requests for data search in such a way that useful data available on the periphery of the search are not ignored simply because the search parameters are too "tight" and inflexible. In the same way, the specialized staff must understand the potential importance of such data and avoid becoming inflexible.

Data Not Available Electronically

The apparent ease of having data available through computer access and of being able to retrieve it using automated systems can be seductive to the analyst pressed for time. However, for all the advantages that such technological advances have brought to the world of intelligence analysis, there are still other matters that have to be considered. Much of the data relevant to strategic study—and to other intelligence probes—is not usually committed to a computerized form. These sorts of data include:

- in-depth interviews and their reports;
- informant reports of some types;[1]
- published reference books and material (by both government and private authors) in hard-copy format; and
- other material available from specialized sources such as peak organizations and industry groups, often published in-house but not normally distributed through (or catalogued by) library systems.

All of this material may be relevant to a strategic intelligence assignment. For example, a major study on illegal drug threats in a particular region may require the analyst to do the following, or cause it to be done in furtherance of the project. The purpose in doing so is to elicit information about using/buying habits. This is information not normally included on official databases focusing on import/export/marketing of drugs and paraphernalia or on arrests and laboratory seizures.

- Conduct interviews with prison inmates.
- Interview and gather qualitative and quantitative data from drug referral centers and shelters.
- Interview drug user circle members.
- Search published books and articles available through public and specialized library systems and from drug treatment agencies.

The aim in all of this additional searching is for the analyst to go beyond the bare facts as recorded in official databases. In generating a full understanding of the problem being researched, the analyst will need to access and gather qualitative information that "informs" the process rather than necessarily proving everything that is of interest. To achieve this, the analyst not only has to develop a suitable data gathering plan, but also has to deal with the mechanical challenge of gathering, reading, and storing such material systematically so that it can be called forward again when needed. This is collation of the old-fashioned sort, and although some of the process can be computer assisted, it is the analyst who has to make the collation system work.

Collation for Strategic Research

Effective collation of intelligence and information is fundamental to efficient retrieval by the intelligence staff involved in carrying out analysis. Strategic intelligence places additional, special demands upon the collation activity. The system chosen will have to cope with larger volumes of different types of data than normally experienced in tactical intelligence. Cross-referencing and access issues pose more challenges that have to be compensated for. Finally, the sheer volume of unsubstantiated, qualitative data provides its own set of problems for those involved in sorting and filing this information.

THE EVALUATION PROCESS IN STRATEGIC INTELLIGENCE

Introducing Evaluation

As with the previous section on collation, this section assumes you have some knowledge of evaluation from previous experience in an intelligence unit. This section will review some basic issues about evaluation of data, and then focus on the impact of strategic intelligence on this part of the overall process.

In the course of the intelligence process, you will receive a variety of information as a result of the collection plan going into force. Much of this may or may not be of value in helping you to interpret the picture and develop conclusions and recommendations. This is because the usefulness of the data is dependent upon both its validity and its reliability. There is, in this, a constant challenge for the analyst. It is not simply to gather enough appropriate data; what is important is that you are able to reach a decision about the usefulness of the information that has been collected, keeping an open mind, but at the same time applying some stringent checks on the quality of what has been provided.

In considering the evaluation process and its implications for the conduct of strategic intelligence studies, the underlying question for you in this section is: Does strategic intelligence create a significantly different set of challenges when you come to the evaluation step in the process?

The Need for Evaluation

It is too facile to think of information as being simply just true or false. Rather, since information input comes from a variety of sources and is communicated in a wide range of ways, these factors have an effect upon how we view the information when we get it. The analyst cannot reasonably expect to know enough about a topic to be an "expert" in evaluating every piece of information. Just as gathering the information for an intelligence project is a group endeavor, so too the process of evaluating the pieces is a product of the efforts and input of potentially many people. These considerations do not, however, detract from the importance of the analyst's need to have the data provided as completely as possible, and in a timely fashion.

Evaluation is not a step that is performed just once. The underlying idea of data evaluation is that it concerns determining the usefulness of any piece of information based on two factors: the reliability of the source, and the believability of the information when compared to other knowledge on the same topic. As you gain more knowledge of the source of the data, the access that source had, and his or her capacity to provide useful information without significant alteration or embellishment, your reliance on that source will undergo a change. It is likely that you will come to rely more on that source. Conversely, depending upon your experience, you might lose any sense of trust and belief you previously held in the source. Whatever the change in your thinking, it is essential is that you see this as part of the learning process, helping to shape your capacity to evaluate the source.

Similarly, as you acquire more information about a topic—and, as a consequence, grow in understanding of the issues involved—your capacity to make better judgments about the level of belief in that new information will likewise grow. In sum, the more you, as the analyst, learn and understand about the topic, the more likely it is that individual pieces of information will be able to be reviewed. In light of this experience, you will be able to regrade the information to a newer, better level of acceptance.

One final point on this issue: Much of the information received by an analyst does not lend itself easily to testing for accuracy at the time of assessment and integration with other data. You should not conclude from this, however, that evaluation of information is not possible before you are able to use it. You can certainly make use of information even when you cannot guess how likely it is to be true or comment on the reliability of the source. The information can still be a useful component of a larger intelligence picture, if only to provide a benchmark for testing against other, known information and views you hold.

Evaluation Systems

It is useful to review some basic ideas about evaluation systems. Most organizations use some form of standardized grading systems to identify their opinion of the worth of particular information. Two terms have special meaning in the field of data evaluation for intelligence analysis. In a somewhat purist sense, the words have connotations of *truth* and *trust*, respectively, but when applied to intelligence their meanings can be even further focused. The terms used are:

- *reliability*, or the index of the consistent quality of the source reporting the information; and
- *validity*, or the index of the perceived accuracy or truth of the information, no matter who supplies it.

The evaluation process is aimed at estimating some index of both of these features for each item of information that is collected. The overall task, though, is not simply to provide some dual notion of validity or reliability. What is essential to further use of the information in the analysis process is

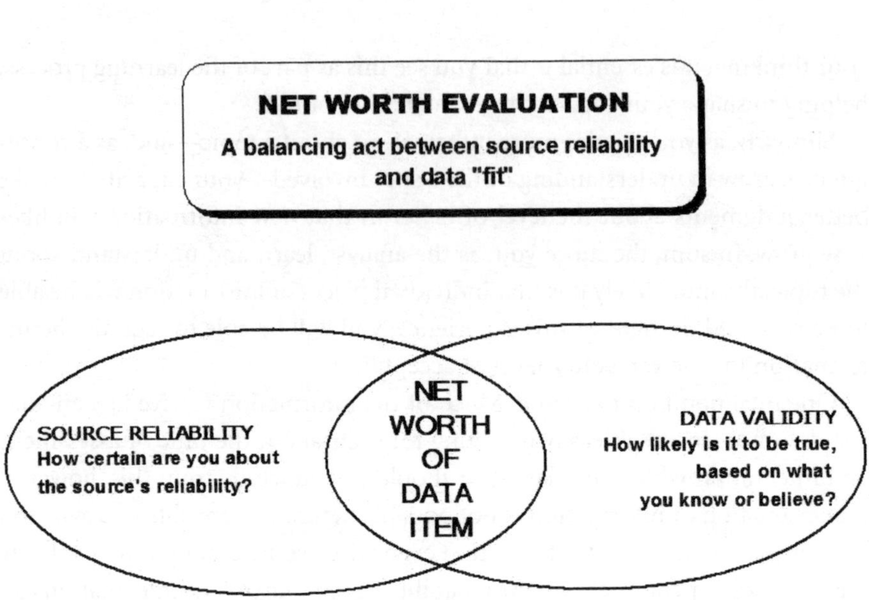

FIGURE 14.1
Net Worth

that the analyst can take these ideas and consider them in the context, simply, of whether or not the information has some worth to the analysis task. By grading the information item, you are, in effect, citing a specific opinion about just how much net worth it has.

The appraisal of reliability and validity can take on a number of forms. Most agencies in the international intelligence community use a multiple-choice grading system that separates reliability and validity, providing a choice of gradings against each aspect. These gradings allow the analyst to select values that range from believable through to unlikely, and true through to false. All provide some sort of numbering that identifies "unknown," when your lack of knowledge—about either the data itself or the source—prevents you from making any sensible grading.

> Evaluation is the assessment of an item of information in terms of its credibility, reliability, pertinence, and accuracy.

The following diagrams (figures 14.2 and 14.3) are typical of evaluation grading systems in widespread use. They are not all the same, but many use this type of model—a variant on the more traditional 6 x 6 "Admiralty System" common throughout the latter half of the last century—as the basis for setting in place a standard protocol that is easy to remember. Because of the number of grading possibilities in the schema shown, it is commonly referred to as a *four-by-four (or 4x4) system.* It is interesting to note that the original Admiralty System, because of its six tiers of grading under each heading, allowed for more possibilities between the highest levels (confirmed) and the lowest or unknown levels of source and validity gradings.

All multitiered alphanumeric systems, like this one, use a very similar means of grading the various levels of reliability and validity. However, the number of levels chosen as the basis for evaluation grading and tabulation often varies according to the needs of a particular agency.

Evaluation and Strategic Assessments

Information evaluation takes on an added set of difficulties in the area of strategic assessment. While the principles and considerations involved in data evaluation techniques remain constant, their application in an environment in which a great proportion of the data is likely to present particular difficulties because of its lack of measurable reliability creates problems for the strategic analyst/evaluator. Increasing experience of strategic intelligence study will demonstrate that gathering a wider range of what is often more unfamiliar and complex data, from a larger community of potential sources, creates its own problems of acceptance and trust.

Does the analyst take the data, including the opinions and inferences drawn by apparently reputable sources, to accept them as they have been given? Adding to the difficulties is the very fact that a study into a topic of wide proportions—typical of strategic intelligence—means that the sheer volume and complexity of data to be gathered, sifted through, and considered will surpass any traditional experience you have in operational intelligence. It is these considerations that impact upon standard evaluation processes. The principles outlined in this section may well have stood the test of time, but the modern information revolution (or "explosion") and the growing array of interested agencies and stakeholders, whatever the topic, mean that you have to become both tenacious and selective in locating knowledge of the topic. As a result, the analyst has to learn to apply the evaluation principles very flexibly indeed, given the diversity of sources and the sheer volume of data likely to be gathered in this process. Holding on to a rigid concept of evaluation, one in which you assume that all sources will approach your requests in predictable and familiar ways, is an unwise choice. Instead, you need to develop an approach of flexibility and adaptation to match the range and complexity of the data being gathered and presented.

The analyst's role in preparing the strategic project plan and the collection plan leads logically to concurrently considering how the data gathered should ultimately be collated and evaluated. Collation is a particular challenge for strategic assessments, because of the wide range of data being collected against the broad and often unfamiliar scope of the project, as discussed previously in this chapter. On the other hand, it is the type of data being gathered—not merely its breadth and scope—that presents a specific difficulty for evaluation. Where the information is measurable and quantifiable, it becomes relatively easy to use appropriate checking routines to establish its bona fides. But data that defies measurement, that provides clues and descriptions and anecdotes, and that may be the fundamental key to understanding essential elements of the strategic problem poses a unique challenge for whoever is responsible for evaluation. Preparing the groundwork for the evaluation process

GRADING	LABEL	DESCRIPTION
A	Reliable	Source's reliability is unquestioned or has been well tested in the past.
B	Usually Reliable	Source's reliability can usually be relied upon as factual. The majority of past information has proven to be reliable.
C	Unreliable	Source's reliability has been sporadic.
D	Unknown	Source's reliability can not be judged. Authenticity or trustworthiness has not been determined through either experience or investigation.

SOURCE RELIABILITY - 4x4 Grading System

FIGURE 14.2
Source Reliability

GRADING	LABEL	DESCRIPTION
1	Confirmed	The information has been corroborated.
2	Probable	The information is consistent with past accounts.
3	Doubtful	The information is not consistent with past accounts.
4	Cannot Be Judged	The information can not be evaluated.

DATA VALIDITY - 4x4 Grading System

FIGURE 14.3
Data Validity

in strategic intelligence can commence even while the analyst is finalizing plans for collection.

This type of "strategic" information will arguably be difficult to evaluate during its initial receipt and recording. However, it must be treated with at least balanced neutrality pending the availability of other, more reliable information. What is important is that the analyst anticipates this problem and prepares to deal with it by not demanding an instant evaluation on every piece of incoming data. This just may not be possible because of what it is, where it comes from, and the volume of it. The earlier collection-planning phase is precisely the point at which the strategic analyst must consider and prepare for this eventuality—well in advance, even to the extent of developing likely indicators for some of the "soft" data that will probably be received.

CONCLUSION

Evaluating information is an essential step in the intelligence process. It is designed to help place the net worth and usefulness of the data that is being gathered in a clear contextual setting. As such, it is an essential adjunct to the data collection phase of the entire intelligence process. Evaluation takes some time to do properly, and this workload increases as the data is regularly reviewed so that the evaluation can be upgraded to meet changing circumstances. However, the effort invested in evaluation and reevaluation is worth the resource cost, particularly to the intelligence analysis phase that follows. Without the sort of formalized system described in this chapter in place, individual analysts would be influenced by their own most recent and case-specific experience and become vulnerable to their own individual biases. Unfortunately, data evaluation is in some danger of passing into misuse as time goes on. In some areas of enforcement intelligence practice, the fundamental principles of source and validity evaluation have already been changed to reflect an impatience and frustration with the intellectual difficulty of blending the two elements. Evaluation grading systems are progressively being simplified. The focus is on two elements still, one of which remains an assessment of the data source. But in place of the long-established data validity estimation principles outlined in this text—plausibility of new data, based on the analyst's depth of subject knowledge—there is growing reliance on concepts of "proof" and evidentiary soundness as the preferred and easier to gauge measure of validity.[2]

NOTES

1. Some informant reporting is entered into enforcement databases only in summary form (a) for reasons of security and (b) because entry-point staff emphasize material that is contextually interesting at the time and in that unit, minimizing or rejecting other included information.

2. These changes have largely been noticed in the European enforcement community in recent years.

15

Deciding on Analytical Approaches

For several decades, intelligence practice worldwide has been focused upon merging the several components of the intelligence process: collation, integration, and analysis.

Traditional intelligence skills training since the beginning of the Anacapa era[1] has increasingly passed on the almost subliminal message that the more intelligently and carefully you manage your data, the more obvious the answer becomes. Any potential real-life difficulties in actually analyzing a given picture have tended, in the cloistered training environment, to be minimized and even trivialized so long as the right data are being collected and summated. However, in this book, the term *analysis* is used in a more traditionally based professional intelligence setting: Analysis is taken to be a catchall term that encompasses the integration, analysis, synthesis, and interpretation of data.

The analyst needs the good data that should come from an appropriate and efficient collection regime. But no amount of good data will, by itself, lead to sound analysis unless the analyst has competent command of the skills, techniques, and approaches necessary to achieve this. In strategic intelligence work, as elsewhere, the analyst will encounter many instances in which mere data management will not solve problems and where even the synergistic result that comes from adding data items together just will not provide an answer without careful and talented analysis.

The focus in this chapter is on what it takes to set you up to facilitate doing the analysis phase effectively. We will examine the process and thinking implemented in providing you a clear understanding of the activities involved in breaking down the data, gaining a view of what it means—its worth and its relevance—interpreting it, and providing answers that include both conclusions and interpretations. For every strategic problem, there are several analytical approaches that can and should be blended together to provide the analyst with a collection of "tools" to enable examination of the topic in depth. In earlier sessions, we noted that every strategic problem comprises many individual components. In the same way, each problem needs to be addressed using analytical techniques that are chosen specifically because they suit the specific challenges of each component.

I have not set out to use this chapter to provide specific hints and directions on analytical processes and techniques. Instead, it encourages the analyst to think about *how* to carry out the analysis phase of strategic assessments. By emphasizing the benefits of considering these issues early in the life of the strategic intelligence project, you will be able to prepare yourself mentally for the analysis phase well ahead of time.

The key lesson here is to ensure that you think through the analytical challenges posed by each and every element of the strategic problem. Using the Terms of Reference document as a guide, it is important that you consider each of its headings and subheadings, then relate them to the way in which you extended these into becoming indicators and the collection plan. Think through this picture and try to visualize exactly what sort of data you will be getting, in what format, and covering what types of issues. For each group of data, you will be easily able to see that such-and-such a group will be mainly tables of figures (for example, drug amounts, prices, etc.) that can be statistically modeled. Other data sets may be the collection of interviews with drug users about how they finance their consumption of various types of drugs. This sort of data represents a different challenge, rarely capable of being modeled mathematically, but certainly able to be explored at a more sociological level. Unless the analyst possesses the knowledge and skill to do so, then this too is a challenge of investing time and effort, or, alternatively, of locating and accessing a suitably qualified person to assist.

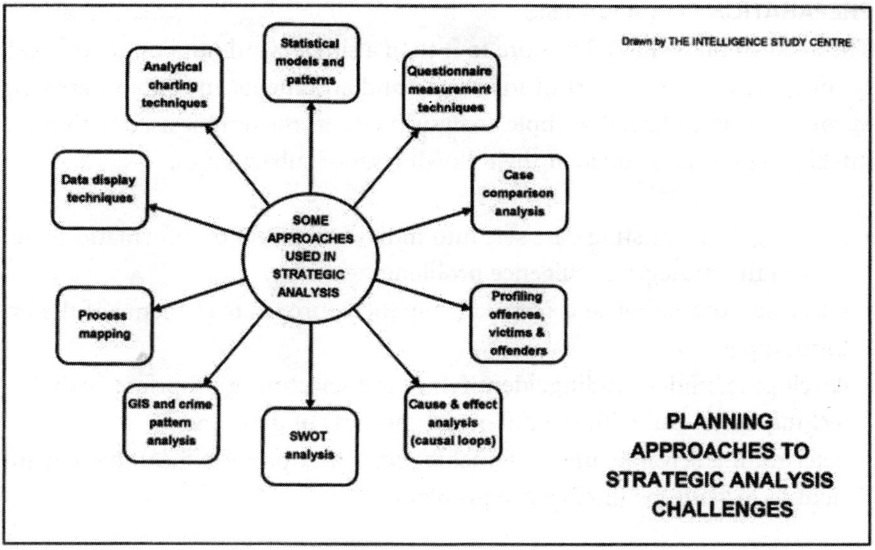

FIGURE 5.1
Planning Approaches to Strategic Analysis

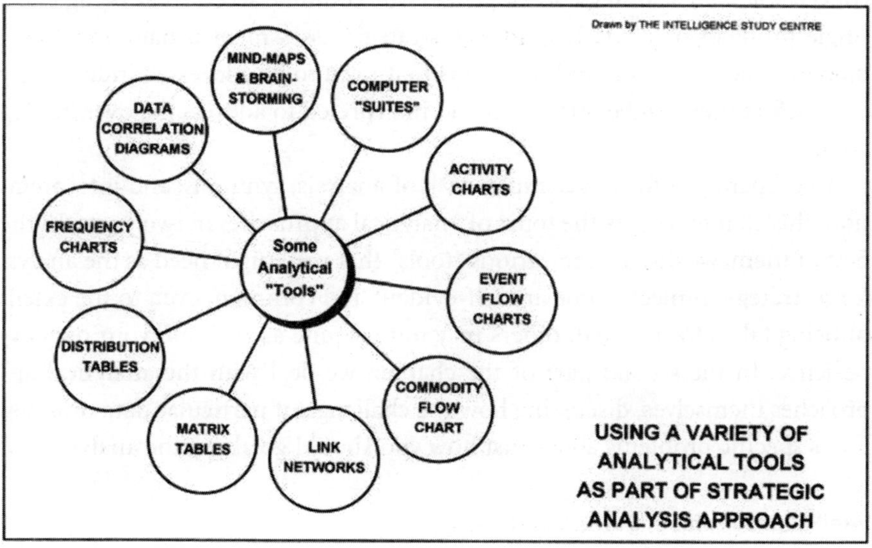

FIGURE 15.2
Analytical Tools

PREPARATION FOR ANALYSIS

The analysis phase has a lot more to it than a single word implies. It goes well beyond merely a statement of inferences and arguments en route to arriving at conclusions. In fact, the whole analysis phase, as the term is used within the intelligence cycle, is aimed at the following set of subactivities:

- breaking down existing data sets into individual pieces of information relevant to the strategic intelligence problem;
- selecting, correlating, and restructuring the appropriate elements of the information;
- developing, understanding, identifying, and selecting appropriate analytical techniques to deal with the differing types/sets of data; and
- determining sensible and sustainable views that provide meaning and insight to explain the intelligence problem.

It is difficult to accept that an apparently simple question posed to a strategic intelligence unit will result in an equally simple answer. It is similarly inconceivable that a strategic intelligence issue could be accepted as being just a single problem or issue. Instead, the strategic assessment usually involves a myriad of subproblems and questions that need to be addressed individually first, before they can be integrated and interpreted to address the overarching issue.

To prepare you for this complex task of analysis, synthesis, and interpretation, this chapter covers the topic of analytical approaches in two parts. In the first of them, we discuss the various "tools" that you might need as the analyst for a strategic project. Some are self-evident and common, even to the extent of being taken for granted; others may not fit quite as well into your own experience. In the second part of the chapter, we deal with the analytical approaches themselves, discussing how the challenge of particular data or issues poses specific problems about just how you should go about the analysis.

Intelligence Problem Solving and Logic

None of the problem-solving activity that you are likely to use in the strategic intelligence process can take place unless you apply logical thought. Without it, the process will be hindered and the outcome will be flawed. So what is logic? In a broad sense, the term refers to a set of principles about how to reason, infer, and evaluate. But for a more detailed view, you should consider that logic refers to an explicit set of procedures for solving problems. In intelligence analysis work, we always seem to assume that a systematic approach to problem solving is the source of much of the analytical "power" used in intelligence work. Logic is, in turn, important in the analysis and generation of real "intelligence" because it is the foundation on which systematic problem solving rests.

If you understand logic, then you may avoid the various thinking traps and biases that inhibit the problem-solving process. If so, this will help you to expose the flaws in otherwise supposedly sound arguments. To achieve this, you need to understand several aspects of the analytical task:

- the role of *facts* versus *values*;
- the nexus between *concepts* and *facts*; and
- how you can generate and test a hypothesis on the intelligence problem.

Intelligence problem solving is a systematic process comprising a series of distinct, separate analytical steps. Logic is hardly just a simple problem-solving tool. It provides you with a unique capacity to bring your own perspectives to the strategic intelligence process. The special, individual perspective that you will bring and apply throughout the strategic intelligence process needs to be as realistic as it is functional. Above all else, the process must be driven by a logical and objective appreciation of the potential analysis methodology you might use and, of course, of the issues themselves and what is at stake. If you think subjectively, not logically, then your application of the intelligence process will inevitably lead you toward misconceptions and misperceptions that infest and distort your intelligence responsibilities.

RESOURCES FOR ANALYSIS

All intelligence officers and analysts use a set of physical and analytical resources or "tools" to help them design, manage, and implement the intelligence process. These aids include the issues in the list that follows, covering the key components of what you might think of as an analyst's "toolbox":

- expertise and knowledge of the problem topic;
- the data appropriate to addressing the problem;

- methodologies that can properly cope with both quantitative and qualitative information;
- options for approaching intelligence problem-solving challenges;
- time;
- logical thinking;
- computer aids; and
- other support resources.

Expertise and Knowledge

Expertise can be thought of as special, high-level experience in a particular subject or skill. The salient questions to be considered are: What is needed? Who has it? Where, and from whom, can it be obtained? Further questions of importance are: How much expertise is required? And how good is the level of expert knowledge that is available? Finally, the question that will challenge both the intelligence supervisor and the analyst is: How are you to best use the expertise that is available?

Self-knowledge is a critical element in this consideration. It is one of the analyst's greatest strengths: Knowing what you are good at and—equally—where you are deficient in some way allows you to make sensible choices about selecting the right resource for the assignment. Similarly, as each intelligence task is assessed at the planning stage, you will quickly be able to identify the sorts of special experience and training required and make appropriate choices in the work plan. If the choice is not about what sort of specialty but, rather, about the competence of the intelligence officer being considered, then making this choice calls for honesty, tempered with some tact and sensitivity. Competence is not always merely a matter of skill; it may be a question of application to the task at hand and motivation to be a contributive member of the intelligence team. Disruptive behavior or a lack of willingness to work within the environment of the team may mean that the choice has to be made to exclude a particular officer, regardless of talent.

Another element of the issue of specialist knowledge is whether or not the intelligence unit should actively seek to encourage its officers to become specialists in their own right. Certainly, there are plenty of examples of units in which analysts have worked for considerable periods of time focusing on specific problem areas—for example, illegal drugs, child pornography, illegal migration, or organized crime. Somewhat inevitably, as these individuals become known for their special levels of knowledge, their units increasingly become dependent upon them for this knowledge and insight. Some agencies take this further and actively create an organizational environment in which work is allocated within functional specialties, thus creating a group of specialist intelligence officers. Note that the word *expert* has not been used in this context: The concept of assigning officers to work within a single specialized area is not necessarily going to result in such officers becoming experts. The point here is that there are differences in the degree to which specialized assignments create heightened awareness and knowledge within the context of the intelligence setting. Contrast this with other individuals who may have had opportunities to study a particular phenomenon thoroughly, academically, and practically in a variety of circumstances.

If strategic intelligence assignments look like they will extend into exploration of a wider range of issues than those normally experienced by intelligence officers and other staff of the agency or corporation, this is a clear sign that those doing the analysis will need access to expert help. Such help will provide the means by which unfamiliar data can be explained and clarified; interpretation of what specific signals or clues mean may come much more naturally to someone with special expertise. While these ideas are surely not unfamiliar or unusual, many enforcement agencies still insist, for a variety of reasons, on trying to carry out all the "important" aspects of the intelligence assignment in-house. To do so when the level of understanding currently available on an issue may be less than optimum in an intelligence unit is to carry out analysis under significant difficulty. As an example of changing ideas in this argument, it is noticeable that many enforcement groups increasingly use sociologists, psychologists, and criminologists as part of intelligence teams, helping to interpret criminal action and reaction to various events.

Information

Intelligence analysis and production is absolutely dependent upon the nature, quality, and quantity of information collected in response to the developed set of intelligence requirements in the collection-planning phase of the process. The importance of data is not unique to the problem-solving processes of intelligence; indeed, all problem-solving mechanisms demand data input at some stage.

In strategic intelligence activity, we commonly encounter the problem of pitting "hard" data against "soft," trying to evaluate just how to integrate these two seemingly incompatible types of information. In fact, many analysts believe that collecting and considering soft data is anathema to the intelligence process—but nothing could be further from the truth.

While intelligence tasking may always seem to focus on hard issues of specific interest to the client, soft information is as likely as hard data to be gathered about these matters. Like it or not, an analyst has to attempt to weave an interpretation of events in the present and the future from the mass of soft information likely to be available. Any form of strategic phenomenon research carries a wide range of inherent issues that go beyond the simplistic identification of the core problem. Such research may need to explore human traits of victims and perpetrators, conditions that encourage misbehavior, and intentions and feelings—issues that might superficially appear to be imponderable. Worse, such issues are often considered to be irrelevant because they do not seem to manifest any discernible links to the day-to-day realities of the enforcement agency. It is commonly the case in strategic intelligence activity that requests by the analyst to explore "beyond the boundaries" are often seen as proof of how unrealistic the analyst's approach really is.

A common opinion encountered within government and enforcement circles is that soft data are suspect, largely because of the source. At a primary level, there exists a fairly strong belief in the usefulness and reliability of data garnered from one's own sources, and thus, departmental and official information is valued more than may be the case for other information. The concept of *source* forms a strong central theme in data gathering, and even though information can be derived through rumor, gossip, anecdote, impressions, other people's opinions, and so on, a value may be placed on this related to the source of that data. Investigators, for example, routinely work up contacts to provide just this sort of data and, once received, evaluate it against their perception of the value of the source.

In the intelligence arena, however, collection of information needs to be driven largely by need for specifics, not by the opportunistic collection of whatever happens to be available. Data necessary to a strategic research project may best be sourced from what are often unfairly considered to be soft sources, such as newspapers, academics, and public lobby groups. Any culture—in enforcement or elsewhere—that denigrates data simply because it does not come from official sources is hardly one conducive to insightful intelligence research. Such cultures all too often cite arguments against the notion of using qualitative, soft data on the basis of assertions that the only useful data are likely to be that which is already proven or at least which enjoys a high degree of perceived certainty. This has been discussed earlier in the book and underlines just how limiting the "culture of evidence" is to potential intelligence. For many who have been working in intelligence for much of their professional lives, it may be unthinkable that such cultures survive, given how damaging they are to the cause of intelligence research. If one draws the threads of these difficulties together, then it is possible to assert with a high degree of certainty that a fundamental difficulty in introducing strategic intelligence into enforcement circles has been the argument that intelligence can not be trusted if it relies upon qualitative, soft information.

Strangely enough, this argument has resulted in the development of a relatively common view that strategic analysis is strong and viable only when it equates to statistical reliability. This is simply not true. Strategic intelligence is always directed toward taking a penetrating and comprehensive look at specific phenomena—to understand them and determine the shape of both risks and opportunities over what can sometimes, though not always, be lengthy time horizons. In these circumstances, judgment, knowledge, and wisdom all play a significant role in analytical thinking and speculation. Gathering and modeling statistical data to establish trends and patterns can be extraordinarily useful, but the analyst should never assume that such data would always be complete, reliable, or even representative of the whole phenomenon under scrutiny. Statistical information is to be much prized where it is available and directly relevant to the research. It is never likely to be the central focus of phenomenon research; rather, it is just another special source of insight.

These issues of type and reliability and validity of data are as relevant to soft information as they are to hard data. Information evaluation is essential, no matter what the difficulty. The difference that most strategic intelligence officers encounter is that finding some persuasive basis for evaluating soft data is much harder than it seems to be for hard data. In fact, this is somewhat illusory, since both types of information can readily be accommodated within standard evaluation systems for later testing and review. This is perfectly feasible so long as the analyst retains some useful level of objectivity to ensure that the availability of hard data automatically allows information to be upgraded beyond those levels granted to soft data.

Methods of Analysis to Suit Quantitative versus Qualitative Data

There is a continuing, traditional debate within strategic and other intelligence circles about the pros and cons of qualitative versus quantitative methods for intelligence analysis and production. A first point of consideration should be to understand the differences between both.

- Quantitative methods refer to those involving a measurement of any kind. While measurement technology in the physical sciences presents no real problems, such measurement within social and behavioral sciences becomes increasingly problematic.
- Qualitative methods refer to those that handle some types of data in nonempirical ways. That is, these methods use a reliance on wisdom, judgment, intuition, and experience to produce intelligence about risk, intentions, and capabilities.

The argument/discussion on this issue takes on other dimensions. Some intelligence practitioners hold views that suggest that quantitative methodology—"real measurement" techniques—are unsuited to what is, after all, an art form rather than a science. Even if one could assume that all intelligence could be predominantly categorized as an art or craft, rather than as a scientific pursuit, the reality is that all intelligence problems include issues and features that are both quantitative as well as qualitative. Remember that the key objectives of intelligence interest are *capability*, *vulnerability*, *limitations*, and *intentions*. One should realize that, for some of these issues, many intelligence impressions will inevitably be qualitative, even though, in other cases, the balance will shift toward being quantitative.

In essence, where the particular feature in which we are interested—for example, intention—is a product of human behavior, then for all practical purposes, qualitative methodologies are usually all that are available. In contrast, where the issue to be considered is capability, it is much more likely that one will be able to examine it in quantitative, not qualitative, terms. The intelligence officer must learn to differentiate and choose the appropriate mix of approach techniques that will interact best with the problems being addressed.

APPROACHES TO INTELLIGENCE PROBLEM SOLVING

There are several kinds of analytical approaches, some of which are anchored in formal academic disciplines. Decisions about which approach to adopt are as important as the earlier decisions regarding the methodology, but what is an analytical approach? It is worth remembering that since many practitioners use the words *approach*, *technique*, and *method* interchangeably, with little attempt to accept any precision in their different meanings, discussion of the choices creates some difficulty.

In practice and as used in the context of the processes and experiences outlined in this book, an analytical approach consists of a set of criteria for selecting the perspective that you wish to bring to the problem-solving situation. Sometimes, this will be a historical approach; on other occasions and in different circumstances, a sociological approach may be more relevant. In addition, using these examples as a guide, other approaches might be categorized as economic, psychological, or even geopolitical. All of these types suggest a particular academic discipline, but it is equally logical to consider approaches derived from particular features of the area of study—for example, a legal or organizational approach.

What do these approaches do for the intelligence process? At its simplest, selection of a particular approach allows you to see the entire problem through one set of parameters, a single perspective on the matters under examination. However, it is almost certain that sticking to one particular view will not answer all the questions that you need to ask in reaching for an interpretation of the matters at hand. However, it is useful to at least determine, through initial study of the problem area, a suitable approach that seems to be more relevant than others. If it is possible to say about any given intelligence problem, "This is a social issue" (or cultural, or economic, etc.), then the approach and the applicable techniques that go with it should follow that line of thinking.

Time

Time is a limited but manageable resource. It can be an asset, but, if misused, it can be wasted, and this will undermine the whole intelligence process.

Time is such a common management consideration that it is frequently overlooked as a real problem-solving tool. Yet there can be no doubt that the proper use of available time is critical to the overall process. The problem solvers in this discussion are people like you—analysts—and you have to make yourself aware of the amount of time available as well as the amount necessary to solve a particular problem. On the other hand, you must remain aware that it is not the quantity of available time that is important, but your effectiveness in managing your time.

The intelligence community is no stranger to people generating time-wasting opportunities. This is not because the community is necessarily less efficient than other professions or because intelligence officers are less competent than other professionals. The problem is that the very nature of intelligence work is such that it is a people-intensive activity. It often involves the search for consensus among a number of participants. Almost always, it carries with it a responsibility for countless procedures to maintain effective control and balance over the elements of the process—data gathering, access, security, and the like.

All of these activities take valuable time, and whether it has been properly used or not, the reality is that time has been expended. Proper allocation, planning, monitoring, and self-control are essential tools of the intelligence analyst.

Logical Thinking

As discussed earlier in this section, logic plays an important role in developing perspectives about the intelligence problem or topic. Logic is also rightly a "tool," in the sense that it is an integral component of the measurement and structure of arguments. It is an essential component in their presentation. Ultimately, the proper use of logic affects the validity of the arguments being presented and the plausibility granted them by the audience.

As an example, when we attempt to determine whether arguments are valid or not, we attempt to "reason." However, our reasoning is not always objective and, left to its own devices, reflects our biases. There is thus a clear need for us to use logical techniques in assessing the strengths or weaknesses present within the arguments we generate. The use of logic is pivotal to the success of the intelligence activity and to the usefulness of its outcomes.

Most intelligence product involves providing judgments. If you consider that the intelligence community prides itself on providing a fully professional service, clients have every right to assume that the intelligence product will be based upon solid reasoning. An awareness of the elements of logic and an ability to apply them will help in the building of better arguments and more soundly based conclusions. At the same time, logical reasoning will actively help the analyst in identifying arguments and conclusions that—on careful reflection—appear unable to be sustained.

Computer Aids

Without doubt, computers can play an enormous role in the total problem-solving process. They can be used to store, retrieve, and manipulate data, and in addition, they can conduct statistical analyses of all kinds. As problem-solving tools, computers can be thought of as resource multipliers, since they can extend human resource capacities and capabilities throughout the analysis and production process. The increasing availability and sophistication of computerized aids to the intelligence process has changed the conduct of assessment activity for all time. This is not to say that the intelligence process and the principles that govern it need to change. What is important, however, is that the intelligence analyst understand just what a help the computer can be in allowing each of the process's subroutines to be conducted quickly and efficiently.

On the one hand, there can be no substitute for a trained analyst using personal skills to think through the complexities of a typical strategic intelligence problem, and determine the most appropriate way of approaching the problem-solving task. Conversely, it also is clear that much of the traditional work of the analyst—and the investigator, for that matter—has relied upon heavy, manual methods of dealing with various facets of the intelligence process. The traditional reliance upon hard copy, private files, manual charting methods, and the like draws down on available resources well beyond the modern necessity to do so.

In every aspect of the strategic intelligence cycle, the analyst can make good use of the computer. Indeed, there are no activities within the cycle, other than thinking, that cannot be enhanced by the application of one or more computer software programs. Apart from "creative thinking," there is no aspect of the intelligence process that cannot be assisted or facilitated by the appropriate use of suitable computer applications.

Since the widespread introduction of computers throughout the intelligence communities in most major countries, there has been an understandable preoccupation with using them for intelligence work. This thought process has tended to focus principally on computers as automated aids for data recording, access, and retrieval, generally the highest area of human resource input. In recent years, though, it has become obvious that many software programs can handle or at least aid in the conduct of the individual activities that form the intelligence cycle. These technological developments have the potential to provide a dramatic change in the way in which analysts will apply themselves to carrying out their assignments. Indeed, the changes are already being felt. However, and despite the obvious advantages for the intelligence process, there are two salient lessons for you in your analyst role to bear in mind. Both sound a note of warning for the future.

First, it is the analyst's role to retain control over determining what data is needed and how it is to be recorded and sorted. The reason for this is simply that many data-providing agencies will store their information in standardized formats to suit their needs, and will provide the data to the intelligence unit in that form. This has the potential to inhibit your project work and limit your capability. The format itself may not match the systems used in your project. Of even more importance may be the fact that receiving data in a form to suit the giving agency, rather than yourself, may inhibit your ability to cleverly read and assess the information's value. The lesson in this is that no matter how complex or sophisticated are the presentational aspects of the data being received, unless you can access it to suit the project's needs, then these data serve little real use.

Second, and perhaps more seriously, the analyst—and the whole intelligence community—must remain constantly aware of the fact that computer programs are tools available to all users, honest and criminal alike. Just as we can use these aids to solve problems, so can others use them to design and create what we would come to regard as criminal opportunistic behavior. In addition, because these computerized tools rely upon sophisticated electronic hardware, they are vulnerable to intrusion, intervention, and failure, either through accident or by deliberate acts.

Other Forms of Support

There are other forms of support, too, that are just as important as those mentioned so far. Without personnel support, even the most well-structured analysis may well not solve the problem. As a responsible analyst, it is your function to pay close attention to identifying and negotiating for the provision of all forms of tangible and intangible support, ranging from people, to machinery and equipment, funding, information, and, in the area of intangibles, the mandate to proceed with the intelligence task.

For those readers who prefer to have a formalized checklist, the following might be typical—but should not be treated as being an exhaustive list:

- access to specially trained personnel (e.g., people with skills in accounting, psychological profiling, geographical information systems [GIS]);
- "subject experts" (e.g., specialists on drugs, environmental crime, tax law);
- computers and software and other communications equipment;
- funds for purchasing information (both from legitimate Open Source Intelligence sources as well as from covert informants);
- surveillance equipment;
- transport facilities (vehicles, garaging, operating budget, onboard equipment); and
- budget coverage for overtime and travel.

ANALYTICAL APPROACHES TO SPECIFIC PROBLEM ISSUES

Intelligence Problems That Demand Predictions and Forecasts

The most constant challenge facing the strategic analyst is to produce predictions about future developments in the topic being considered. But this objective cannot be addressed in isolation. Whatever the problem being examined, strategic intelligence assessment and practice generally covers a time continuum that ranges from the past to the future, as shown below.

- Descriptive strategic intelligence examines and concentrates on past events and conditions to describe what is being observed—an "encyclopedic" view of the topic or phenomenon.
- Current (explanatory) intelligence concentrates upon present events and those conditions which are currently unfolding, trying to explain their impact against the background already described in basic intelligence.
- Future (estimative or predictive) intelligence uses the knowledge and perceptions gained through the previous phases (basic and current intelligence), and is deliberately focused on forming views on the future risk or status changes surrounding the situation.

One cannot forecast the future of a strategic intelligence problem in isolation from its past. Production of background intelligence, current commentary, and interpretation are fundamental to the forecasting effort. It is this latter activity that is the mainstay of strategic intelligence work.

Predictive or estimative problems come in a variety of guises. Some issues are long-standing and even repetitive. The requirement to keep current the forecast of the state of threat posed by a particular group could, for example, focus on terrorism. Since forecasting the future is obviously neither easy nor exact, it is small wonder that intelligence efforts in this regard demand considerable study. Such examination will include study of past and present, to provide the essential basis for evaluating changing circumstances.

Further, there is a need to assess changing circumstances in the context of their impact on the intentions of those posing a threat, their likely or developing capabilities and vulnerabilities, and changes that may be developing in terms of the limitations imposed on the threat groups.

Objective and Scientific Problem Solving

Problems that ask you to predict or estimate the future can be helped along by the use of analogies, historical examples, precedents, templates, and models developed precisely for that purpose. These allow you to do some problem restructuring with a certain level of confidence in the particular benchmark that you have chosen for comparison and development. Using case study analysis methods allows you to conduct a very detailed examination of an issue, problem, or situation in an environment that is clearly defined in terms of its extent and the data involved. Historians and anthropologists are both particularly apt examples of professionals who are well used to conducting detailed case study-based deduction.

Another general and arguably objective approach is the use of comparative analytical techniques. These allow you to take a particular situation and consider all its detailed aspects in the light of comparison with relevant, similar situations already known to you.

Finally, there is the use of statistical analysis techniques to take quantifiable data and model, or correlate, them against different sets of variables in order to establish and explore the trends that may be observed. This is of immense use in establishing some expectations of benchmark norms for behavior or incidents observed thus far. However, statistical analysis is not the basis for all intelligence activity, nor is it a synonym for strategic analysis. Where countable or measurable data are available, one outcome of analyzing them will be to develop a statistically driven understanding of the patterns. It is not the only outcome, though, because the individual data elements may help the analyst understand behavior, motivation, or methodology. The point to bear in mind is that statistical analysis is an extremely useful tool where the data sets allow this technique to be used effectively. However, it is not a substitute for other forms of analysis, but rather a complement to them. It is a highly specialized field of analysis in its own right, and properly so, to the extent that analytical units should try to avail themselves of the services of qualified statisticians.[2]

All of these useful and familiar techniques have in common their ability to convince the analyst that subjectivity is being kept to a minimum, since they draw on observed data to establish justifiable conclusions. It is precisely because they do not rely on impressions or "best guesses" that these techniques are considered to be both objective and "scientifically defensible."

Subjective Methods

Subjective forecasting methods rely principally on data or information generated by individual "experts," providing structured—or unstructured—opinions or judgments. As the analyst, you may find it appropriate to take a reasonably formalized approach to this technique by identifying, locating, and encouraging input from respected experts and specialists. In this search for a subjective but "acceptable" view of a given set of circumstances, the idea of seeking consensus is pivotal. This is because these subjective techniques have the potential to gain strength through agreement among a number of participating observers/analysts and their individual judgment calls.

Consensus Techniques: The Delphi Method

Just one example of consensus methodology is the Delphi method. This involves the collection of views and opinions on a given problem from a number of "experts" and commentators, providing their input separately to the central point. At the completion of that round of information gathering, the individual group members are provided with feedback about the group's overall judgments, and a second round of opinions is called for on the same problem. This stimulates review and response conditioned by the feedback each has received and internalized in the previous round. This process continues to narrow the estimates until the tasking unit is satisfied that some form of agreement has been reached—an agreement gained through sharing of individual expert opinions based on differing levels and types of experience, all brought to bear on a common problem.

- While some observers might think of this process as simply brainstorming, the reality is that the development and sharing and review of opinions takes place in a highly structured environment. It can be argued that typical brainstorming sessions often lack this desirable level of formality and structure, becoming instead loose discussion groups.
- In the Delphi method, the participants most often conduct the business distant from one another, ensuring that feedback occurs within a controlled system. This is designed to make the activity one free from the emotional and dynamic interaction likely to result from personal contact among all members of the chosen sample group.[3]
- The Delphi method can be used for problems that are either "hard" or "soft," and may be particularly useful when the problem area defies precise definitions or lacks hard, useful data.
- The drawback to this methodology for intelligence practice is twofold. First, it is expensive in both time and effort. Second, it may be difficult to assemble an array of expert participants who are "free" from organizational conditioning and conformity, or at least enough so that they can contribute without organizational bias.

PROBABILITY THEORY: A BRIEF COMMENT

Another major category of subjective forecasting methodology relies upon the use of mathematical techniques that, notwithstanding their scientific basis, deliberately employ judgment about values. Application of mathematical law such as Bayes's Theorem of Conditional Probabilities is one of these techniques. Others include probability diagramming, influence diagramming, and hierarchical influence structuring.

These techniques are, at heart, subjective in that they rely heavily on *assessing* the influences acting on given situations to change them and then allocating numeric levels of probability or certainty to the outcomes. The techniques are popular in certain circles of intelligence analysis because they allow analysts to fully use their accumulated wisdom and experience in a subjective-quantitative way, giving assumed probability values to the likelihood of events in situations where no real measurement is capable of being applied.

As an example, in some agencies particularly in defense circles, decision tree analysis is used as a form of generating not only ideas but of determining potential event outcomes in probability terms. The technique has well-established validity in assisting analysts to generate ideas. However, when it comes to being used for probability purposes, it is a questionable technique because there is a strong reliance upon subjective possibilities allocated to various nodes of the diagram. This occurs because certainty, evidence, and statistics are all absent. Although the allocated possibility values are usually explained in terms of the analyst's accumulated wisdom and value judgment (or similar explanation), the fact is that such diagrams can hardly claim to be mathematically instructive or persuasive if the level of speculation at various points has been high.

Overall, there are drawbacks in applying the various common probability techniques. These are principally related to the complicated nature of the techniques themselves, where they are mathematically based. Moreover, as a matter of principle, some intelligence officers make a point of choosing *not* to become involved in ascribing numerical values of "certainty" where none can realistically be measured. These individuals argue persuasively that the approach is rather more spurious than useful because of its subjectivity, and difficult to do, in any case, because of the somewhat sophisticated nature of the methodologies themselves.

In many cases, the more simple and acceptable answer for the analyst is to apply knowledge, insight, and wisdom and simply discuss probability in verbal terms, avoiding numeric values unless there is some component of the picture that lends itself to statistical modeling.

CONCLUSION

As a strategic analyst, you have a range of tools available to you to use in carrying out the whole process of handling a strategic project. These range from data, to time, to the use of logic and more. But they are only props or resources that, when used intelligently, will allow you to become efficient in your activities.

Of more importance is the issue of deciding which one—or several—analytical approach methods you could use to solve major strategic issue problems. Since each strategic topic contains many separate component issues, it is likely that you will need specific approach techniques to deal with each one of them. The task that calls for you to examine biker crime in your state or province, for example, will almost certainly result in the gathering of many types of information. Some of it will be descriptive, some statistical, some confidential, and some overtly obtained.

Faced with this collection of different data types, you will need to adopt different techniques to analyze and interpret them. This chapter has been designed to show you that each strategic problem actually contains a larger number of smaller, separate—but linked—problems. Each has its own set of information, and each demands that you work out just how to analyze it when the time comes.

The analysis phase of the strategic intelligence process draws on several resources that every analyst possesses or, at the very least, has access to. At a very simplistic level, you can readily identify and acquire the skills and resources to apply to the problem-solving case. These are issues that are easy to address, even though the actual acquisition of expertise or resources (or whatever resource is needed) may pose obvious practical—but never theoretical—difficulties.

The fundamental question facing you is the very one that poses the most difficulty: the selection of appropriate methodologies and techniques for actually carrying out the analysis of the data and the subsequent synthesis of the conclusions and interpretations. It is unlikely that any strategic intelligence problem will simply be able to be answered by the application of a single analytical methodology.

The nature of strategic assessment topics is such that it will be normal for them to consist of a wide range of analytical tasks, many of which call for different analytical techniques. The role of the strategic analyst is to identify each analytical component, to select the appropriate analytical methodology, and to know how to integrate the "solutions" that you arrive at for each component. The end result will be that, if you follow this detailed approach to selecting structured ways of dealing with the strategic project, you will be able to better develop an appropriate set of conclusions that goes directly toward answering the original strategic assignment.

The key to selecting the right analytical approach rests not with technology or techniques. These are merely tools that aid the analyst in achieving the strategic assignment. What is essential in the analyst is an ability to think through the challenges, plan to avert failure, and conceptualize approaches to data gathering and interpretation. It is this thinking ability—with its fostering of creativity, insight, and foresight—that makes the ultimate difference between the true analyst and an analytical technician.

NOTES

1. Intelligence training in a formal sense first became available to law enforcement communities in North America in the mid-1970s, and later that decade to other countries. The training doctrine was codified by Anacapa Sciences Inc. of California, and has since become the intelligence profession's benchmark for basic, process-driven, intelligence, and investigative analysis practice worldwide.

2. It is not recommended that every analyst should try to become a statistically qualified analyst. This is a specific field of academic study of its own. What is important, though, is that analysts should be trained in the basic concepts of statistical modeling, sufficient to make them better "clients" of the services of a statistician. Only by being so trained can the analyst instruct the statistician about what is wanted and what is important in the wider context of the phenomenon setting.

3. Note that Erasmus University in Rotterdam, the Netherlands, utilizes custom-designed computer software that avoids the burdensome communications cycle inevitably involved in Delphi experiments. This involves bringing together the "expert panel" in a controlled physical and electronic environment similar in concept to "language laboratories." This system allows for the compartmentalization of participants who nonetheless remain electronically connected to the exercise controllers in a manner that enhances their capability to react to input and so provide quick response via additional questions and provocative feedback.

16

Developing Strategic Reports

This chapter concentrates on preparing written reports for a wide, demanding, and often critical readership. While it acknowledges the importance of verbal briefings as an aid to presenting the results of strategic research, that is a specialized skill set for which there is other training available.

Intelligence officers in tactical and operational environments probably already have some—maybe even considerable—experience in writing reports and giving verbal briefings. After all, this is a common feature of intelligence practice. The requirement in those cases is usually to provide timely input to managerial decision making. The sorts of reports you have to give may often be brief, and the purpose is to impart the best intelligence you can produce, concisely and urgently.

Strategic intelligence assessments are different. They start off with a demand for long, broad views of specific crime activities so that upper-level executives can be informed in their function of making policy, preparing programs, and developing strategies. As a result, the types of reports most often wanted in the strategic intelligence environment are those that address the whole picture. They are meant to summarize the essential outcomes and to provide in-depth detail where the presentation of argument is a necessary part of convincing the audience—your managers and clients. It is certainly possible that strategic assessment studies may be accompanied by verbal briefings to introduce the report, explain its detail, and lay out or respond to questions by the readers. In this setting, good oral communication skills will adequately equip you to carry out this aspect of the reporting role, providing that you alter your style to fit the topic and its scope.

GENERAL CONCEPTS AND PREPARATION

Basic Issues

Given the nature of strategic research, it is probably inevitable that the results of the strategic intelligence project have to be presented to the client through the submission of written reports.

There is always the likelihood that the analyst preparing the report will also have to give verbal briefings in order to explain issues, to provide answers to questions, or merely to introduce the written report. For example, it may well be appropriate to provide an oral briefing that covers the key features of the findings, backed up by your well-written and comprehensive report. This allows listeners to grasp the outline of your results and then refer to the greater detail of the written report separately.

The presentation and communication of your report must meet a high standard; this is essential if the findings and outcomes are to avoid becoming unappreciated, unwelcome, or even perceived to lack relevance and applicability to the client's needs. This is, in fact, a "selling" activity aimed at providing and presenting the intelligence product in the best way possible. To do this effectively, you must take account of two key factors:

- The message must be relevant to the client's needs (*message* in this context means the content, methodology, data, conclusions, and recommendations). Indeed, one would hope that the report content will largely match the client's expectations. The report must not only deal comprehensively with the agreed project objectives but it has to be structured so that it clearly indicates that every item is covered.
- The presentation techniques used by the analyst in preparing the report must be of sufficiently high order that they enhance the credibility and acceptability of the product—and of yourself. This will overcome any hidden or obvious consumer resistance to the views that you are presenting.

Preparing the Strategic Report

1. Timing

There is no better time to start preparation than during the early problem definition and projective directive phases of the strategic process. The plan that you develop early on in the life cycle of the project can—and should—include your preliminary thoughts on the outline of the report. You can certainly start to consider outlines for the sort of report you envision, complete with headings and subheadings, all derived from your early work on starting up the project. You may not consider that this will save you much time or effort, but in reality this exercise is part of that overall form of mental discipline we have mentioned, encouraging you to plan every possible step of the project in detail. Nothing in doing so will inhibit your flexibility to adapt to changing situations, but it is important that you have some developed ideas about what you will be doing and how you will be presenting the results.

One suggestion that works very well is to draft the report skeleton at the outset, then amend that as necessary through the collection/collation cycle, as information is coming in and being initially assessed. Then, as analysis commences, many analysts find it useful to merely enter notes on individual issues into the appropriate part of the skeleton report, fine-tuning the structure if necessary. In doing this, you develop the report as an ongoing exercise, albeit in rough note form, and you are not left at the end of a long project with the task of starting afresh to write for several hours, days, or even weeks. This approach was outlined in the session on project planning.

2. Matching the Report to Expectations

Regardless of your conclusions, the report must deal with the issues and objectives agreed between client and yourself at the outset of the project. It is important that every one of the original features of the case be mentioned in your report—even to the extent of an explanation about why it has become impossible to deal with them, if such was the case. Your study findings can go beyond these limits and explore other issues that you believe are relevant to client needs, though these may not have been mentioned in the original Terms of Reference. In addition, you must meet the expected time-critical targets for the report.

3. Balancing Conclusions and Evidence

Strategic study is about the exercise of long-term judgment of issues that may be obscured from clear view. Nonetheless, it is important that you find a balanced relationship between the findings and the supporting evidence/rationale that you can offer. Your intention must be to satisfy the client that your conclusions are appropriately and convincingly based on thorough intelligence work, even where the data are inconclusive.

4. Making Recommendations

As a result of the depth of study undertaken within strategic research, there is every reason to expect that the strategic analyst is in a primary position to observe the need for change and to make recommendations. These may concern additional avenues for intelligence activity, or, if approved in the earlier negotiations with the client, your recommendations may go beyond intelligence issues to deal with aspects of organizational policy, staff, training, operating procedures, potential legislative changes, and the like.

Not all intelligence units carry out their responsibilities in this way, and in many cases, local protocols may actively direct the intelligence analyst not to make any recommendations. The reasons for such a routine to exist can be quite varied. In some cases, local protocols may simply insist that managers recommend, while analysts clarify. In others, analysts themselves may feel hesitant about pushing themselves beyond the analysis into so-called no-go areas of operational or executive concern. Yet at the strategic research level, it is quite possible that by the end of a project, the analyst is the most knowledgeable person about a given phenomenon.

A persuasive view is that the analyst should fully apply the uniquely gained vision of the subject by not only commenting upon situations and their futures, but also providing comment upon issues that may need to be addressed in order to minimize threat, risk, or harm. This harm-minimizing approach can easily be applied by encouraging the analyst to comment on, for example, loopholes in legislation, operational routines, and data-gathering regimes, where these have been shown to be facilitating the perceived risk or threat. At the same time, my recommendation is that the analyst act maturely and sensitively and absolutely not extend these observations of "areas needing improvement" into the operational and executive realm of specific changes to programs. To do so would be to invite criticism quite properly directed toward pointing out that analysts share neither operational accountability nor, in general terms, operational competence and understanding. Analysts are equipped to explore problems and identify areas of potentially beneficial change: They are neither equipped for nor charged with the responsibility of working out exactly which changes are necessary and how they might best be implemented. To stray beyond the barrier of good sense is to invite being marginalized and even ignored.

5. Writing Up the Findings

It is particularly important that you present the conclusions and findings in their appropriate context. Where the availability of—and reliance upon—certain sorts of data has colored the views reached, then your level of conviction about them should be openly disclosed and discussed. You should be comfortable with disclosing circumstances surrounding why you believe something in the findings and ready to explain the availability, reliability, and measurability of the data supporting each finding or conclusion.

Equally, however, it may be that some required data were not available during the intelligence assignment. If this is the case, it is essential for the maintenance of your credibility as an intelligence officer that these gaps in data gathering and their impact on decision making are also admitted within the report.

Where there is a requirement for you to do an oral briefing on a project—either during it or at the completion—all of the foregoing principles are equally relevant and applicable.

PRESENTATION AND FORMAT

Presentation Issues for the Written Strategic Report

The principal goal of the reporting step in the intelligence cycle is to provide the client with a product that meets the research objectives. At the same time, the presentation of the product needs to be persuasive in convincing the client that the requirements and expectations have been met. By developing a planned approach to report development and presentation—whether oral or written—it is certainly possible to cover all the features in such a way as to focus the client's attention on the substance of the report.

As the responsible strategic analyst, you must keep in mind that "selling" the assessment product is arguably as important, once the project draws to a close, as the analytical effort that went into the earlier steps. There are several key points for consideration in the design of the report's presentation. It ideally should be based on the issues discussed below.

- A logical structure in the presentation and array of ideas and findings is a powerful feature of the report.
- While formatting and report-writing style may well be determined by organizational or client requirements, it is essential that, within any such guidelines, you should prepare a report that:
    1. demonstrates a high degree of language skill, with an emphasis on plain and unambiguous expression, clarity, brevity, and relevance;
    2. is aimed at the client's level of technical understanding and addresses the need for supporting or explanatory detail; and
    3. gains and holds attention and encourages the client to follow the approach being taken, accepting the logic of your development of arguments to support the conclusions and findings.

The format or layout style may be a set feature of the way in which your organization carries on its business. However, it will be readily apparent that the nature of the intelligence cycle itself, with its sense of a logical buildup from data to potential solutions, will impose an inherent requirement for you to prepare the report in a way that builds understanding rather than merely providing an immediate answer. This is particularly true if you are to convince the client to accept not only the outcomes and predictions your report offers, but also that the intelligence product is soundly based on the meticulous and logical way the intelligence officer proceeded with the task.

The length of the report is important for several reasons. All the information that needs to be presented and available for the reader's reference has to be included. However, it is a matter of your judgment whether or not all the data actually do need to be presented within the report. As an optimum solution, the report should be used to display key points, conclusions, suggestions, and a synopsis of the supporting rationale. You should not slavishly offer every piece of information gathered in the course of the strategic probe.

The length of a report is not one of rule. It is a function of the complexity of the subject, coupled with the need to meet the client's expectations.

- Determining the final level of detail that is to be included calls for fine judgment by the analyst, bearing in mind all the needs of the client. On the other hand, the concept of sensible topic coverage may not necessarily sit alongside the wish to achieve brevity.

- In some organizations, there are established expectations that briefings, verbally or by note, should be limited to short presentations of the order of "two minutes" or "one page," for example. In such cases, you need to understand that the strategic intelligence report and the briefing are two entirely separate presentations. Both need to be prepared so as to meet quite separate but complementary goals.
- In essence, the report must fit both the subject matter and its inherent complexities, and the expectations of the client. The question of length is a question that needs to be addressed by the analyst each and every time a report is being prepared.
- Preparing a report to meet these objectives does not necessarily mean that the process is an onerous one, nor does it mean that the report itself will be long. What is important is the arrangement of items to be presented so that the reader or listener is taken through the steps in a manner calculated to build and reinforce knowledge, interpretation, and understanding of the topic.

Report Layout

There are many ways of laying out a report. Academic reference books suggest methods; organizational training manuals suggest others. I am not inclined to recommend one single approach as "best practice," but in the following notes you will find a list and ordering of the sorts of headings that ought to be included. The idea behind these suggestions is to give you a framework to use as the basis for thinking about how your own reports might be structured. Remember that every topic is different, and, as a result, your strategic analysis reports may well need to be individualized to suit the circumstances of the topic, your client's needs, and your own feelings about presentation.

Treat the suggested list of headings, then, as merely a guide, albeit one that has been well and truly tested over several years. If you allow yourself to always retain a sense of flexibility in how you use it, then this list will be useful to you. A sample model report layout is given at the end of this chapter for use where an established "house style" is not in use.

Although not part of the report itself, you should also review and reevaluate the way in which the assignment was carried out as an extension of the strategic intelligence process. In fact, some of the lessons learned may impact

A SUGGESTED REPORT LAYOUT (IN THE ABSENCE OF AN ESTABLISHED "HOUSE STYLE")

EXECUTIVE SUMMARY

This statement dentifies the topic, the reason for examining it, the main findings, and the significant recommendations.

BACKGROUND

This section provides a situational backdrop against which the client's focus of interest is described, and sets out the original directive given to the analyst.

AIM

This is a specific statement of the aims and objectives of the intelligence assignment. It summarizes what has been negotiated and agreed between the practitioner and the client.

APPROACH

This describes the methodology taken in both the task itself (the application of process) and the report (the order of components and inclusions in the report). This is a useful inclusion since it highlights just how the project was organized, and why.

MAIN BODY

This is not a heading; it merely describes the section that summarizes—and provides detail where applicable—the following issues:

- the history of the topic; and
- the current situation—main players and activities, methods of operation, locations, relationships, motivations, previous related activities, and so on—each of these being dealt with under separate subheadings

CONCLUSION AND FINDINGS

Included in this section are the reasons for reaching each conclusion, the level of probability associated with it, any misgivings you have about any conclusions (for example, the lack and poor quality of data), and the implications that flow from each of them.

RECOMMENDATIONS

These elements will flow naturally from the whole assignment, and they will generally focus on additional work that may need to be done to collect focused data to validate one or another of the conclusions. Recommendations may also be made concerning potential extensions to the scope of the existing topic.

ANNEXES

These can contain detailed data that is useful but unnecessary within the body of the report.

the report's final recommendations—in terms of extending the scope for further intelligence probing, for example. An important point for the review, though, is to gain the widest possible understanding of exactly what the lessons tell you and your colleagues and managers that might be of use in future intelligence work.

Finally, where the nature of the report topic deserves it, additional information should be included by means of annexes and appendices and even, where appropriate, a bibliography and reading list.

FINALIZING THE REPORT FOR DISTRIBUTION

The eventual and final product must be your own work, since the report is a mirror image of what you have examined and the conclusions you have drawn throughout the process. Others have a role in the research project, and your seniors, your peers, specialists, and the client will wish to examine and provide comment upon the report as it is being drafted and finalized. You can always learn from this process, since it provides a trial run of the report past other readers, with the obvious opportunity for feedback to you as the writer. The experience of your senior staff members—and their association with higher levels within the organization—often provides an opportunity for valuable mentoring and advice to you on these issues.

Other important issues that need to be handled include matters such as security and special handling of data. Finally, one important issue that needs to be dealt with at this point is that you must determine who else should receive the report, apart from your manager and your client.

Many strategic studies examine issues in such as way as to provide a wealth of reference material to other readers who might not be directly concerned with your organization. An example would be a report on illegal drugs in your state or province. Assuming that you have completed this report from a police perspective, the fact is that many other agencies that deal in drug issues, directly or indirectly, would nonetheless find benefit in receiving your report. Its function in those circumstances would not be to feed directly into operational decision making, as might be the case within your own organization. But you should actively seek to disseminate your report as widely as possible if will provide benefit to them, however indirectly. The return on this investment on your part will be the capacity you thus have to follow up with those "consumers" (not clients) and request feedback—critical comment, suggestions, and additional data—that will ultimately help you in your role as strategic analyst.

CONCLUSION

Preparing reports is not difficult providing that, at the earliest possible moment, you take care to think about the intent of the report and the most appropriate structure for it. This may not be particularly true of operational intelligence, but it is certainly so in the case of a strategic intelligence assignment.

The time spent in setting out the skeleton of the report prior to beginning will be worth it when the end of the strategic intelligence process is in sight. In fact, the mental discipline in working out the probable/possible layout of the report will positively help the analyst plan and conduct the whole intelligence process.

The early stages of the strategic intelligence probe involve you in designing mental models and negotiating a clear and unequivocal statement of what it is that the client wants covered, and what sort of issues need to be explored if useful options and recommendations are to be made. It is precisely during these phases that you can commence drafting the main headings and sub-issues of the report, setting up the framework on computer for you to later input information and findings.

Finally, it is important for the analyst to accept an essential truth about strategic reports. Where the assignment has been to produce a study of a particular phenomenon, the report will be comprehensive and perhaps bulky. This may be the most appropriate way to represent the complexity of the topic and the thoroughness of the research and the intellectual rigor that has been invested in its implementation. That some of the executive/client readership may not want to wade through a voluminous report is no reason to avoid writing one; rather, there are two needs, and both must be met by intelligence:

- The research itself has to be written up as a reference work for immediate and continuing use by the many different sorts of interested consumers and researchers of the topic.
- A summarized version addressing the major points must be written up for use in briefings and to satisfy manager/client requirements.

These two ideas are not exclusive; it is a waste of time for the strategic analyst to carry out a comprehensive project and then produce a report of minimal length that only addresses the latter needs and ignores the wider audience of continuing interest.

V

THE ANALYST

17

The Role, Responsibilities, and Functions of the Analyst

THE ANALYST'S ROLE AND FUNCTION

In this chapter, we will discuss the many facets of an analyst. It is not all that common for analysts as a group to get the opportunity to reflect upon just how demanding is the job of analysis. While we all understand the concepts of "work overload" and the "not being fully appreciated" syndrome, complaining about common issues is no substitute for actually identifying what it is the analyst's role is supposed to be. Only by doing so clearly can we expect to move on to the next step of articulating our difficulties in a way that helps to find solutions.

Much work has been done over the past few years to try to identify and categorize the core competencies of analysts so that a planned approach can be developed toward meeting the training and education needs of all intelligence officers, not just analysts. However, neither the mainstream agencies nor the professional bodies have yet addressed in detail exactly what it is that the analyst should be, as opposed to what she should be doing.

The discussion that follows lays open just some of the issues that need to be recognized and discussed openly within the community of intelligence and analysis: the role of the analyst, the analyst's responsibilities, and analyst's functions.

Identifying Organizational Needs

Any judgment about intelligence product is always linked to its relevance. If the client or customer cannot see the significance of the assessment, warning, or forecast in terms of his or her responsibilities, then it is small wonder that it is the reputation of the intelligence unit and the analyst that suffers as a result. Two things are paramount here:

- The analyst has to make the links so that they are obvious to every reader. This is not just a question of intelligent use of language, but strikes right to the heart of the analysis itself. Unless the way in which the problem or task has been addressed is consistent with—or at least complements—the organization's role and responsibilities, then it will be unclear why the analyst is doing such work.
- Even if the work is perceived to be relevant from the analyst's perspective, it is the analyst's role to explain this persuasively—to "sell" the idea of relevance so the product will not be trivialized—or, worse, ignored.

It is not particularly important in this context whether the task has been set by organizational clients, the customers, or managers, or whether it is work derived from initiatives from within the intelligence unit itself. What matters is that these questions of organizational need and relevance are paramount. The easiest way for the analyst to test this is to pose the question: Does this issue impact upon our responsibilities and are we the legitimate stakeholder or at least one of them?

What are the outcomes if intelligence resources are applied to issues that are irrelevant to core organizational interests? The easy answer is, of course, that time and effort are wasted, but there is more to this question than just that simple result. Rarely is intelligence activity wholly and genuinely embraced by government or corporate organizations; instead, as a result, it usually finds itself energetically pursuing understanding and acceptance of its role. To spend time focusing on issues that are peripheral, at best, to central organizational concerns may well impact adversely on its image and standing in the organization.

Without doubt, the best way for intelligence to prove its case for legitimacy is to illustrate its worth by producing assessments and warnings that are timely, accurate, and relevant to organizational focus. The intelligence officer or analyst cannot always expect organizational executives to lay out the details of what is—and what is not—relevant to changing organizational needs. Beyond the basic established charter of the organization, this level of shifting detail is something that the intelligence analysts have to work out for themselves. The onus here is on the intelligence staff to maintain constant vigilance for indicators of threat, risk, opportunity, or change that may impact the organization. Once identified, the analysis of such indicators can then be persuasively argued as being relevant to organizational interests and worthy of intelligence resource input. Working out what to do—not only how to do it—is a role that the analyst cannot afford to overlook.

Having a Necessary "Research" Focus

One feature of intelligence work is its capability for seducing its practitioners toward the "exciting" activities normally associated with investigation, not intelligence. The obvious exception is in those agencies that are solely devoted to intelligence work and that have within their structures their own investigative resources. These are not dealt with in this chapter. Part of the difficulty of maintaining focus in analytical work—particularly in enforcement but also in competitive (business) intelligence—lies in the enthusiasm intelligence staff bring to their jobs. Such enthusiasm can create a longing to "get out and do things" that are more in line with field investigative work than the creative thinking that more normally ties the analyst to the office.

Strategic analysis is far removed from operational intelligence in many ways, and this book has covered and emphasized those differences, as well as acknowledging the fact that the outcomes of each have an impact on the other. What was stressed throughout part 4 is that the analyst must control the whole strategic intelligence process and demonstrate a commitment to the orderly and disciplined application of the analytical processes and methods outlined.

What is most helpful is if analysts are encouraged—and positively reinforced by supervisors and managers alike—to consider themselves researchers, perhaps the archetypal "armchair detectives" of fiction. Only by emotionally accepting this requirement to work assiduously at applying intellectual analytical skills will the analyst be able to establish and maintain the necessary research focus.

Early in the introductory chapters, the idea of phenomenon research was used as a means of explaining the essential difference between strategic and operational intelligence. The underlying theme of that concept stresses that this is an activity of serious research, requiring the talent to remain objective throughout the strategic assignment, and not to succumb to the potential excitement more often associated with tactical or operational intelligence activity.

Understanding Data Sources

Chapter 13 highlights the effort involved in developing appropriate strategic intelligence data collection plans. Readers will note that the analyst first has to work out what exactly is needed, in terms of detailed information, and then consider all the appropriate sources that might be able to provide some or all of the information being sought. The role of the analyst here is not just to determine which agencies or individuals potentially have access to the type of data being sought. That is clearly a crucial concern, but the analyst has to get beyond that awareness to the point where there is also an understanding of the nature and quality of the source's access. Many source agencies may well have access to certain sorts of data in which the analyst is interested. But it is just as crucial to know how they gain their access, how they record their observations, and whether there is a particular focus or skew in their observation and data collection routines that is consistent—or inconsistent—with that required of the strategic analysis. These and similar issues are rarely, if ever, written down and passed into the organization's institutional knowledge banks. Rather, each analyst learns through experience that, regrettably, is likely to be reiterated again and again without being passed along to others with similar interests.

So what should be the role of the strategic analyst in this context? Every strategic assignment offers the opportunity for the analyst to learn from experience of data collection just what contribution each of the selected sources can make. Part of the outcome will necessarily rest with the way in which the analyst couches the requests for information, but we will assume that the analyst can consistently apply care in framing the data requests in such a way as to extract the best possible response from the provider. The response, then, can be judged by the analyst against some sensibly standardized criteria, something along the lines of the following:

- Did the level of detail that was provided match the requirement spelled out in the communication between analyst and source?
- In what respect was it deficient?
- Was lack of clarity in the communication likely to be the cause?
- Is there a discernible "flavor" in the way the source has structured or written up the data provided?
- Does this suggest a particular focus on the part of the source?
- Does the source acknowledge this?
- Can you deduce a pattern of focus or limitation that is helpful in determining future use of this source?

It is important, as part of both the ongoing strategic project and the following review, that the analyst rigorously consider these issues with an eye to future use of any source. Moreover, a commitment to recording and sharing this information is advisable if the intelligence unit as a whole is to learn from each analyst's experiences. Only by this pooling of information—even with hindsight—will analysts be better equipped to design the data-and-source matrix of the collection plan.[1]

Performance Measurement

It is an inevitable outcome of the analyst's work on strategic assessments that all the stakeholders will, in time, come to some form of judgment of the project and the intelligence effort. Bizarre as it may seem, this has always been the case, and yet even now, after almost a quarter of a century of formalized intelligence practice in enforcement, there has been no concerted effort worldwide to develop intelligence doctrine to cover the issue of performance criteria. This is a likely area for thoughtful exploration and development of doctrine for the whole profession to engage in.

In the absence of established and well-tested principles of performance measurement of intelligence activity, what, then, is the role of the analyst conducting strategic intelligence projects? The "players" in this context are the analyst, the supervisor/manager of intelligence, and the client or customer. These are the most important persons involved, although it is obvious that every single reader of a strategic assessment inevitably forms a view about its worth, a process akin to developing a "performance opinion."

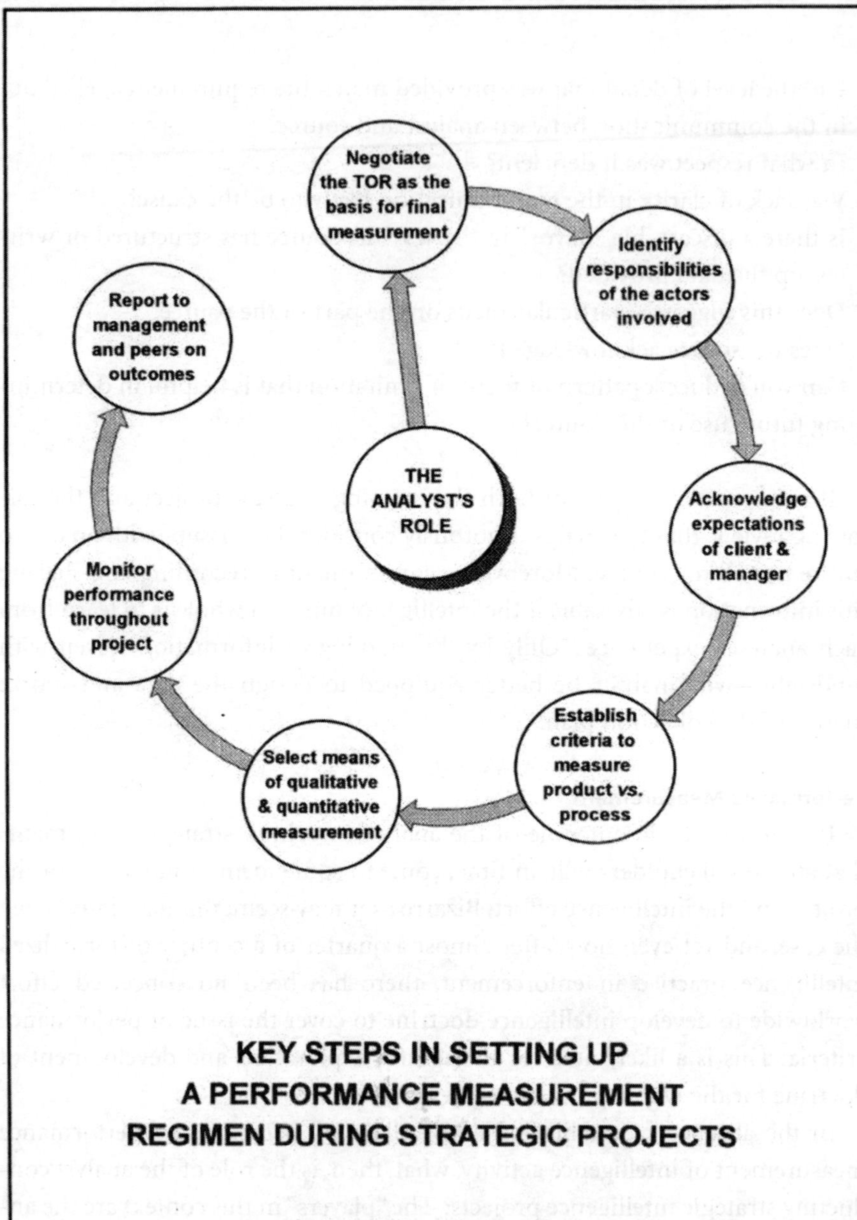

FIGURE 17.1
Performance Measurement Steps

There is little that is so destructive to the long-term conduct of intelligence work as unnecessary, ill-founded criticism derived of ignorance or private agenda. Avoiding this is not always easy, but there are some simple steps and principles for the stakeholders to follow.

- It is essential that the intention to appraise the quality of the strategic assessment and measure or otherwise judge the performance of those involved is recognized at the outset of each intelligence project.
- The criteria by which any project is to be judged should form part of the joint negotiations between the intelligence staff and the client in the early stages of the project. This has already been mentioned in chapter 9 in the discussion about benefits of negotiating the project's Terms of Reference.
- The criteria should be developed so that there is a clear distinction between the expectations of the client and the need to internally review intelligence practice within the analytical unit.
- There should also be a clear distinction between those criteria and benchmark expectations that are quantitative and those that are qualitative.
- All these issues should be arrived at through rational discussion among the parties, agreed upon, and endorsed as part of, or an attachment to, the Terms of Reference.
- The actual conduct of the review should ideally involve the three key participants—analyst, client, and manager—but may also involve a facilitator or mediator. No single party should have primacy in this activity, and those examples of agencies that employ an independent arbitrator to "find fault" run the risk of losing sight of the genuine need for improvement and instead focusing on finding blame and sowing mistrust.
- In writing the strategic project report itself, the analyst should ensure that the project directive is clearly presented in sufficient detail to ensure that performance measurement and judgmental action by other readers is taken with full knowledge of what was originally intended by the project.
- It is a good idea for the post-action review to be written up and the report publicized among intelligence staff—and, where appropriate, to others—for the benefits they will gain from considering the lessons learned in the project.

An inadequate strategic intelligence assessment is no credit to anyone involved and, indeed, rarely is it the sole fault of one individual. If we acknowledge that there are three key players involved in the enterprise, then all have a responsibility to ensure that they contribute to its success. It is up to the analyst, however, to provide the impetus for this to happen in an orderly way.

Managing Upward and Laterally

Throughout the book, I have stressed my strong belief that it is the strategic analyst who actually "runs" an assessment project. Certainly this cannot be argued against in terms of the intellectual control necessary to a good final outcome. Even the practical control issues over resources, direction, speed, and so on are almost certainly best left to the analyst in charge of the project, instead of to some third party. Only by this means can it be assured that the project stays on track and that all of the relevant considerations are taken into account.

This does not mean that your accountability as analyst is solely to yourself—far from it. The analyst is simply the focal point for the entire analytical project activity and, in this vein, is answerable to both the unit manager and to the client equally. Yet running the project calls for skills that are not necessarily inherent in each and every analyst. Some agencies have experimented successfully with the concept of an analyst-in-charge for individual projects; others have provided the opportunity for analysts to access training in project planning and management. Each solution is a worthwhile and well-intentioned approach to equipping analysts to do the best they can in conducting major research projects.

The analyst has another function to perform in this area, though. Controlling the project is not enough unless the analyst can convince others above and outside the immediate project area that such control is appropriately vested in and exercised by the intelligence specialists. Enforcement and other uniformed cultures,[2] for example, generally regard "rank" as the arbiter of power, and it is no mean feat for the intelligence staff to assert their legitimate professionalism even in matters of intelligence practice. In some cases, the organizations are so hierarchical that intelligence staff may not have the influence or the opportunities to exercise responsible independence and speak out as the professional voice of intelligence. Worse still, you may find that this situation is exacerbated within those organizations in which there exists a mix of uniformed and civilian staff without cross-cultural acceptance. These are a minority of cases, but they serve to point up the difficulties the intelligence discipline faces in trying to gain acceptance to carry out its tasks enthusiastically and well, rather than under sufferance.

It is precisely because of these sorts of difficulties that the expert intelligence staff—including the strategic analysts—must learn to "manage" their lateral and vertical relationships. Only by accepting this responsibility can the analysts and others constantly reinforce the message of professionalism and the organizational dependence upon intelligence for good advice. In this context, many readers will be fortunate enough to work within organizations in which intelligence is a legitimate and credible "equal" of other functional groups. Other, less fortunate readers will have firsthand experience or knowledge of organizations that have not yet fully embraced the intelligence function.

THE ANALYST'S RESPONSIBILITIES

The strategic analyst has several roles to play in carrying out an assignment. Moreover, analysts generally find that the "image" and status of intelligence and analysis within and beyond their organization is something that needs to be constantly worked on. The discussion that follows deals with the key responsibilities the analyst must bear as part and parcel of the notion of professionalism.

Selling the Ideas and Concepts

There can be no doubt that part of the role and function of intelligence staff is to "sell" the ideas and concepts of a professional intelligence service. This is because intelligence analyses generally—and strategic intelligence particularly—are still relatively new concepts and do not yet enjoy the ready acceptance of, for example, investigation activity.

If strategic intelligence practice is to gain credibility, then there are various means by which this can be achieved, and strategies should be developed by organizations to suit their particular cultural needs. It seems inevitable, though, that good performance to produce interesting, relevant, and helpful research of the strategic kind is probably going to be the best element of such a strategy. This comes down to the analyst's role and responsibilities, coupled with the way in which the manager and others in the organization support and encourage strategic analysis activity.

Part of the answer lies, however, in a continuing program of proselytizing the value of having a strategic intelligence capability. These selling activities that are incumbent upon the analyst have, as their core content, a dual message: the focusing of attention on the mandate of strategic intelligence, and the need for acceptance of analysts as professionals in their own right. The analyst has a key role to play here and should lose no opportunity to generate a positive and professional image, one of both confidence and competence, to all those within and outside of the organization with whom contact is regularly made. This is the stuff of "selling" the image. It is unfortunate that some analysts and other intelligence practitioners doubt this requirement and feel "uncomfortable" with the very idea that their work needs to be bolstered by advertising of any sort. One frequently hears comments suggesting that the quality of the work should speak for itself. Yet every policy developer, researcher, investigator, and intelligence officer knows that generating credibility rests, in part, on one's ability to shape the presentation of ideas and new products.

If there is a principle here, it is that quality, by itself, is not enough unless the potential user is persuaded to objectively consider it. The analyst has a legitimate role in ensuring that this happens, through report writing and even daily routine contact and communication, and should not shirk this responsibility. Indeed, a positive mindset to actively promote the image and reality of strategic intelligence would be much more helpful and, at the same time, would help reinforce the confidence of the analyst.

Maintaining Intellectual Rigor

If the analyst is to properly establish and maintain control over the strategic project, then there is a concomitant responsibility to do so with utmost professionalism. This means not only being expert in the field of strategic research, but also in demonstrating this by maintaining a continuing high standard of such expertise. This is not about knowledge per se, but about thorough and disciplined conduct of the orderly research process. It is not acceptable behavior for any analyst to become so preoccupied with his own level of knowledge that it takes on a life of its own and supplants hard, detailed research work. The maintenance of intellectual rigor is what sets strategic research apart from many other forms of intelligence activity, and the analyst cannot afford to let any need for quick and popular answers overcome the requirement for responsible research effort.

Developing Preparedness: The Value of Conceptual Models

One aspect of research still not well understood or practiced within intelligence circles is that of developing and maintaining appropriate conceptual models. The doctrine is quite simple and has been discussed in chapter 8. The challenge is to convince intelligence staff that there is merit in going beyond the mere intellectual understanding of this step in the process, putting it into organizational practice as standard routine.

The pros and cons of conceptual model development are generally well understood, and, indeed, quite a lot has been written elsewhere on this topic. The nature of intelligence work, however, is such that it is often understandably accompanied by extreme pressures of deadlines to provide answers. While this seems logical in the context of operationally urgent activities, running a strategic intelligence unit with the same pressures is arguably likely to become self-defeating, particularly if the time-critical targets are laid down arbitrarily rather than for reasons of common sense. In these circumstances, there can be strong pressure on the analysts to simply assume a level of prior knowledge about topics, avoiding what are seen as intrusive process steps that do not appear to have substantial and direct outcomes.

Throughout this text, I have stressed the need for commitment to the orderly process that research demands. All the steps that appear to "spend" time actually do so wisely, and conceptual model development is that crucial phase that establishes the structure of any given phenomenon or concept prior to commencing planning for the research project. Without it there are only two possible outcomes: Either the analyst ignores the opportunity to establish a reasonable basis for subsequent progress, or, instead, she opts to use her current level of knowledge as the conceptual baseline, assuming there is no need for critical self-examination. Both approaches have the potential to provide an inadequate basis for project planning and neither is a substitute for careful development of a more appropriate model.

One further aspect of conceptual modeling that is often overlooked is the need to realize that this step need not wait until an actual project topic has been assigned. In many cases, the nature of the work of an organization, its interests, and its focus, are such that it is not difficult to project likely or at least possible areas for intelligence analysis and probing in the future. Departments of defense, national security, and foreign affairs are examples. Corporate organizations involved in competitor scanning and risk/opportunity assessment, and other government departments that deal with changing patterns of social, economic, and trade activity, are examples of areas in which future tasking for intelligence is akin to scenario development. If this is the case, then there should be no impediment to analytical staff using "spare" time to explore and develop possible scenarios to at least progress to the point of establishing the conceptual models that are applicable. These might have to be updated as time elapses, but this is better than simply accepting that each new task represents an absolutely new and strange challenge.

As an example, customs organizations worldwide handle dumping complaints,[3] in which the generally accepted routine under customs law is for no action to be taken unless there is a complaint. Thus, industry in the disadvantaged country becomes the means of identifying and reporting on noncompliant practice by other countries. Consequent investigation by customs is usually limited by regulation that specifies time constraints. One might argue that this is not the most effective means by which a country can protect itself from economic impact of such trade. Moreover, a telling feature of current practice is that, because of the way the law is read, most customs agencies assume that they have no obligation to be prepared to deal with such complaints, so they make little or no effort to assess the likelihood that commodity X might become the subject of a complaint. The argument often made is that to conduct preparatory scanning of potentially disadvantageous commodity flow would be time-consuming and, in any case, far too difficult to do. Yet many private companies and government business enterprises find considerable benefit in providing exactly this sort of service to those organizations whose interests focus on making profit on commodity exchange. This is the sort of example that shows that scenario development is both possible and, given the stakes for a national economy, highly desirable.

Similar examples abound in those organizations that deal with value-added taxation, in which strategic risk assessment activity is often hampered by the lack of understanding of how specific industries work. In such cases, targeting can often be relegated to determining which industry areas have shown most problems, with scant regard for examining the potential for revenue loss among those industries that have limited or negligible incident records on file. It is here that scanning, to establish potentially useful conceptual models of the structure and arrangements of such industries, will pay dividends at a future time and will, in fact, lead to a greater understanding of whether or not to devote time to a particular industry on some basis other than track record.

It is in these sorts of areas that analysts can use their skills to develop appropriate industry or commodity or scenario models, with the specific aims of saving time and developing more educated ideas about what future analytical projects might encounter in data terms.

SPECIAL CHALLENGES FOR THE ANALYST

Risk Taking, Speculation, and Courage

In much of what has been discussed in this chapter—and throughout the book—we have acknowledged the latent power and influence of the analyst in making sure that everything to do with strategic intelligence activity is carried out with a high degree of professionalism. Balancing this has been the acceptance that this is not necessarily an easy role to perform, partly because the analyst may wish to avoid a level of commitment that could lead to confrontation with peers and seniors, and partly because organizational culture often inhibits good practice.

What is necessary is that the analyst realize and accept that being expert and professional carries with it the responsibility to confront challenge and deal with it. Depending upon the way in which an organization works, so also will the potential level of confrontation facing the analyst change. This, of course, is not limited to the analyst alone, and intelligence supervisors and managers will always feel much of the same pressure to conform to what is expected of them. But whereas their roles are affected by the organization's expectations of them in their managing roles, it is the analyst who tends to remain separated by the intellectual nature of the research and, to some degree, the mystique that often surrounds intelligence activity. Handling this responsibility—and dealing at the same time with what can appear to be the isolation of the strategic research from the "real-world" activities of others in the organization—is not easy. It calls for the analyst to develop a strong sense of purpose, a self-awareness of competence and its attendant confidence, and an ability to act with courage to promote what may be new ideas and unconventional conclusions.

Moreover, the analyst has to realize that intelligence products will not necessarily always please all audiences. To maintain a sense of conviction that the research has been thoroughly carried out and the conclusions reached are appropriate is dependent upon not only courage, but on a sure knowledge that intelligence is about speculation. This is not investigation, with its search for conclusive evidence, but a research activity that aims to explore issues to their fullest and give the best interpretation possible in the circumstances. The levels of judgment are high, but so is the intellectual rigor that has been applied to the process, and analysts must develop a sense of self-worth about the quality of their speculation, estimation, and prediction.

Professional Development

It is not intended in this chapter to deal in detail with the issues of selecting and training analysts for strategic intelligence work. This book outlines the sort of environment that surrounds strategic research and, in so doing, identifies what will be the desirable attitudes, behaviors, and skills required to carry out this work successfully. Many agencies in Europe and North America have and continue to explore ways and means of making sure that the appropriate people are selected to work in strategic analysis. That some consistently assume that an academic education is the arbiter of performance potential is, in this current era of managerial thought, understandable. Nonetheless, one can easily find the grounds for argument that strategic analysis is, after all, a fairly simple set of processes that can be learned. It is the issue of personal traits and mindset that becomes more important in this discussion, and few agencies in my experience address this aspect comprehensively. In fact, most of the current models of intelligence standardization established back in the late 1990s still focus upon the skills-giving process and less, unfortunately, on the need to shape the behavior and thinking involved in their application.

One relatively new development is the trend toward providing academic training and education in the intelligence doctrine and practice.[4] It is this inclusion of the education component that holds some hope for developing in analysts a sense that the mere application of standardized processes, without too much additional thinking, is insufficient for the challenges of modern analysis. Many universities and colleges in Europe, North America, and Australia are now experimenting with courses designed to address the needs of intelligence practitioners, and it is to be hoped that some, at least, will move to providing education wholly by distance-based methods if the needs of the intelligence community "market" are to be met. This is a development that has been slow in coming, and while many institutions work to provide interesting and useful programs, the fact is that organizations often cannot wait for three or more years for the required outcomes from a study regimen. An aspect of these changes to training and education is the growing assumption within some agencies and at many universities that practical, vocational training courses are a thing of the past and that academic education will adequately replace them. This, too, is a misconception, and there is a continuing and high demand for quick, expert training that can be complemented—not supplanted—by tertiary education.

The Analyst as a Creative Thinker

One of the hallmarks of strategic analysis, as with any other, is that the analyst is required to be able to think in leaps and bounds and not be circumscribed by precedent or conformity. Any reasonable observation of investigation practice would highlight the fact that the chain of logic and evidence must be impeccable if the result can withstand scrutiny, whether this is in the courts, the boardroom, or on the stock exchange. In contrast, while intelligence supports investigations in some settings, that does not make it a form of investigation practice. As mentioned elsewhere, intelligence relies on clever interpretation of data and events to identify what might be happening, what might occur next, who might be involved, and what could be the impact of such actions. This is a service provided to decision makers to allow them to focus on problem solving and opportunity taking. It is not an investigation with a finite, provable endpoint. History is the proof of good analysis.

There is a clear need to educate and train strategic analysts to use their minds creatively. Only by raising their awareness can the intelligence unit be assured that their operatives will avoid the traps in being slave to conformist thought, precedent, and imposed cultural values—all enemies of objective analysis. That the analyst can get exposure to what is involved in becoming a creative thinker is unarguable. Courses exist for this very purpose, and many books, tapes, and videos are available dealing with the skills and techniques involved in creative thinking. What is necessary is for the culture that surrounds intelligence practice within an organization to change—if necessary—to allow for a spirit of creativity to emerge and prosper. This does not mean that analysts, their peers, and their mentors should lose their grasp on reality—far from it. Rather, what is needed is an atmosphere that accepts that creativity is not the enemy of logic, and that imagination does not replace process. As most of the popular authors on thinking practice observe, creative thinking is akin to learning to better use a particular organ or muscle—in this case, the brain—and teach it to comfortably adopt new tricks.

CONCLUSION

One view of the intelligence community asserts that all intelligence officers are equal, and that at best, analysts—like the CEO or managing director of a corporation—are only the first among equals. For those who come from a strong military or similar background, such a view is not uncommon. After all, the nature of an intelligence career is often one in which movement between different postings to carry out various functions within the intelligence spectrum is a logical outcome of the service's requirements. Conversely, this practice—and the view that surrounds and supports it—is not as common in the world of enforcement, nor is it common in competitive intelligence activity operating in a corporate environment.

Analysis has, in its own right, become a generic specialty within the field of intelligence. Insofar as intelligence activity is conducted in different environments that call for the application of highly specialized techniques, analysis itself is becoming somewhat functionally divided and compartmentalized. The language and culture surrounding analysis has undergone change, and, for example, job descriptions of analytical positions can vary significantly, as can the defined selection criteria.

How does this relate to the area of strategic intelligence and analysis? The answer is that analysts undertaking strategic research need, above all, to be mentally robust and intellectually equipped to cope with the demands of the sort of research described throughout this book. The processes and techniques used are different from those applied in tactical and operational intelligence, and the training programs for both understandably have little in common. The type of research request, the client's purpose in wanting the strategic product, the type of technical effort required to produce it—all these are "special" to strategic intelligence.

Basically, though, strategic analysis arguably calls for the same sorts of benchmark skills, qualities, and traits required of analysts everywhere. These core qualities include the ability to conceptualize problems, to consider and select the appropriate problem-solving tools, and to apply those techniques skillfully. Moreover, the analyst has to carry out this chain of activity with honesty and integrity, with care and attention to detail, being imaginative and creative, and all with discipline and orderliness in the way one behaves. These central qualities are basic to all analytical work in the intelligence field. Being able to apply them in those circumstances that demand different and particular skills and focus is what separates the various types of analytical functions.

The analyst's role in strategic intelligence research is just one of the many applications of analytical skill. In this particular setting, the analyst must be able to show a personal capability to undertake the type of research regime demanded. Moreover, as has been stressed several times earlier, the strategic analyst has to accept the intellectual responsibility for "ordering" the entire research project to ensure that all the complementary elements—project design and data collection, for example—fall into place. While one might consider that this is a fanciful and unworkable concept, the past fifteen years of strategic intelligence practice in enforcement shows just how fragile and fraught the analytical work is when this leadership role is not allocated to the analyst and, for whatever reason, the notion of centralized intellectual control is sacrificed. To be wholly effective as the lead strategic researcher in a project, the strategic analyst must spare no effort to find the means of convincing managers and clients of the benefits that accompany placing "control" of the research project in its entirety with those who, from an analytical standpoint, run the project.

The responsibilities and obligations of a strategic analyst are not trivial. Apart from the workload volume stress that obviously goes hand in hand with this form of research, there is the additional burden of carrying the responsibility for conducting research on issues that may have such far-reaching impact.

While this chapter is clearly not intended as the complete answer to defining analytical qualities per se, its purpose has been to raise awareness and focus attention on some of the key features that need to be addressed concerning the strategic analyst's role. These issues are no less important than is the acquisition and implementation of the appropriate research processes and routines.

NOTES

1. While such meticulous practice is not commonplace, H. M. Revenue and Customs (UK) successfully use this model/routine as part of their intelligence standard operating procedure.

2. Nor would this be unusual even in business circles. Indeed, there is a concerted effort within corporate intelligence circles to overcome the "lack of power" syndrome

that is all too commonly observed of intelligence in the corporate sector. It is significant that in recent years several large corporations in Europe and the United States have moved to "legitimize" intelligence in their organizations using strategies that include the allocation of important functional titles, assumedly to establish a corporate recognition of the importance of the function.

3. Dumping is the export of goods to foreign markets, where home-country production costs have been subsidized in order to gain competitive export advantage.

4. My own companies—the Intelligence Study Centre (www.intstudycen.com) and the College of Intelligence Studies (www.intelligencecollege.com)—provide just such a range of intelligence education opportunities through distance-based learning programs.

Final Thought

The purpose of this book has been to provide direction, guidance, and encouragement about strategic intelligence research in four ways:

- to inform managers, clients, and practitioners about strategic intelligence;
- to educate analysts about the processes and standards of strategic research;
- to encourage managers and executives to adopt the concepts outlined in the book because of what strategic research can do to help them achieve success, avoid failure, and minimize risk; and, finally,
- to show that the processes are simple enough of themselves, but need to be applied with robust intellectual discipline, creative flexibility, and open-mindedness if they are to provide a successful outcome.

Of course, this book does not cover the whole story of strategic intelligence and analysis. Other volumes are in preparation. One focuses on taking the processes described here and showing their application in corporate and government environments broadly. Such a work is necessary since, although the enforcement community needs the sort of service described in this book, that community is only one of many potential client groups. The second is a more broadly based reference for the intelligence community: an annotated dictionary of intelligence.

Further Reading in Intelligence Analysis

Compiled by the Intelligence Study Centre

Andrews, Paul P., and Marilyn B. Peterson, eds. *Criminal Intelligence Analysis.* Loomis, CA: Palmer Enterprises, 1990.

Bozeman, Adda B. *Strategic Intelligence & Statecraft: Selected Essays.* Washington, DC: Brassey's (US), 1992.

Bridgeman, Cressida. *Crime Risk Management: Making It Work.* London: Home Office Police Research Group, 1996.

Bruce, Christopher W., Steven R. Hick, and Julia P. Cooper, eds. *Exploring Crime Analysis: Readings on Essential Skills.* Charleston, SC: BookSurge, 2004.

Crime Analysis through Computer Mapping. Workshop presented by the Illinois Criminal Justice Information Authority, August 22–25, 1993.

Criminal Intelligence Program for the Smaller Agency. California Peace Officers Association, Organized Crime Committee, October 1988.

Dey, I. *Qualitative Data Analysis: A User-Friendly Guide for Social Scientists.* London: Routledge, 1993.

Dintino, Justin J., and Frederick T. Martens. *Police Intelligence Systems in Crime Control.* Springfield, IL: Charles C. Thomas, 1983.

Ekblom, P. *Getting the Best out of Crime Analysis.* London: Home Office Police Research Group, 1987.

Farrington, D. "Quantitative Criminology in the UK in the 1990s—A Brief Overview." *Journal of Quantitative Criminology* 12, no. 3 (1996): 249–63.

Friedman, George, et al. *The Intelligence Edge.* New York: Crown, 1997.

Gottlieb, Steven, with Sheldon Arenberg and Raj Singh. *Crime Analysis: From First Report to Final Arrest.* Royersford, PA: Alpha Publishing, 1994.

Harris, Don R. *Basic Elements of Intelligence*, rev. ed. Washington, DC: Law Enforcement Assistance Administration, 1976.

Heuer, Richards J., Jr. *Psychology of Intelligence Analysis.* Washington, DC: Center for the Study of Intelligence, Central Intelligence Agency, 1999.

Intelligence: The Ultimate Managerial Tool. Sacramento, CA: Law Enforcement Intelligence Unit, 1983.

Issues of Interest to Law Enforcement. Sacramento, CA: Law Enforcement Intelligence Unit, 1995.

Kahaner, Larry. *Competitive Intelligence: From Black Ops to Boardrooms: How to Gather, Analyze, and Use Information to Succeed in the Global Marketplace.* New York: Simon & Schuster, 1996.

Kedzior, Richard. *A Modern Management Tool for Police Administrators: Strategic Intelligence Analysis.* Ottawa, ON: Criminal Intelligence Service Canada, 1995.

Khalsa, Sundri. *Forecasting Terrorism: Indicators and Proven Analytic Techniques.* Lanham, MD: Scarecrow Press, 2004.

Maguire, M., and T. John. *Intelligence, Surveillance and Informants: Integrated Approaches.* Crime Detection and Prevention Series. London: Home Office Police Research Group, 1995.

Marshall, Peter. *Research Methods: How to Design and Conduct a Successful Project.* Plymouth, UK: How to Books, 1997.

McDowell, Don. *Fundamentals of Intelligence: A Reference Manual for Analysts.* Cooma, NSW, Australia: Istana Enterprises, 2003.

———. *Strategic Intelligence & Analysis: Guidelines on Methodology and Application.* Cooma, NSW, Australia: Istana Enterprises, 1997.

———. *Strategic Intelligence & Analysis: Selected Writings.* Cooma, NSW, Australia: Istana Enterprises, 1998.

———. *Wildlife Crime, Policy and the Law: An Australian Study.* Canberra: Government of Australia Publishing Service, 1997.

Morris, Jack. *Crime Analysis Charting.* Orangeville, CA: Palmer Enterprises, 1982.

Oldfield, R. *A Review of Crime Pattern Analysis in the UK Police Service.* London: Home Office Police Research Group, 1992.

Paton, Michael Quinn. *Qualitative Evaluation and Research Methods*, 2nd ed. Newbury Park, CA: Sage Publications, 1990.

Peterson, Marilyn B. *Applications in Criminal Analysis: A Sourcebook.* Westport, CT: Greenwood Press, 1994.

———. *Criminal Intelligence: A Vital Police Function.* Issues of Interest to Law Enforcement. Sacramento, CA: Law Enforcement Intelligence Unit, 1998.

Peterson, Marilyn B., Bob Morehouse, and Richard Wright, eds. *Intelligence 2000: Revising the Basic Elements.* Lawrenceville, NJ: Law Enforcement Intelligence Unit and International Association of Law Enforcement Intelligence Analysts, 2000.

Prunckun, Henry W., Jr. *Special Access Required: A Practitioner's Guide to Law Enforcement Intelligence Literature.* Metuchen, NJ: Scarecrow Press, 1990.

Ratcliffe, Jerry H., ed. *Strategic Thinking in Criminal Intelligence.* Annandale, NSW, Australia: Federation Press, 2004.

Read, Tim, and Dick Oldfield. *Local Crime Analysis.* London: Home Office Police Research Group, 1995.

Sadio, Sefton. *Intelligence: The Way Forward. The Proactivity Paradigm in a National Police Force.* PhD diss., Manchester Metropolitan University, UK, 1998.

Sources of Information for Criminal Investigators. Santa Barbara, CA: Anacapa Sciences, 2001.

Sun Tzu. *The Art of War.* Translated by Samuel B. Griffith. Oxford: Clarendon Press, 1963.

Tilley, Nick, and Andy Ford. *Forensic Science and Crime Investigation.* London: Home Office Police Research Group, 1996.

van der Heijden, T., and E. Kolthoff, eds. *Crime Analysis: A Tool for Crime Control.* The Hague: Ben Baruch, 1992.

Viljoen, John. *Strategic Management: How to Analyse, Choose and Implement Corporate Strategies.* Melbourne, Australia: Longman Professional, 1991.

About the Author

Don McDowell is a specialist adviser, researcher, teacher, and consultant on intelligence matters, particularly on strategic analysis and research. With a long intelligence career in defense, international relations, national security, and law enforcement, he has for the last several years been providing consulting services in Europe, Australasia, and Canada. He has written extensively on strategic intelligence as a tool for management and on the doctrine and teaching of its techniques. He continues to conduct strategic and operational research for various governments and lectures extensively worldwide.

Don is the author of two books on strategic research processes—*Strategic Intelligence Analysis: Guidelines on Methodology and Application* (1997) and *Strategic Intelligence & Analysis: Selected Writings* (1998)—and one on their application to the issue of wildlife crime, *Wildlife Crime, Policy, and the Law: An Australian Study* (1997). When originally published in 1998, the present book was the first major reference work on strategic intelligence doctrine and applications in the civilian, nonmilitary intelligence community. Don is active professionally and works in academic circles internationally on intelligence analysis curriculum development; in this respect, he runs the College of Intelligence Studies, which is devoted to encouraging distance learning for the intelligence community.

As a lifetime member of the international Society of Certified Criminal Analysts, Don also holds active membership in several related professional associations. He is also active in providing advice on strategic development issues to various corporate groups, and is involved in computer software development and adaptation to intelligence uses.